TRANSLATING INTO SUCCESS

The American Translators Association Scholarly Monograph *Series* is published periodically by John Benjamins Publishing Company. Since contributions are solicited by the Editors, prospective contributors are urged to query the Managing Editor or Theme Editor before submission. The theme and editor for volume XI is *Language Management*, Robert Sprung.

Back volumes of the ATA *Series* may be ordered from John Benjamins Publishing Company Amsterdam (P.O. Box 75577, 1070 AN Amsterdam, The Netherlands) or Philadelphia (P.O. Box 27519, Philadelphia PA 19118-0519, USA). Volume I (*Translation Excellence*, edited by Marilyn Gaddis Rose), Volume III (*Translation and Interpreter Training and Foreign Language Pedagogy*, edited by Peter W. Krawutschke) and Volume IV (*Interpreting-Yesterday, Today and Tomorrow*, guest editors: David and Margareta Bowen) are out of print. The following volumes are available:

Volume II *Technology as Translation Strategy*. Guest editor: Muriel Vasconcelles, Washington, D.C.
Volume V *Translation: Theory and Practice. Tension and Interdependence*. Guest editor: Mildred L. Larson, Summer Institute of Linguistics (Dallas, Texas).
Volume VI *Scientific and Technical Translation*. Guest editors: Sue Ellen and Leland D. Wright, Jr., Kent State University.
Volume VII *Professional Issues for Translators and Interpreters*. Guest editor: Deanna L. Hammond, Washington D.C.
Volume VIII *Translation and the Law*. Guest editor: Marshall Morris, Puerto Rico, Rio Piedras.
Volume IX *The Changing Scene in World Languages. Issues and challenges*. Guest editor: Marian B. Labrum, Brigham Young University, Utah.
Volume X *Translation and Medicine*. Guest editor: Henry Fischbach.

Managing Editor: Françoise Massardier-Kenney, Kent State University (Kent, Ohio). Editorial Advisory Board: Marilyn Gaddis Rose (Binghamton University NY); Deanna L. Hammond (†); Peter W. Krawutschke, Western Michigan University (Kalamazoo); Marian Labrum, Brigham Young University (Provo, Utah); Marshall Morris, University of Puerto Rico (Rio Piedras, P.R.) and Sue Ellen Wright, Institute for Applied Linguistics, Kent State University (Kent, Ohio).

Translating Into Success

Cutting-edge strategies
for going multilingual in a global age

AMERICAN TRANSLATORS ASSOCIATION
SCHOLARLY MONOGRAPH SERIES

Volume XI 2000

Robert C. Sprung
EDITOR

Simone Jaroniec
CO-EDITOR

JOHN BENJAMINS PUBLISHING COMPANY
AMSTERDAM/PHILADELPHIA

The paper used in this publication meets the minimum requirements of American National Standard for Information Sciences — Permanence of Paper for Printed Library Materials, ANSI Z39.48-1984.

Library of Congress Cataloging Serial Number 87-658269

© 2000 John Benjamins Publishing Company, Amsterdam/Philadelphia   ISSN 0890-4111

ISBN 90 272 3186 9 (Eur.) / 1 55619 630 X (USA) (Hb.; Alk. paper)
ISBN 90 272 3187 7 (Eur.) / 1 55619 631 8 (USA) (Pb.; Alk. paper)

Printed in The Netherlands

v

Contents

Foreword

The transformations in the language industry following the groundswell of globalized trade are nothing short of revolutionary. In under 10 years, the translation and software-localization businesses have evolved from a cottage industry into the global business imperative. According to the European Commission, the translation-services market is valued at over US$30 billion annually and is growing at 15–18 percent per year.[*]

By the early '90s, the major US software companies were averaging seven languages per each product shipped internationally. They were learning that the longer it took to enter foreign markets with translated product versions, the greater the revenue loss. Today, with an emphasis on simultaneous shipment, the larger companies publish products in over 30 languages. By 2005, Microsoft alone predicts increasing this number to 80 languages.

Ever more companies are beginning to understand the complexity and commitment behind going global—which permeates every facet of an organization's structure. This includes language-investment strategies, language-processing technologies, translation systems, quality-assurance guidelines, and market education. The Web is only accelerating this trend.

Despite such growth, the language industry is experiencing a severe shortage of talent and information to meet this demand. Major professions like accountancy, medicine, and law enjoy well-established educational paths, certification and professional standards, trade organizations, and savvy consumers. Meanwhile, the equally quality-critical language industry is struggling to develop all these trappings of a profession, and to establish standards and best practices for conducting its business.

Translating Into Success is a landmark publication. It documents the strategic importance of translation and localization in the global marketplace. Through case studies and process reviews, readers can learn from the experts, and benchmark their own operations to those of companies with leading language solutions. This is a collection of hard-won, real-world solutions for the language professionals—ranging from practitioners like linguists, designers, and software engineers, to project managers and purchasers of language services—who are helping fuel this global revolution.

—Michael Anobile, founding member and managing director,
Localisation Industry Standards Association (LISA), Geneva

---

[*] 1996 MLIS Program, *Translation Market Study.*

Introduction

These are heady times for the language industry. Riding the wave of globalization, companies are finding that to sell beyond their borders, they must communicate in their customers' language.

A surprising amount of ink is spent on the premise that translation is on the way out. English is the world's *lingua franca*, the argument goes, particularly after the arrival of the English-dominated Internet. Most people can speak English, and translation adds large expense and time to product development and international commerce.

The facts say otherwise. Consider these touchstones of a booming language industry:

*   The worldwide market for translation and software or Web localization services is large and growing. Market watchers at Allied Business Intelligence peg it at US$11 billion for 1999, growing to US$20 billion in 2004.[1]

*   Non-English-speaking Internet users will exceed English-speaking users by January 2001. According to Forrester Research, business users on the Web are three times more likely to purchase when addressed in their native language.[2]

*   In fiscal 1998, over 60 percent of Microsoft's revenues came from markets outside the United States. In that same period, revenue from translated products exceeded US$5 billion. Microsoft executes over 1,000 localization projects a year.

*   *Newsweek, Glamour, Discover, People,* and *Rolling Stone* magazines are now available in Spanish or Portuguese. *Reader's Digest* reached 600,000 Brazilian readers in 1998, with 1.7 million reading the publication in Spanish and Portuguese; *Glamour en español* now sells 500,000 copies. *Time, The Wall Street Journal,* and CNN have Spanish editions as well.

*   The world's population of translators is flourishing. According to a study for the European Commission, there are practically 100,000 people translating professionally in Western Europe.[3] A separate study estimates 317,000 full- and part-time translators worldwide.[4] Translator

1. Allied Business Intelligence, *Language Translation,* 1998.
2. Rose Lockwood, "You Snooze, You Lose," *Language International,* August 1999.
3. Rose Lockwood, "Bigger Than a Bread Box," *Language International,* June 1999.
4. Allied Business Intelligence.

organizations are thriving: the American Translators Association (ATA) has 7,000 members in 58 countries—double the total of seven years ago.

Much of the translation performed today is required by regulatory authorities or prompted by liability and safety concerns. An Italian sedan in Madrid requires a Spanish service manual. An American mutual fund in Luxembourg may require a German prospectus. A French medical device in Tokyo requires Japanese instructions and labeling.

Much of the remainder is required by a simple marketing analysis. Once a product exists, translating it—typically a small percentage of the total product cost—may open up new and lucrative markets. Twenty years ago, IBM might have gotten away without translating technical manuals, claiming that the engineers reading them spoke enough English. Today, most exporters face local competitors—consumers in Taipei or Moscow will gravitate toward the product in their own language, not the one in the strange packaging. Companies are finding that *the cost of not translating* poses too great a risk to international sales.

These are some of the foreign-language-related services for which demand has skyrocketed in recent years:

- *translation*—the core skill of converting text from one language to another, whether on hard copy or electronically.

- *internationalization*—designing a product (e.g., software) so that it supports usages around the world (e.g., number, date, and currency formats) and can be easily adapted and translated for individual local markets.

- *localization*—taking a product (ideally, one that has been internationalized well) and tailoring it to an individual local market (e.g., Germany, Japan). "Localization" often refers to translating and adapting software products to local markets.

- *cross-cultural consulting*—booming areas are marketing to ethnic minorities in a given country (e.g., Hispanic or Chinese communities within the US) and name verification to ensure that a proposed product name is effective and inoffensive in other languages. A name is *de facto* accessible to *all* other language communities when it appears on the Web.

- *multilingual design*—typesetting and desktop publishing in foreign languages.

- *multilingual technology and tools*—these range from automatic hyphenators in different languages to terminology-management tools that ensure consistency in translated documents.

- *machine translation*—using a computer to perform a first-pass translation.

A note on usage: companies that specialize in software localization are quick to distinguish themselves from "translation companies." However, those outside the language business proper are not as likely to draw such distinctions. In this introduction, "translation business" and "language industry" encompass the entire range of services listed above.

WHY THIS BOOK?

The emerging language industry is sorely in need of "best practices"—standards of excellence which can assist in communications between clients and vendors, and also aid in the training of those entering the industry. This book aims to help fill that gap. Each case study strives to capture actual achievements, not merely theories or opinions, that have broader relevance in the language industry. Case studies are written by recognized authorities and leading practitioners, including those who helped pilot the multilingual effort at Microsoft, Hewlett-Packard, Time Warner, Ericsson, and the European Commission.

These case studies help answer the fundamental questions in global communications today:

- How do we control language costs while maintaining quality?

- How do we reduce translation cycle time to improve time-to-market?

- How do we develop a scalable language process that can keep up with our company's growth?

- How do we stay on top of language-technology developments?

- How do we look at language strategically, to leverage our brands and products worldwide?

The "language industry" is largely an industry in name only—a convenient rubric for a patchwork of sole practitioners, in-house language departments, and small translation companies. Translation is often literally "mom and pop," with husband-and-wife teams of translators operating from home. Although a recent wave of mergers and acquisitions has created a half-dozen US$50-million companies, the market remains highly fragmented, with no player holding much more than one percent.

One result of this fragmentation is a lack of accepted quality standards. Despite the inherently cross-cultural nature of their work, translators are not held to any international standards for quality. Since the translator or localizer in Amsterdam and the one in Tokyo are doing *exactly the same thing*, the industry seems tailor-made for such professional standards, particularly given the inability of the general public to evaluate language work. Some national standards or "certifications" do exist, but they vary radically from country to country in both rigor and enforcement. A translator in Germany or Argentina may meet nationally accepted requirements in education and professional practice—the term "publicly sworn translator" means something very specific both to language practitioners and to the broader public. In many other countries, however, meaningful standards are either absent or so new and inadequately promoted that consumers are unaware of them. The customer is thus usually left to fend for himself in selecting a language solution and evaluating a foreign text.

The educational system certainly plays a role. In Europe, which has been translating successfully for centuries, educational institutions are more firmly entrenched than in the US, where translation is largely fueled by a relatively recent boom in global trade. In the United States, one of the largest purchasers of translation services, a handful of educational institutions offer degree programs in translation. It is difficult to hold translators to rigorous standards when so many are needed and so few are trained.

Part of the problem, too, is that translation professionals have long had an image problem. The portrait of translators derived from most reference books is not flattering—you might find that the Italians coined the catchphrase *traduttore, traditore* (translator, traitor). Purchasers of language services are often unaware of the skill needed to recast text in a foreign tongue—the typical response to a translation request in many US corporations used to be: "Get a secretary to do it." Translation is often thankless; ask a dozen marketing managers for their experience, and their only memories will be of translation errors. A professional translation does not enjoy praise—it merely avoids criticism.

The tide is turning, however, largely because of the strategic nature of translation. Billions of dollars are spent each year on translation and related services—a tiny fraction of the value of the actual products being sold. Poor translation means lost revenue through lower acceptance abroad, or even a potential product recall. Inefficient translation means lost revenue through slower time-to-market. Given the importance of the multilingual versions we create, the market is quickly raising the bar on translation quality.

On the customer side, professional organizations like the Society for Technical Communications (STC) and the Software Publishers Association (SPA) have raised awareness of multilingual communications for their members. Leading trade publications increasingly feature serious stories on translation (not merely rehashing apocryphal gaffes such as Chevy's decision to market the "Nova" in Latin America, where "no va" means "doesn't run" in Spanish). Consider that *Adweek* now stresses global branding, with regular features on pitfalls in international advertising. Crossing cultures and languages has become a mainstream obsession: consider recent cover stories in *Newsweek* (on the booming Hispanic and Spanish-language market within the US) and *National Geographic* (on "global culture").[5]

Trade and professional organizations have made progress in industry standards. Many countries have professional translator associations (e.g., the American Translators Association in the US, SFT in France). The ATA, sponsors of this book, have made great strides in promoting the profession of translator, and have taken on the daunting task of developing a standard for translation certification in the United States. The Localisation Industry Standards Association (LISA), based in Geneva, helps bring together customers and suppliers in the software business. One case study in this work features the LISA Quality Assurance Model, which several companies have successfully implemented to set standards for language projects. Translators in other countries are striving to organize and establish new quality standards, while broader international organizations such as Germany's DIN are pushing for international translation standards.[6]

Educational institutions have broadened their offerings in the language professions. In the United States, the Monterey Institute of International Studies and Kent State University both offer degree programs in translation and related fields, and are training a generation of translation producers and consumers with cutting-edge strategies and techniques. And publications such as *Language International*, for which the present writer serves as editor, strive to provide a written record and forum for this emerging profession.

The language industry has started appearing on the radar screens of major market-research companies like Forrester Research and Gartner Group. A few translation market-watchers have emerged—which implies that there is a growing market worth watching. Rose Lockwood, who is represented by a case study in this volume, has helped elevate the discourse surrounding language professionals, by situating their work within the context of an

---

5. *Newsweek*, July 1999; *National Geographic*, August 1999.
6. DIN preliminary standard 2345; Web site: www.din.de.

InfoCycle—the creation of a company's information and its subsequent life cycle as it appears in varying forms and versions. Lockwood's *Globalisation* study was the first to analyze and quantify the industry formally.[7]

THE CASE STUDIES: A ROADMAP

Translating into Success may serve as a casebook for those already working in the industry, or those seeking to enter it. We have organized the book into five thematic sections, which give a cross-section of a complex industry in rapid growth and transition.

Section I: Cross-Cultural Adaptation

Effective translation bridges the gap between cultures, not merely words. The case studies in this section show that the most effective way to make a product truly international is to make it look and feel like a native product in the target country—not merely to give it a linguistic facelift by translating the words of its documentation or user-interface.

Bernhard Kohlmeier describes how Microsoft effectively localized *Encarta Encyclopedia* into several languages, by creating and adapting content so that it would appear to be a native product. The foreign versions of this online encyclopedia actually differ from country to country; the achievement was not only gathering the appropriate resources to make editorial decisions, but also developing and managing complex work processes so that the project could be completed in a very short timeframe. The technical and procedural innovations in managing this project—which included some 33,000 translated articles totaling 10,000,000 words—serve as an invaluable source of best practices. Kohlmeier offers memorable examples of the way Microsoft modified its foreign-language versions to increase sales and avoid potential embarrassment abroad.

Robert Sprung writes about *Time* magazine's first appearance in a foreign language. The key to success was that the publication did not merely duplicate its English version, but tailored contents specifically to Latin America. The case study illustrates the challenges of recreating the voice and style of a text for a different culture—the same principles apply, whether the text is journalism, marketing copy, or technical documentation. The project required a robust, scalable work process that could convert 10,000 words every week into Spanish and Portuguese in little over 48 hours, which required not

---

7. Rose Lockwood, *Globalisation: Creating New Markets with Translation Technology*, London: Ovum, 1995. The current version (1998) is published by Equipe Consortium (www.equipe.net).

only a top-notch team of language experts, but also cutting-edge communications and publishing technology. The case also illustrates the potential for international brand leverage—*Time*'s series on Leaders for the New Millennium included multilingual content in its English magazine, the Latin American edition, CNN en español, and the Web.

Susan Cheng shows cultural adaptation at work in a small, cutting-edge e-commerce company, chipshot.com. When this firm decided to market golf equipment to Japan via the Internet, they used specialized software and work processes to localize their e-commerce site. The case study illustrates the importance of understanding current marketing idioms in a given culture, and applying these in the localized version of a Web site, regardless of the language of the user-interface. Cheng illustrates how Web translation differs from translating for traditional media, and gives us an inside view of workflow and resources used, with copious graphical examples.

Section II: Language Management

Smart companies understand that translation is a strategic imperative. It requires complex planning and analysis, with significant investment of time and resources to achieve the ultimate goals of lower translation costs, higher quality, and shorter turnaround time. These cases show how some companies are lifting decision-making for translation and language issues to the highest levels, rather than treating it as an afterthought or low-end administrative work. Given that the success of their core products is riding on translation quality, the move seems long overdue.

David Brooks describes Microsoft's efforts to bring translation and localization costs under control. Microsoft spends hundreds of millions of dollars each year on localization, with translation in the critical path to product delivery. Finding an optimal way to cut costs and time was thus hardly optional, but a key to survival and success in the global marketplace. In spite of its mammoth size, the company takes a very entrepreneurial and creative approach to problem-solving, and the innovations it employed, which are outlined here, apply to small companies as well as large ones—with implications far beyond the software industry. Brooks, who helped craft the localization effort at the world's largest software company, focuses on the need for true global design of products, and for cost-basis accounting to rein in skyrocketing localization expense. He discusses the application of quality and cost metrics to translation at Microsoft, applying Andrew Groves's dictum, "If you can't measure it, you can't manage it." He also steers the reader's gaze toward cutting-edge solutions that have not quite arrived: "Linguistic technologies such as speech recognition, natural-language-based search engines, and machine translation will redefine the scope of localization. These technologies are being commercialized, and will soon become mainstream utilities."

Cornelia Hofmann and *Thorsten Mehnert* describe language innovations at Schneider Automation. Multilingual efforts there break down the traditional categories of "translation" and fit into the broader context of "multilingual information management." The authors argue that "the information of tomorrow is quite different from the documentation of today." Consider these examples:

- Information is increasingly integrated into products (e.g., online help or on-screen messages).

- Products are increasingly "information-intensive" (e.g., car navigation systems containing large volumes of translatable data).

- The Web is blurring the distinctions between traditional documentation categories (technical documentation, marketing literature, or customer support).

The authors advocate abandoning a "silo perspective" that processes individual "documents," and propose an integrated approach that thinks in terms of recyclable "information objects." The real-world examples in this case study have far-reaching implications for translation in a wired world.

Andrew Joscelyne introduces another facet of the language business—translation for public and quasi-public institutions. Organizations like the European Commission, the IMF, and other international bodies are among the largest employers of translators and language services in the world. Many of their problems are specific to the nature of such organizations, their needs and decision-making structures. Others are similar to the challenges faced by firms, large and small, in the private sector. Joscelyne shows that international organizations like the Organization for Economic Cooperation and Development (OECD) can innovate as well as their private-sector counterparts.

Section III: Localizing the Product

This section offers three facets of the complex processes of "localization" and "internationalization." Internationalization means designing a product so that it can be easily adapted to local markets. Examples include developing a computer operating system so that it can support complex foreign character sets like Chinese or Japanese, international date formats, and sorting sequences. A product that takes into account the various *possibilities of adaptation around the world* is said to be internationalized. Localization is commonly defined as the process of taking a product—hopefully one that has been well internationalized—and adapting it to a specific *locale* or target market or language group (translation is thus a subset of localization). An example may help illustrate the point: designing an automobile chassis so that the steering wheel could be installed on *either* the right or left would be a case of internationalization. The decision to actually make a given batch of cars left-steering would be a case of localization.

Localization is most commonly associated with the software industry, since it is one of the largest consumers of such services. However, we define it more broadly, to include the adaptation of any good or service to a target market, since the principles applied in both cases are similar. These three case studies offer invaluable insights with application far beyond the computer desktop.

Karen Combe outlines Hewlett-Packard's approach to localization. HP experienced dramatic growth in international sales, and with it a rising demand for language and localization services. The case study is particularly interesting in its illustration of the principles of partnership and communication between a customer and a language vendor. The innovations here point the way for a truly collaborative and strategic effort in tackling complex language problems. We also see how managing the human aspects of language projects under intense pressure is as critical as managing the technical complexities. Combe describes how Hewlett-Packard strove to apply founder David Packer's classic "management by objective" philosophy to localization and translation—HP's Information Engineering department benchmarks its language program based on cost, on-time delivery, and quality. The results are impressive.

Suzanne Topping turns our attention to cutting time-to-market at Kodak, where she helped implement new approaches in use today. "Indeed there will be time," T.S. Eliot once said. Clearly, he was not writing about the localization industry, where "yesterday" often seems too generous a deadline. As soon as word spread that a new Kodak camera was available or soon to be released in the US, consumers in other markets were impatient for delivery—which would be impossible without translated instructions and associated software. In the not-too-distant past, consumers abroad felt like a younger sibling receiving a hand-me-down: their brethren in the US would enjoy version 4, while they had to sit by patiently with version 3. The Web has changed that for good: since the world knows the instant a new product or version is available, the goal is to come as close as possible to *simultaneous release* of foreign-language versions of a product. Topping shows how Kodak worked toward this goal, which entailed reengineering product development to accelerate translation. Her study is a blueprint for many technology companies seeking to cut time-to-market.

Ricky Thibodeau shows how localization is a strategic imperative for small companies no less than for the big players. He reveals the techniques in use at MapInfo, a smaller but no less potent software developer. His is a lesson in the sheer economic power of localization: although MapInfo has only 450 employees worldwide (three quarters of them in North America), its products are available in 58 countries and 21 languages. He provides comprehensive analysis of MapInfo's decision-making as it refined its localization strategy. He shows how MapInfo transitioned from a model where translation was performed by its distributors to a hybrid model involving other third parties and a shored-up internal team. Thibodeau provides detailed descriptions of the company's tools and techniques—useful in an era when many firms keep such competitive advantages hidden from public view. Perhaps this is with good reason, given the impressive results MapInfo has achieved: they cut localization costs by 25 percent, in addition to reducing cycle time and improving quality.

Section IV: Language Tools and Techniques

This section covers language technology and process. Advances in these areas have been impressive, ranging from specialized tools for language professionals (electronic dictionaries and terminology management, for example) to specialized models for project management, budgeting, and communication.

Siu Ling Koo focuses on innovative approaches to controlling quality. LISA has developed a quality-assurance model for language projects, including standardized methodology for classifying errors. Koo's firm has supplemented the model with sampling techniques, so that portions of a language project can be tested, saving time on QA. If a sample has fewer than a predetermined number of errors, it passes; if not, it fails. She has been applying the model for a significant period, and illustrates the potential application of quality metrics to translation—a sign of a maturing industry embracing modern management techniques.

Gary Jaekel describes terminology management at Swedish telecom giant Ericsson. His case study offers an object lesson in the benefits of controlling the words we use. Terminology management typically involves a system for cataloguing, updating, retrieving, and managing terms. Without it, there would be far greater danger of using incorrect or inconsistent terminology. Terminology management is critical for reducing cost and turnaround time on translation projects: if translators are given standard, approved glossaries of terms on which to base their translations, quality will be far higher with greater consistency. Jaekel here outlines how he helped create a terminology department that ultimately produced a product with over 15,000 core terms. Terminology is blossoming as its own discipline. Kent State's Sue-Ellen Wright, for example, oversees a growing number of graduate students pursuing this field. Terminology management is hardly an ivory-tower theory: Microsoft recently took a significant share of Trados, a prominent maker of commercial software for exactly that purpose.

Robert Sprung writes on technology and project-management innovations in regulated industries—those with a high degree of oversight or which must translate text that is subject to strict standards or regulatory audits. Consider the large volume of text translated for medical, pharmaceutical, automotive, legal, and financial firms—quality is obviously critical, but pressures continually mount to translate in ever shorter timeframes while containing costs. This case study focuses on cutting-edge solutions crafted for two Johnson & Johnson companies, ranging from ISO-compliant language processes to a custom corporate intranet to manage and control the translation cycle.

Section V: Language Automation

"Can't you get a machine to translate it?" This question seems to be on the lips of many vice presidents in charge of international sales and marketing. Do the math: a company with 10 user manuals totaling 1,000,000 words in English contemplates a move into 10 foreign languages; the price-tag for translation could easily top $3,000,000. With the stakes this high, and with the price of computer processing speed and storage dropping dramatically, pressures have been considerable to automate the language process.

Using computers to perform translation has been one of the holy grails of artificial intelligence (AI) since its inception. A machine that can translate is a machine that can think and write like a person. Easier said than done, it turned out. Although commercial machine-translation systems have been around for about 30 years, the vast majority of translation performed in the world today is still done by those pesky humans. This often surprises American marketing executives who are new to language and translation. Take the sentence "Mary had a little lamb." How do we know that "had" means "possessed" and not "ate" (as in, "John had a little beef and Mary had a little lamb"), "taught," "took advantage of," or, heaven forbid, "gave birth to"? The answer is that we don't know—cognitive scientists don't sufficiently understand how our brain places this particular lamb in a nursery rhyme and not a butcher shop. Since each language has unique "mappings" of words to meanings, the computer can easily end up linguistically mistreating Mary and her lamb. And if the computer has a problem with Mary, what sorts of problems will it have with legal contracts or technical specifications for a nuclear power plant? Douglas Hofstadter, a pioneer in artificial intelligence, thinks that the computer might never be able to produce a reliable translation that reads coherently.[8]

Meanwhile, commercial pressures continue to impel innovations. Some think part of the solution lies on the *output* side, in the form of lowered user expectations. The search engine Altavista pioneered a Web-based machine-translation (MT) solution by partnering with Systran. Click on a Web address listed in the search engine, select a language, and *voilà*: a "translated" Web page free of charge. Don't expect a polished or even a particularly accurate translation, however. The system is good for "gisting"; by having most key words translated accurately with reasonably understandable syntax, you can often understand enough of the text to determine its basic meaning or at least context. If you need a polished translation or one on which the accuracy is verified, humans will have to get involved.

Another angle of attack is to refine the *input*. If you can simplify the text to be translated, the computer's problem will be greatly simplified. *Rose Lockwood* outlines such a solution implemented at Caterpillar over the course of years. This leading international manufacturer of heavy equipment looked at the cost and time involved in translation, and helped develop the concept of "controlled authoring." By dramatically limiting the vocabulary and sentence complexity, the company has achieved impressive results with machine translation.

Carmen Andrés Lange and *Winfield Scott Bennett* offer another machine-translation case study, this time from Baan Development in the Netherlands. Baan has successfully combined machine translation with translation memory, software used to store and manage terminology usage on an enterprise-wide basis. The authors also demonstrate that much of the challenge of implementing MT rests as much on the human as the technical side: many technical writers view their craft as more art than science, and are resistant to writing in a manner that they consider stilted or to using automated means in general. For machine translation to be viable in the long term, those who review the machine's output ("post-editors") are typically skeptical, and need extensive coaching and training if they are to support the effort.

---

8. See Douglas Hofstadter, *Le Ton beau de Marot: In Praise of the Music of Language*, Basic Books, 1997.

Finally, language-technology watcher *Colin Brace* offers a glimpse into the European Community's implementation of Systran, a large-scale machine-translation system. Brace explains how the EC has gathered terminology and "trained" its system over the years, and has effectively customized Systran for specific types of EC documents. The case illustrates the extensive preparation involved in any MT implementation. There is currently no "all-purpose" MT solution on the market; one must invest in technology and human capital for a specific use. It may take several years and substantial investment to recoup the investment in an MT system—cautionary words for that overly optimistic US marketing manager we mentioned above. But as these three case studies illustrate, it may be worth the trip. And as the Internet further heightens demand for rapid translation, the coming years will no doubt bring us other dramatic developments.

ACKNOWLEDGMENTS

This volume is part of the American Translators Association Scholarly Monograph Series. The ATA provided invaluable support, particularly through Professor Françoise Massardier-Kenney of Kent State University. Professor Kenney was an ideal project supervisor, offering constructive criticism throughout that greatly improved the balance and focus of the book.

Assistant editor Simone Jaroniec, a seasoned language professional, was an inspirational colleague. She managed the overall production of this volume, on top of a full workload. She continually held the team to the highest editorial standards, while her keen insight and dedication made the project a pleasure to work on for the team.

Graphic specialists Ted Assur and Sean Mahoney breathed life into the text, giving it an attractive design and format. Kristin Padden, who also serves as the associate editor of *Language International*, offered her usual inspired editorial assistance. Special thanks to Adela Hruby, Adriana Lavergne, Liza Loughman, Natalia Mehlman, and Peter Torkelsson for attentive proofreading.

Thanks also are due Sue-Ellen Wright of Kent State University, Dean Diane de Terra and Jeff Wood of The Monterey Institute of International Studies, and Walter Bacak and Muriel Jérôme-Okeeffe of the ATA. Each of these valued advisors plays a critical role in educating the broader public to translation issues, as well as training the next generation of language professionals.

Ingrid Seebus and Bertie Kaal of John Benjamins offered critical assistance in printing and organization.

Any errors that remain are my own. We hope you will find valuable insights in the present volume. A second is already under consideration; if you are aware of appropriate case studies or wish to correspond on language issues, do drop a line.

—Robert C. Sprung
Cambridge, Massachusetts
October 1999

Microsoft Encarta Goes Multilingual

Bernhard Kohlmeier
Bowne Global Solutions

THE CHALLENGE

Since 1993, Microsoft has been distributing the US version of *Encarta Encyclopedia*, a digital reference title based on a US print encyclopedia. In 1995, Microsoft was the first to take an electronic encyclopedia into several foreign tongues, including German and Spanish. Bowne Global Solutions was contracted to carry out the project and provide ongoing updates.

From the start, it was obvious that a plain translation of the US version would have no chance in the international market, because all content (articles, style, media, and features) was targeted to US users.

From a German or Spanish perspective, local content (locale-specific biographies, historic events, and geographic entities) was missing, while content developed for the US audience might have confused local customers. Examples, institutions, laws, and other frames of reference were US-centric. Further, the manner of presenting facts and judging these facts was problematic for a non-US audience, particularly in articles concerning historical, legal, or political matters.

The challenges of executing the project rested in the following areas:

* Content adaptation and creation

* Very large project size

* Project management

* Budget tracking

* Media selection and production

* Management of updates throughout the project

* Paper management

Below is a chart giving a sense of the mammoth project scope. Figures are approximate.

	Version 1	Version 2
Articles	27,000	33,000
Words (depending on language)	7,200,000/9,000,000	8,200,000/10,000,000
Media Elements	10,000	11,000
Photos and Illustrations	7,000	7,600
Audio Elements	2,000	2,000
Maps/Charts	1,000	1,250
Videos and Animations	100	110
Web Links	0	1,500
Bibliographical Entries	0	3,500
Yearbook Builder	25 articles monthly	25 articles monthly

In this case study, "content entities" refers to articles and media elements (videos and animation), as well as maps and charts.

THE SOLUTION

Project Management

A carefully defined project-management procedure, with close monitoring of all aspects of the project, was crucial for success. Tracking each content entity with utmost accuracy at any stage was one of the greatest challenges. Workflow-management tools based on SQL Server and written in Visual Basic allowed the management team to monitor the project at any time. Each content and media entity had to be tracked, along with its status, history, class, and workflow. Assignment rules allowed automatic resource assignment without manual interaction.

With a production time of 18 months (first version) to 10 months (subsequent versions), a project like *Encarta Encyclopedia* localization seems quite long. But as soon as the project manager started to break down the total time available into time available per entity, the schedule became very tight indeed. Each content entity was tracked based on a detailed and carefully controlled throughput model. An intranet-based system tracked individual performance and status of each content entity.

An editor could not reasonably be expected to produce the same volume each day or week. Content editing and creation is not a conveyor-belt operation. Besides the human factor (people's metabolisms differ from day to day), each article differed significantly in complexity. Some needed extensive research. Others could be edited without additional investigation. An article with a few words might require a trip to a library while one of multiple pages was straightforward. Project management needed to account for this; a simulation was created to calculate projected throughput based on actual, accumulated data. This model allowed for real-time simulation of the time left in the project, and empowered the project- and content-management teams to adjust to the parameters. This process of schema and correction can be graphically depicted as follows:

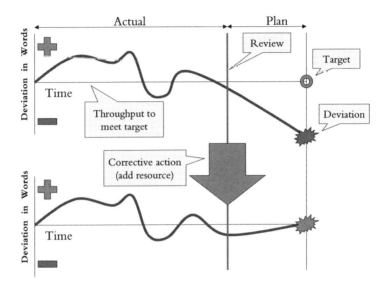

Making Decisions

The editorial team had content authority for the project, while project management controlled scheduling, budget, and production. Conflicts between the major areas had to be resolved throughout the entire project, requiring creative solutions at all times. What should be done if there was a last-minute change due to breaking news? How important was the change to the product and how would it be introduced? Key factors in the decision-making included the trade-off between content requirements and the risk of jeopardizing a process or build (compilation of an executable software application), or simply the potential for introducing new problems by addressing another.

Budget Tracking

In a project with several hundred team members, budget tracking of both internal and external resources is essential to financial success. Tracking of the project progress and associated costs incurred was supported by custom and off-the-shelf tools. The entire process, from managing costs to generating invoices, can be very time-consuming, and on a management-intensive project, it can sidetrack the project manager from proactively managing the project. Therefore the selection of the proper tools to support this process was critical.

The project team was able to share real-time data on budget spent versus progress made, including tracking of all expenses. This allowed the project manager to make strategic decisions based on cumulative experience and data on the project. Monitoring and managing the quality of several hundred contributors required strict accounting and resource-management standards. Incoming work needed to be analyzed against quality guidelines, and contributors often had to rework text to bring it to the required quality level. A financial process triggering payment had to be linked to final acceptance of a contributor's product.

Managing Paper

At some stages of the project, printouts were necessary for both articles and media. Given the volume of content entities, printouts quickly exceeded 100,000 pages. Not only did the paper have to be tracked and the electronic version locked, but hard copies also had to be archived in a way that allowed quick retrieval while preserving a complete paper trail. Revisions marked on paper had to be proofed against the corrections entered by text-prepping staff. Another important aspect was the differentiation between a *live* hard copy currently being processed and a *dead* copy used for personal reference by team members. The need to mark copies as live or dead becomes clear by imagining the scenario of two paper copies of the same article with different sets of markups. Here it would be difficult to determine the valid copy, and the older the copy is, the more difficult to determine the revision history.

We found a solution to this challenge in a place that tracks many different physical entities: the supermarket. We implemented barcoding on all printouts, and used a print routine that distinguished between system-controlled and individual printouts. The barcode not only simplified data entry for resources dealing with paper, it also eased inventory and archiving. In addition, it provided a watermark that could not be easily reproduced. Barcoding significantly reduced the time required to access electronic versions of paper copies, and also minimized the potential for data-entry errors.

Testing the Results

Testing a project the size of *Encarta Encyclopedia* brings with it a complex set of challenges. A single build cannot be completely tested before revisions are made to the content, as those cycles would produce unacceptable delays in time-to-market. The solution developed included an ongoing testing and revision cycle closely integrated with the workflow-management system. At any given time, multiple revisions were tested against a new build while editors and media-production staff were working on revisions. Locking content entities assigned to a specific resource was mandatory to avoid confusion in the workflow and to preclude simultaneous access by different people or computer processes.

Harnessing Consistency

An encyclopedia project requires the creative contribution of many individuals, which poses the risk of inconsistencies in style and detail. Each team member has preferences for what is correct, ranging from macro details like proper representation of historical fact, to micro details such as formatting and stylistic guidelines.

Here are but a few potential hotbeds of inconsistency:

- Spelling of proper names

- Format of date ranges

- Format of the first paragraph of an article

- Guidelines for the type of information to be included

- Manner of referencing media in articles

- Choice of appropriate media entities for articles

To ensure consistency in these and many other areas, a custom style guide was created that outlined the content and media requirements in sufficient detail. The key is *sufficient*. Although it is easy to create style guides of several hundred pages, the information must be sufficiently concise to be usable for translators and copy editors.

Constant updates to the style guides and requirements documents reflecting the latest input by copy editors allowed for corrective action throughout the project, continuously improving the quality. This loop allowed the project manager to steer the project's quality in close to real time.

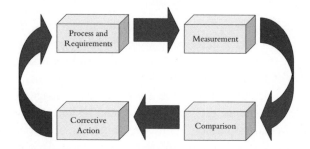

Editorial Subtleties

The value of electronic publications rests on their accuracy and timeliness. With each passing day, many changes in our world potentially influence a product like *Encarta Encyclopedia*. New discoveries, changes in geopolitics, and biographies are a few examples. Historic events must be monitored and all related content entities kept synchronized with the latest information.

When Yitzhak Rabin was assassinated at a peace rally on 4 November 1995 in Tel Aviv, the news affected not only the statesman's biography but also many articles about Israel, the Middle East, and international politics. The workflow-management system efficiently located the related entities and reassigned them, according to classification, to the responsible editors, and changed their status within the workflow.

The editorial process needed to include clear style guidelines on how to edit an article. Editors had to continually monitor the length of the article—predetermined through the headword list review at the beginning of the project—while balancing time allocated to that task in the overall project plan.

Editors also had to let go of content entities at a reasonably predictable rate, otherwise project and editorial management could not effectively plan the project and monitor throughput. Thus, a key to the project's success was constant coaching of editorial staff on how to successfully close articles on a regular basis, and how to perform a self-evaluation of their work using various tools. The support of the editors in monitoring their own performance and in evaluating their own throughput on an ongoing basis reduced the project-management overhead.

It turned out to be important to reassure editors that if a headword was influenced by a news event, they would be able to revisit the headword and related articles. This is critical for topics subject to frequent updates, and to the editors' peace of mind.

Cultural Adaptation

Adapting a product to various cultures is very complex and requires deep and timely knowledge of the target markets. The content of the entire encyclopedia had to be analyzed based on a thorough review of the headword list, with input from the best subject-matter experts.

Advisory Boards

Two advisory boards were established to review content, write articles, recommend authors and consultants, and suggest new articles and features. One board comprised 38 academic advisors from Argentina, Brazil, Chile, Colombia, Mexico, Peru, Spain, and Venezuela, ensuring that this version of the encyclopedia encompassed the 22 Spanish-speaking countries in the Americas and Europe. Seven academic advisors staffed the German advisory board. The advisors had many ideas and suggestions, although it was not always easy to find a common realistic and practical approach. Direct communication was established either through visits to their respective countries or regular meetings of the entire board.

Headword List Review

Content balance is a key factor in producing an encyclopedia. Although the original version provided a great level of detail in some areas, the team had to ensure the proper balance of headwords for the target locale. Numerous topics and categories needed expansion. For example, a Spanish or German user expects a more detailed treatment of European and national history than is provided in the US version.

Editorial management and subject editors reviewed the headword list. During this phase, decisions were made whether to keep or omit certain articles. The next step was to decide on a process for determining the proper course of action for an article associated with a given headword: adaptation of content, completely new material, or a full or partial translation.

For all articles authored locally, length and content requirements were defined. The article was then written by authors specialized in the respective subject area and edited internally. Translated articles were classified according to the magnitude of the revisions necessary.

All the factors mentioned above were reflected in throughput projections, assignment rules, and revision cycles. Appropriate approval processes for articles of high cultural sensitivity in the respective market were also defined.

Fact-Checking and Research

There are many sources for facts in the world, many of which differ significantly from each other. Geopolitical issues are referred to in different ways depending on the local standpoint, for example. These phenomena influence large parts of a product such as *Encarta Encyclopedia*, which necessitates extensive fact-checking throughout the editorial effort. The goal, from the outset, was that the product should represent the generally accepted view of the locale that would be found in the most widely accepted reference material. In numerous instances, editors performed additional research to gather information that could not be translated in a straightforward manner. A good example is the way in which titles of movies and books are referenced in a German encyclopedia, where the title of the original work is given along with the local title. As the local title is only rarely a literal translation of the original, research was needed to identify the correct translation: the Spielberg film *Saving Private Ryan* is entitled *Der Soldat James Ryan* in German ("the soldier James Ryan"), for instance.

Tailoring Content to Locale

Areas of high cultural sensitivity required specific attention by the editorial team. A certain fact or name used in one language and locale may be inappropriate or even insulting in another. Geopolitical issues are particularly sensitive due to their close relation to a nation's or people's history and sense of identity.

Additional coverage of content areas sometimes required additional media work. The introduction of the euro was deemed so important in Europe that a link in the Timeline had to be added in the German product, to cite one example:

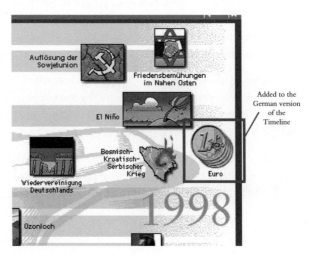

A typical case of differing geopolitical perspectives comes from the Spanish *Encarta Encyclopedia*. Although the headword "Falkland Islands" is used in English-speaking locales and is acceptable in the US, it cannot be used in the Spanish product due to its unacceptability in Argentina where the product is sold. The Spanish product refers to the island group as "Islas Malvinas."

The same principle applies to disputed geographical areas such as borders, where it is often necessary to consult numerous subject-matter experts and even governmental institutions in the target countries. Historical events are another major source of problems, as different cultures will often have varying viewpoints on methods of classifying "reality."

Depending on the target market, adaptation of wording is sufficient in some cases. In others, completely new articles must be created, resulting in new content relationships. This approach effectively leads to a new hyperspace of content relationships specific to the locale. The content that the user reads is different, and the approach to linking and associating content entities is redefined.

An example of this challenge is the case of German reunification. Although the US version of the product covers the topic in several articles, it does not exist as a separate headword. Given the importance of the topic to Germans, a separate headword was created that added substantial information about the political situation leading to reunification. This included videos and a new map of the occupation zones following the Second World War as a result of the Potsdam Conference.

Screenshot of German-Adapted Content

Another example is Bovine Spongiform Encephalopathy (BSE), or mad-cow disease. The scientists who discovered it, Hans-Gerhard Creutzfeldt and Alfons Jakob, are German and their biographies are separate headwords in the German version. Creutzfeldt and Jakob were considered sufficiently covered under one headword in the BSE article of the US product.

Here are some additional changes made in the German version:

- Due to fundamental differences between US common law and German civil law, most law articles were replaced and several new headwords added. Examples include: Role of Jury, Role of Leading Cases, Role of Cross-Examination.

- German sign-language conventions differ from US standards. The relevant media element had to be completely modified, as illustrated below:

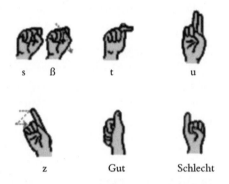

- Because of the extremely sensitive nature of articles on National Socialism and Adolf Hitler, related content had to be heavily adapted to the German market. Special attention was given to the latest research and current discussion in Europe and Germany. Given the critical nature of this period of German history, articles had to added due to their significance to the locale. Examples include: *Arbeitsdienst* (forced labor), *Arier* (Arian), *Bücherverbrennung* (book burning), *Dolchstoßlegende* (the belief that the German army of World War I had been "stabbed in the back" by the nation's civilians), *Entnazifizierung* (denazification), *Ermächtigungsgesetz* (Enabling Act), Roland Freisler, *Gleichschaltung* (nazification), *Hitler-Stalin-Pakt*.

For the German user, the depth of the original US articles concerning National Socialism was insufficient (background, connections, developments, ideology, etc.). By contrast, articles on American history (biographies, events like the American Civil War) were too detailed. Editorial changes needed to reflect the needs of the locale with an extremely thorough review process to avoid the slightest ambiguity in articles covering such topics.

- In the subject area of Biology, several locale-specific animals had to be added. Examples include: Black-Throated Jay, Common Otter, Grass Frog, Greyleg Goose, Common Viper.

CONCLUSION

Globalizing a multimedia product with over 30,000 articles and 10 million words presented challenges in project management and cultural adaptation that were new to the parties involved, as well as to the language industry in general. In a sense, the project itself entailed the adaptation of the language vendor's process and corporate culture, in order to deal with the highly topical content produced under tight deadlines. In the end, the product on which we collaborated and innovated would itself play a role in educating people around the world on issues of history, science, and culture—an accomplishment which we could all find satisfying and fulfilling.

Note: Images from Encarta Encyclopedia *are* © *Microsoft Corporation.*

Adapting Time Magazine for Latin America

Robert C. Sprung
Harvard Translations, Inc.

Alberto Vourvoulias-Bush
Time Latin America

OVERVIEW

This case study examines *Time* magazine's first foray in a foreign language—a weekly news supplement in Spanish and Portuguese for Latin America.

We explore the business decisions behind the move, and outline the innovations employed by Time, Inc. and its language partner, Harvard Translations. The challenge was unique for these reasons:

- Time hoped to preserve its signature style in the foreign-language copy, and not merely provide an accurate translation.

- Harvard Translations needed to provide a robust, scalable work process, converting 10,000 words every week into Spanish and Portuguese in little over 48 hours.

- The tight timeframe required novel application of technology, with remote access to sophisticated publishing software and electronic download of final pages by Time's Latin-American partners.

This collaboration—which has produced over 75 weekly issues to date—is a success story that yields intriguing and profitable insights for clients or language-service providers, both within the publishing sector and beyond.

THE MARKET OPPORTUNITY

Purveyors of information—whether print-, broadcast-, or Web-based—are going global no less than their brothers who hawk hard goods. Some have broadened international distribution by expanding English-language readership: *The Economist* and *The International Herald Tribune* have long been staples for innocents abroad and for natives wishing a distinctive global perspective. What is new is the intensity with which the major media are going multilingual. *Reader's Digest* publishes in many languages, *National Geo-*

graphic has just launched a French edition, and translated Web sites for major publications are gaining momentum.

With the US newspaper market sluggish, Latin America presents particularly fertile ground for international publications, according to a recent feature in *The New York Times*. *Newsweek, Glamour, Discover, People*, and *Rolling Stone* are now available in Spanish or Portuguese, cashing in on a thirst for their distinctive US spin. Says *Fortune* magazine's Gary Neeleman, "People in Ecuador want to read about Bill Gates."[1] Each *Reader's Digest* reached 600,000 Brazilian readers in 1998, with 1.7 million reading the publication in Spanish and Portuguese; *Glamour en español* now sells 500,000 copies.

The Wall Street Journal chose a publication vehicle that would ultimately be chosen by *Time* as well: a newspaper supplement in local newspapers. The *Journal*'s Portuguese supplement has appeared since 1997, and its Spanish version, which reaches 2.2 million, since 1994. The investment in Spanish and Portuguese is particularly efficient: "It is the only region in the world we can cover entirely in two languages," says Hugh Wiley, president of Time's Latin-America division.[2]

Time Warner is no stranger to multilingual publishing: it offers *People en español*, *Fortune* appears as a Spanish and Portuguese newspaper supplement, and CNN broadcasts in Spanish (with an associated Web site). *Time* magazine itself has long had local editions in Asia, Europe, and Latin America. These English-language publications offer differing editorial content and balance, while preserving the magazine's "look-and-feel." Cautious about potential impact on its flagship magazine, the company decided to "walk before it ran," and adopted the supplement approach, partnering with leading newspapers throughout Latin America. Time would supply content— final pages in the local language—while the partner would provide the printing and distribution. The partners would share responsibility for ad sales. Time's partner network includes:

Ambito Financiero	Argentina
Folha de São Paulo	Brazil
Reforma/El Norte	Mexico
El Tiempo	Colombia
La Tercera	Chile
El Nacional	Venezuela
El Comercio	Ecuador

1. "American Publishers Add Readers in Booming Latin America," *The New York Times*, May 11, 1998, first business page.
2. Ibid.

El Diario de Hoy	El Salvador
Gestión	Peru
Listín Diario	Dominican Republic
Siglo XXI	Guatemala
La Prensa	Panama

Sample Supplement Covers in Spanish and Portuguese

CHALLENGES AND SOLUTIONS

Marketing Challenges

Time's local-language supplement is managed by Time Latin America, a division of Time, Inc. based in New York's Time & Life Building. Hugh Wiley, president of the division, is responsible for overall business and marketing decisions for the supplement. George Russell, editor of the English-language Latin-American edition, oversees content and production of the local-language supplement. Alberto Vourvoulias-Bush, a published author and former college professor originally from Guatemala, directs the supplement's day-to-day operations in Spanish and Portuguese.

The personal involvement of these decision-makers illustrates the importance Time gave the local-language supplement from the start. They decided not only on the overall direction and positioning of the supplement, but also on editorial content and its translation into Spanish and Portuguese. This contrasts markedly with many publications where translation is perceived as a more mechanical or even secretarial endeavor.

Once the decision was made to bring *Time* to Latin America in local languages, the first challenge was in designing a publication. Each week, Russell and Vourvoulias-Bush select articles to be translated from the story list of Time's Latin-American edition. These stories are then re-edited, due to the different size and format of the Spanish and Portuguese publications. The story selection reflects the magazine's commitment to covering Latin America and the week's top world and US news stories. Care is also taken to preserve the balance of topics characteristic of *Time* and to appeal to a broad range of readers with varied interests. Included in each issue are articles on business, discoveries in science and medicine, and trends in culture and the arts. Through feedback from its newspaper partners in Latin America, in fact, Time learned that readers were particularly keen on the Time's perspective on social and cultural trends in addition to relying on it for more traditional news stories.

In an age of information overload on cable television and the Internet, Time's most valuable asset was its analysis and distinctive attitude. Diluting or losing these in translation could impair the company's global brand and core product. In an increasingly competitive global market for information, having an edge through superior story selection, content, and style, was considered to be worth the investment.

The Belly of the Beast

Time first sought a translation source. Given the need to assemble a team of a dozen linguists and project managers working within a tight timeframe, Time opted for a translation company rather than freelancers.

Finding linguists who could respectably convert movie reviews by Richard Corliss or book reviews by John Skow into idiomatic Spanish or Portuguese was a tall order. Consider the inherent difficulties in recasting these sample English passages in a foreign language. One such article would be enough to test a seasoned translator. Translating 10,000 words, with an unpredictable mix of subject matter and style, would prove a daunting linguistic hurdle:

> *Who or what owns a public life? Surely not, in an age of celebrity babble, the public person who lives it. And not some over-delicate concept of historical truth.*
>
> *A distinctly sleazy case in point is The Rich Man's Table, an expertly written novel by Scott Spencer, that rips off the life of Bob Dylan. Most readers will recall that Dylan was a scraggly haired harmonica player with an edgy voice and an edgy mind, a Jewish kid from Minnesota who changed his name from, let's see, Zimmerman? The character who dominates Spencer's novel was born Stuart Kramer, transformed himself as "Luke Fairchild," and came from "the Midwest," not specifically from Minnesota. Otherwise, the fit is exact.*

The translator who insists on finding the right translation for "let's see" is doomed from the start. In the memorable guideline of editor Alberto Vourvoulias, "Let the translation sparkle where it wants to sparkle." This might entail recasting a hip, staccato syntax into a periodic style more appropriate to Spanish, or leaving out altogether English quips or catch-phrases that would deflate upon translation.

Especially challenging were passages where you could hear America singing. Latin partners expressly wanted the latest perspectives from the States, and the localized version was not to dilute or "dumb down" the original text, which often brimmed with Yankee sound and fury:

> *You're driving from the office, the fuel tank is nearing empty, and so is your refrigerator at home. For Americans ravenous of appetite but starved of time (and in need of an oil change), a quick turn into the Chevron station off Interstate 680 in San Ramon, Calif., is the answer. That's right, Chevron, purveyor of premium gasoline, is serving fresh panini, three-cheese pesto and double espressos along with its usual selection of octanes.*

Or consider these verbal pyrotechnics on consumerism in the US:

And now for a moment of alarmism: imagine a high-school geometry class getting started in Anywhere, USA, sometime in the pre-asteroidal future. Students, outfitted in mandatory Nike uniforms and sluggish from lunch at the Pizza Hut-only cafeteria, lumber into a classroom where the teacher bears a disconcerting resemblance to the Nissan man. He begins his lesson, using a Dorito, one of the school's now required visual aides, to try and explain the Pythagorean theorem.

Or this hip review:

But the largest fun lies in the other characters: jut-jawed Kent Mansley, the funny-dumb government agent who has bought into the whole duck-and-cover thing; Dean the beatnik junk sculptor whose cool helps thwart Kent's heat; Hogarth's mother, an old-fashioned, benignly clueless sit-com mom.

The linguistic dilemma: the more fluent a native Spanish or Portuguese translator, typically the less grounded he or she is in the network of idioms and associations of the source text. More concretely: the translator who can write the equivalent of "benignly clueless sit-com mom" in Spanish probably wouldn't quite get it in English.

Or consider these "winners and losers"—quick "thumbs-up" or "thumbs-down" to people in the news. Many references require explanation for non-English speakers, yet the layout allows no text expansion. Translators would thus need a serviceable telegraphic style for this type of piece. The first example features two basketball players charged with sexual harassment (they played for the Washington Wizards; the untranslatable headline is rendered in Spanish as "crying foul"); the second spotlights a judge in the Clinton case.

WAYWARD WIZARDS
Chris Webber and Juwan Howard investigated; this pair needs more focus, fewer fouls

MARCANDO FALTA
Os jogadores de basquete Chris Webber e Juwan Howard são acusados de assédio sexual

NORMA HOLLOWAY JOHNSON
Exec-privilege judge insists on keeping hearings closed.

Jueza en el caso Clinton insiste en audiencias a puerta cerrada.

JON AMOS

Through sheer will—and wheel—power, disabled British athlete sets world endurance record	*Voluntad de hierro: el atleta británico en silla de ruedas marcó récord mundial de resistencia*

OLIVER STONE

Busted! Stone-d director agrees to enter rehab to avoid jail time in drugs-and-drink case	*¡Deténgase! Director acude a rehabilitación para evitar encarcelamiento por consumo de drogas y alcohol*

Headlines offered a special challenge. Many publications have separate headline writers, and for good reason. The best ones are masters of word-play and allusion—crossword aficionados with a poetic touch. *Time*'s original headlines are often untranslatable; a "faithful" translation would yield gibberish or unsightly copy given the page's geometry. The New-York team of copywriters would thus style fresh headline for the translated piece. These actual headlines illustrate the problem:

> *The Man Who Would be King Kong* (a piece on Serbian strongman Milosevic, in a multiple allusion to Kipling and a gorilla).

> *Not Fonda Georgia, Jane?* (a short on Jane Fonda's comparison of US state Georgia to a third-world country; the piece ended by mentioning her apology, followed by the equally untranslatable parting shot: "Peachy").

> *Read My Zipped Lips* (a blurb on George W. Bush's silence on whether he took cocaine as a youth, weaving in an allusion to his father's signature "read my lips"—a close translation would be laughable).

Converting the Text

After extensive testing of some dozen vendors, Time chose Cambridge, Massachusetts-based Harvard Translations, Inc. as its translation supplier.

HT assembled a team of language experts and project managers. It was hard enough finding an individual translator to convert a Corliss review into Portuguese. The broader problem rested in finding a team of linguists who could translate *quickly and consistently* over time. Technical translators—those who might excel at medical or computer manuals—only very rarely can double as literary translators who can recreate an author's voice in a foreign language. But technical translators are the ones used to delivering high volumes on tight deadlines. Literary translators typically work on books, often with several months to create a first draft.

Further complicating the issue was the breadth and variety of stories. A Corliss or Skow review required a translator with an ear for the music of language who was also well versed in current English usage. But these literary pieces made up a small albeit critical part of the publication. A given issue would feature longer pieces on politics, economics, or science. Sample cover stories included: money laundering, e-commerce, Latin music, biodiversity, gun control, the shroud of Turin, and Sinatra. And breaking news would routinely provide a last-minute shift in subject matter.

Given the nature of the news business and editorial process (*Time* often goes down to the wire late on Saturday), HT never knows the exact content each week until it receives materials a mere 48 hours before they are due. One week might feature a technical piece on medicine, while the next might have an equally technical piece on monetary policy.

HT found it optimal to recruit and train a rotating team of some eight linguists, with a range of technical expertise and writing styles. But they all had to exhibit certain baseline skills, including:

• ability to work reliably under intense time pressure

• several areas of specialization (one team member, for example, is a medical doctor with a degree in literature and strong interest in classical music)

• strong research skills, with the ability to quickly scan sources like the Web for terminology, but with the intelligence to evaluate the reliability of such sources

• strong fluency in English, with a keen ear for idiom

• a professional, fluid style in the target language, with a penchant for brevity.

A brief aside on the topic of "text expansion." Most who have dealt with translation tell you to prepare for translated text to expand as much as 20 or 30 percent when making the journey from English. There are a variety of reasons for this, including:

• *The explicative nature of translation.* Translators do not translate words, they translate ideas. With a culture-bound text like *Time,* much of the translator's task rests in *explaining or repackaging* the message for a new audience. There might be no easy Spanish equivalent for "mosh pit"; an effective translation might require a half-dozen Spanish words to get the point across.

- *The syntax of Romance languages.* English noun strings ("defense department spokesman") require prepositional phrases in most Romance languages ("the spokesman for the department of defense").

- *Translator sloth or greed.* Many translators go for the path of least resistance: it is easier to write more words than fewer. Technical translators (unlike many of their literary counterparts) are typically paid by the word, which further incentivizes verbosity. "Due to the fact that" garners 50 cents; "because" will only get you a dime.

While we originally budgeted for text expansion of 15 percent, we found that translations did not have to be much longer than their English counterparts. The actual expansion factor would depend on the nature of the text to be translated. Omitting any technical detail on a medical or political piece is unacceptable, and greater expansion is inevitable. Translators have greater liberty with a cultural piece—preserving every Corliss alliteration or allusion would produce a stilted or incomprehensible version in Spanish. Movie or book reviews could often occupy the same amount of space as the English original.

Brevity was critical to preserving *Time's* voice. Translators working under pressure, without the luxury of putting their work aside and reviewing it another day, would require a steep learning curve to "pre-edit" their own translations and omit needless words.

Harvard Translations put each article through three processes:

- *Translation* by a subject-specialized language professional (the week when the shroud of Turin appeared on the cover, the lead translator happened to have a degree in religious studies; it didn't always work so smoothly).

- *Editing* by a second native speaker. This entailed a close review of the text against the original.

- *Mechanical review* by a linguist to verify completeness of text and accuracy of names and numbers. This stage also provides feedback on the quality of the prior two stages.

HT developed detailed style guides and glossaries of key terms to heighten consistency. We also assembled a library of standard journalistic reference works (such as the official style guide of the *Folha de São Paulo, Time's* partner in Brazil). Our custom project style guide, which was available electronically and totaled some 20 pages, included sample translations and common pitfalls. Here are a few samples:

- North America Free Trade Agreement (NAFTA) is translated as Tratado de Libre Comercio (TLC).

- "American" is "norteamericano"; use "estadounidense" for variety.

- The symbol for ordinal numbers (1st, 2nd, etc.) in Spanish and Portuguese must be consistent. On a Mac, type option-9/0 for underlined superscript "a"/"o". Do not use the degree symbol (°).

HT developed a standardized translation process with these features:

- *Documented procedures*, in compliance with the company's ISO quality systems; these include a paper trail of who did what at each stage of the project. In a given week, there might be 30 project components (15 pieces in two languages); since each goes through five or more linguistic or administrative actions, 150 discrete actions must be monitored and managed.

- *Regular feedback loops* to all project team members, including formal project recaps with suggestions for improvement.

- *A proprietary project-management system* that tracks and invoices projects.

Some key lessons we learned from the translation:

- It proved critical to have an English native speaker present at all times; when there was a breaking news story, even the most savvy translator could misinterpret a trendy turn of phrase.

- A translator's apparent subject specialization was no guarantee of quality. We found a number of candidates with degrees in the sciences who would make basic translation errors, or who would provide literal or even inaccurate translations of key technical terms. Seasoned technical translators with subject specialization are much more successful than technical experts who are new to translation.

- Excellence on translation tests is no guarantee of future performance. Those who emerged as star translators did not necessarily appear so at first. Commitment and a strong work ethic proved as important as linguistic skills—late-night and Sunday work were the norm, and a "nine-to-five" attitude would have spelled disaster.

Polishing the Text

After receiving translated copy from Harvard Translations, Time has little over 24 hours to do the following:

- proof the copy

- make corrections to the text where last-minute changes modified the original article after it was sent for translation

- fact-check questions raised in translation

- polish the copy

- edit the articles to fit their redesigned layouts

- write headlines and photo captions

- process the pages

- post them for transmission to Latin America.

The key to making the process work, under these extreme time constraints, is editorial teamwork. There are two in-house editors per language. Each must be fluent (linguistically and culturally) in both English and either Spanish or Portuguese. Working together with the top editor, they share duties for all aspects of the editorial process, from research and fact-checking to copy-editing and proofreading the final pages.

Logistical and Technical Challenges

The graphics below illustrate the overall project timeline each week, along with the roles of key players.

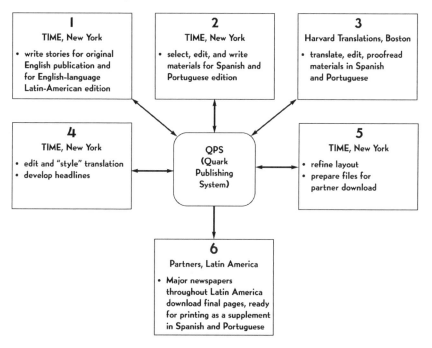

Who	What	When
Time	sends text to Boston	Saturday midnight
HT	delivers translated, edited text to NYC	Monday morning
Time	"style" copy, writes headlines, finalizes graphics and layout	Tuesday evening
Partners in Latin America	can download PDF (Acrobat) files of final pages	Tuesday evening

HT used technology that proved invaluable, notably its proprietary project-management system. Time provided other key technology, without which rapid turnaround would have been impossible. Key components were a high-speed data network linking all parties, and Quark Publishing System software (QPS). QPS includes QuarkXpress, the popular desktop-publishing and layout application, but is customized for a publishing environment. QPS was largely developed for Time, Inc., and it serves as the workhorse for *Time* magazine (other large publications, including *Reader's Digest,* use it as well). It has all the features of QuarkXpress, with these key additions:

- The key working unit of text is the story. Stories can be a long feature, or even a word or phrase (e.g., an individual photo caption or story byline). Anything that needs to be tracked separately may be defined as a story (the person writing the caption or headline may be different from the person writing the article).

- QPS is a networked application, with identified users granted access levels and passwords. One access level might permit the user to erase a file or change access levels, for example.

- Stories go through a customizable cycle, and could be routed in this sequence, for example: writer -> editor -> translator -> proofreader. No two people can work on the same story simultaneously; stories are checked in and out, as in a library.

- The system is real-time: the most recent version checked in by an author can be viewed immediately by anyone with suitable access.

- QPS has a galley view, which allows the author to see plain text (as in a word-processor), with tools to control word- and line-count. The system also has an annotation feature; anyone in the process can add queries or comments. Annotation also lets editors squirrel away extra text, in case a story later runs short. A redline feature retains every past version of a story (i.e., its final state after every action is completed). This ensures a virtual paper trail (who changed what and when), and allows comparison between any two versions. (A paper trail has become critical in journalism, given the potential for lawsuits.)

- A page-layout view allows the author to see the story in graphical context at any time. Since images belong to the layout and not individual text stories, designers can work on graphics while the author writes or edits. Further, there is no danger that an author can alter graphic content.

The high-speed network meant that anyone with access to QPS could work in the same "virtual office." This allowed instant transfer of files between Time and translators. It also allows projects with intense deadline pressure to take advantage of time differences around the world, if a global team were assembled.

Time's New York office also used Quark Passport, a variant of QuarkXpress that includes hyphenation for a number of foreign languages. None of these electronic hyphenators is foolproof; further, Time has particularly high aesthetic standards when it comes to line breaks—no machine can replace the eye of a copy editor.

EVALUATING THE RESULTS

Time has been producing its weekly Spanish and Portuguese supplement for over a year and a half.

From a business perspective, the venture is a major success. Readership is climbing, with a number of major new newspapers in Latin America signing up as partners (this is a major vote of confidence on their part, as they must invest in the production and also sell a substantial part of the local-market advertising). Readership currently totals 1,347,000 per week.

To determine the level of acceptance of the supplement, Time hired an independent third party to conduct a reader survey. Based on 2,000 completed questionnaires, the research firm found:

- 86 percent of the newspaper subscribers saw or read the supplement. Of those, 48 percent read it every week or almost every week.

- 86 percent feel the supplement is a very valuable or somewhat valuable addition to the newspaper.

- 40 percent spend nearly 30 minutes reading the supplement.

- 25 percent spend 30–60 minutes reading the supplement.

- 44 percent read all or nearly all of the supplement.

- 36 percent read between half and three quarters of the supplement.

- The supplement had good pass-through readership, with each copy reaching an average of three readers.

Time has positioned the foreign-language supplement as part of a larger program for Latin America. Consider the following synergies on a recent campaign:

- Time's Latin-American *English-language edition* features a series on "Leaders for the New Millennium," which focuses on 30- and 40-somethings who will shape Latin America in the coming years.

- *The supplement* offers Spanish and Portuguese versions of the feature, bringing it to over a million additional readers.

- *CNN en español* produces television programs featuring leaders profiled in the series.

- *CNN and Time* reinforce the Leaders campaign with local-language Web pages.

Time has been able to sell this package to corporate sponsors such as Compaq, BellAtlantic, and Mastercard—one-stop shopping for reaching a broad segment of the Latin-American market. In the survey referenced above, 93 percent of respondents agreed with the statement, "I would like to see other editorial initiatives similar to Leaders in the future."

The screenshots below come from a full-color and sound CD-Rom demo that introduces the Leaders feature. The first screen shows the cover of the Latin-American edition. Upper right is the supplement in Spanish, and below it is a video clip from *CNN en español*. Note that corporate sponsors also appear in this demo CD.

From the perspective of Harvard Translations, Time's language vendor, the program has been a major success as well. Our contract has recently been renewed, and we see the relationship as a model for a collaborative relationship. In an industry where the typical question asked of translators is, "how much do you charge per word," it is immensely gratifying to work on a project where quality matters—and the client knows the difference.

It is only fitting to end with a word of thanks to the many team members that make the project a success week in, week out. Far from shrinking at the latest twist of fate that will determine this week's cover story—and their weekend schedule—these linguistic gymnasts seem to thrive on it. The team is also proud that, in their own way, they are helping bring news and insight to an engaged audience around the world.

Globalizing an e-Commerce Web Site

Susan Cheng
Idiom Technologies

INTRODUCTION

Enabling a sophisticated corporate or e-commerce Web site to be multilingual and multiregional is a complex and subtle undertaking. A Web site is technology-based and interactive, with text continually changing. Standard approaches to translating text and software are inadequate for this new information vehicle.

This case study profiles the globalization of a dynamic Web site, from conception to implementation. We showcase an e-commerce site that was adapted from English into Japanese, crossing numerous linguistic, cultural, and technical hurdles in the process. We also profile new language technologies and processes tailored to the World Wide Web.

WEB-SITE OVERVIEW

chipshot.com is a midsize e-commerce site that sells custom-made golf clubs via the Internet. First published in 1996, the site is marketed as "the Internet's largest retailer of custom-built golf equipment." Some basic facts about chipshot.com include:

- It features standard e-commerce site layout, including a common navigation bar and multiple product listings.

- Content is displayed within a template.

- The entire site is based on proprietary, noncommercial design and infrastructure.

- Product names and prices are pulled from a live SQL database.

- Content text is updated or added daily (e.g., product names, product descriptions).

- Functional features are updated or added weekly (e.g., a gift-certificate suggestion center).

Given golf's popularity in Japan, Chipshot recognized the opportunity to expand sales there by making chipshot.com fully functional in Japanese.

PROJECT EVALUATION

The project of globalizing chipshot.com for Japanese viewers was evaluated according to: 1) the front end (what the user sees); 2) the back end (the technology and processes behind the scenes); and 3) long-term Web-site development. The table below summarizes the goals identified for chipshot.com globalization:

Front End	**Linguistic**	translated text and graphics
		converted/formatted prices and dates
	Cultural/Marketing	consistent look-and-feel
		brand promoted for target country
		well-advertised site
Back End	**Technical**	foreign text correctly displayed
		character encoding issues addressed
	Managerial	translation integrated with development
		sites synchronized on ongoing basis
Long Term		changing functional features
		future Web-site needs

Front End

Chipshot outlined a set of goals for how a globalized chipshot.com would look, feel, and function in Japan. The existing site design was reviewed to identify front-end initiatives that would make the site a viable revenue-generating site in this new market.

Linguistic

A Japanese chipshot.com needs to contain translations and cultural adaptations of the English site's textual content, including introductory remarks on the home page and components of the navigation bar. Given the commercial nature of the site, language and presentation were critical. Almost all text and graphics would be translated in a culturally targeted way that reinforced the site's marketing message and merchandising functions.

Globalizing the core shopping features required that product prices be displayed in yen with current currency conversions. Prices on the Japanese site would be converted directly from US-dollar counterparts on the English-language site. Instead of presetting the conversion rate, Chipshot decided to pull it from a live source.

Cultural/Marketing

It was important to balance two potentially competing considerations: the site should be culturally appropriate for Japan, but at the same time should have a look-and-feel consistent with the English site. Colors, images, and page-by-page format should be the same, to the greatest extent possible. Chipshot marketing executives aimed to preserve a consistent visual and functional format to promote brand awareness and to foster general visitor familiarity and comfort during page navigation. However, recognizing that the browser standard for presenting Asian-language Web-site material may change in the future (e.g., Asian characters may be displayed vertically instead of horizontally), the company wanted to retain the flexibility of changing page-by-page formatting of the Japanese site.

Chipshot decided not to translate certain product names, product descriptions, and marketing slogans, as these were recognized to have particular American appeal to Japanese golf customers. The same reasoning was applied to the site's "Ask the Expert" section, which contains direct quotes from US golf professionals regarding golfing tips and Chipshot's products. Recognizing that further market research might indicate a need for translating more of the site, Chipshot wanted to have the option of adapting these resources in Japanese at a later time.

Back End

The existing site infrastructure was analyzed to determine what would be required to achieve *full* globalization. Chipshot engineers then decided which alterations they could accommodate without compromising the quality and functionality of the original English-language site.

Technical

Initially, the most challenging back-end issue was the foreign-language text. It quickly became clear to Chipshot engineers that correctly displaying Asian-language text would require experience with character-encoding issues and double-byte characters. Further, the engineers recognized the difficulties associated with embedding Japanese characters in HTML, programs, templates, and scripts underlying the existing site. Many sections of the site required that Japanese text be stored in and recalled from databases. Achieving full technical functionality and presentational accuracy for the

Japanese site, it soon became clear, would require Japanese-speaking programmers or an outside vendor for this portion of project.

Managerial

The project offered significant managerial issues, in addition to purely technical challenges. The initial globalization would require coordinating the work of Chipshot's Web developers and site designers with outside translators and editors. Textual changes, such as product-catalog additions and price updates, were being made to the English site on a regular basis, and these would need to be reflected in the Japanese site in a timely manner. Managing globalization would thus be an ongoing effort, in order to ensure that both native-language and foreign-language sites would always be synchronized.

Long-Term Development

Chipshot anticipated that changes to the site would involve not only textual content but also functional features. A functional feature is an element of a Web site that serves the viewer in an interactive way, often delivering custom content to a particular visitor to the site. Prominent functional features on the site include:

Shopping System. This feature allows customers to add products to an electronic shopping cart and subsequently purchase all shopping-cart items via credit-card or customer-account number through a secure connection.

Golf Club Configurator. The "Perfect Fit" feature allows customers to submit specific information, such as an individual's height and wrist size, for ordering custom clubs.

Order Tracking. Customers enter order numbers and track delivery status of purchases.

Gift Suggestion Center. Customers input information about a person for whom they wish to purchase a gift and then view a list of appropriate suggestions.

Account Accessing. Customers review their transaction history and modify account and billing information.

On chipshot.com, functional features are updated, added, or removed weekly. Since these modifications would be frequent and ongoing, the company opted for a maintenance-system approach to globalization. A *maintenance system*, as opposed to an *ad-hoc nonsystematic* approach, formalizes a process of streamlining and integrating all tasks required to globalize a Web site.

The Web-site classification framework below helps determine the most appropriate globalization approach. The more interactive and subject to change a site is, the more appropriate a maintenance system for globalization. The more static and unchanging a site, the more appropriate an ad-hoc, nonsystematic method.

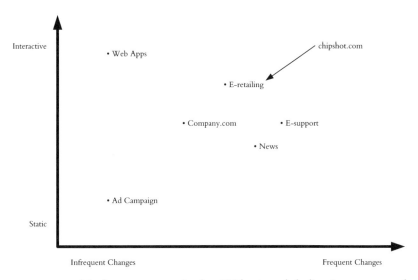

In summary, chipshot.com required a Web-site globalization system that would: 1) consistently deliver quality, up-to-date foreign-language versions of their Web site; and 2) flexibly mesh with their existing Web-site development and management process, even as changes to this process were being made.

OPTIONS

Chipshot considered the following in-house and outside vendor options for globalization:

Machine Translation. The first option was to combine readily available machine-translation and translation-memory tools with in-house Web-development resources. This would mean devoting at least one full-time in-house developer to effectively applying machine translation, and one full-time translation manager to supervise ongoing translation. While machine translation was potentially cost-effective, the company felt it could not rely on such language-automation tools alone to deliver a foreign-language site.

Translation Service Bureau. Another option was to combine in-house development resources with outside human translation services. Outsourcing only the translation necessary for the project would mean devoting significant in-house resources to manage the project and aid with implementation. Chipshot considered this option unfeasible given the company's limited in-house resources and lack of experience with a project of this nature.

Software-Localization Firm. Chipshot considered contracting with software-localization companies. However, the company found it difficult to locate a traditional localization house that could guarantee on-time delivery of a Japanese e-commerce site. The localization companies generally proposed to globalize the site by rebuilding it from scratch, and to incur substantial initial and maintenance costs in the process. For similar reasons, Chipshot ruled out Web-design and development companies.

Web-Site Globalization Company. Chipshot ultimately chose to work with Idiom Technologies, a company that offers technology and service products that enable delivery of end-to-end, integrated Web-site globalization.

Globalization Process

Idiom Technologies' globalization approach involved using WorldServer, a software-based system that facilitates the three main aspects of globalization: translation, workflow, and delivery. Globalization requires that: 1) site content is presented to translators in a way that allows for high-quality, in-context translation; 2) ongoing translation, editing, and validation of content are efficiently managed; and 3) translated content is properly published within a Web context and is delivered on time.

Chipshot selected WorldServer for two main benefits: reduced cost and quick time to implementation. WorldServer eliminates the need to build and manage a foreign-language site separately from the native-language site (i.e., it does not incur the cost of creating and maintaining parallel sites). WorldServer also minimizes the management issues typically involved in Web globalization through the use of integrated and automated workflow. As a result, management of one or many versions of a single site remains centralized and only one Web manager is required for initial and ongoing management of full-scale globalization.

Based on XML technology, WorldServer facilitates the extraction, distribution, and final synthesis of Web content during translation. WorldServer implementation involved leveraging Chipshot's existing Web-site infrastructure while separating globalization issues from the company's regular Web development.

Model Architecture

The WorldServer system includes three main components

WorldTags. These XML tags are added to the original-language Web site at the HTML level to identify all content in need of translation. These directives are also used to specify content for different target languages and countries.

WorldManager. This integrated globalization environment is used by translators, content editors, and site managers. A key component of WorldManager is the Translation Center, the module used by those involved in translating textual elements. Site managers use WorldManager to identify content in need of translation and then monitor the distribution and collection of translation tasks. WorldManager is also used by site managers to review and approve all content for publishing on multiple-language versions of a global site.

WorldPublisher. WorldTags embedded within the original-language site speak to this production server that stores translations and works with existing Web servers to deliver a global Web site.

When a foreign-language user requests a Web page from the original Web server, WorldTags and WorldPublisher together synthesize a coherent foreign-language version of the page. The new version, delivered in real time, is comprised of content (i.e., text and graphics) previously translated and stored in a *translation database.*

WorldServer simplifies the challenge of supporting double-byte characters to correctly display Japanese text. The infrastructure software supporting chipshot.com, like most commonly used Web-site authoring tools, does not support non-ASCII text on its own. Without WorldServer, all hard-coded strings of text embedded in HTML and scripts would have to be moved into a resource database before being translated. Without this new technology, locating Japanese-translated content within the original site would require extensively rewriting scripts and other code.

WorldServer lets Chipshot sidestep these iterative and QA-intensive processes. Within a unified workflow system, WorldServer can support multibyte encoding standards including ucs2, utf-8, and other Unicode standards, and display Asian text using formats such as Shift-JIS, Big5, and GB.

Process

Web globalization often involves multiple translators, editors, local-content authors, developers, and designers—ideally coordinated by an experienced Web manager. Globalization has a cyclic workflow that should consist of a few basic, repeatable actions:

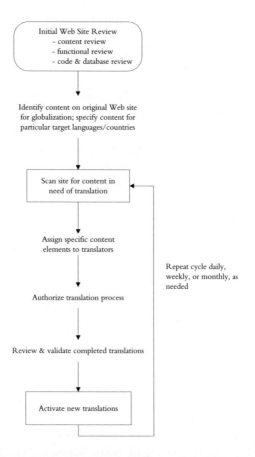

Initial globalization took approximately three weeks. This was the total time required to have the site fully functioning and running live as an electronic retailing site in Japanese. A breakdown of the initial globalization by time and staff resources is shown below.

Task	Human Resources	Time Required
Identify text and graphics in need of translation	1 project manager (using WorldTags)	16 hours (2 days)
Scan site and assign identified content to translators	1 project manager (using WorldManager)	8 hours (1 day)
Translation and editing	2 translators (using WorldManager Translation Center)	128 hours (16 days: 8 days per translator)
Review and validation	1 project manager (using WorldManager)	16 hours (2 days)
	Total:	168 hours (21 days)

Preparing the Site

The project manager first identified translatable items using WorldTags. WorldTags also mark conditional content—items that should appear only in certain language versions of the site. For the initial globalization, Chipshot wanted only the main sections of the site translated, including the navigation bar and all instructions for online shopping.

WorldTags signal content for globalization

WorldTags also mark date and time information for correct display and formatting for Japan. For currencies, WorldTags marked currency for automatic conversion into yen, according to a live conversion-rate source. As WorldTags are HTML-compatible, they were embedded within HTML, CGI scripts, programs, and other WorldTags.

Scanning for Global Content

After marking the original code with WorldTags, the project manager used WorldManager to automatically scan the US site for all text and graphics that had not been previously translated. WorldManager identified items for translation by "crawling" the 25-page site in a logical fashion. Site content was automatically divided into individual translation items, each assigned a unique identifier. A single item could consist of a single graphic, a short string of text, a paragraph, or a whole page. During scanning, the project manager verified items in need of translation and then used WorldManager to store the items, preserve their contexts, record any associated comments, and feed everything to the Translation Center where translators could access it.

Translation

Two translators were assigned to translate the selected text and graphics and then edit each other's work. WorldManager's Translation Center displays newly assigned items, now called translation projects, within an organized interface. Translators were free from code; only text, graphics, and other pure content resources were shown, allowing them to focus on translation and not be distracted by HTML. The Translation Center hides HTML and other programming code from the user without actually separating code from context, preserving functional integrity.

Translators could view items in the context of the original Web page and then preview translated items within a new Web page. These features helped translators perform in-context translation and initiate quality control from the beginning of the process. The Translation Center also integrated and tracked all changes and comments made to a translation project.

A Translation Center interface where translators work with text in context, separately from HTML code

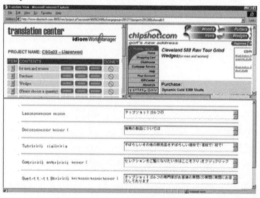

One translator chose to work online within the browser-based Translation Center interface shown above. Items for translation were separated from HTML and listed in the lower left, while translations were typed into text boxes in the lower right. The other translator chose to export and then import translation, working offline using preferred tools and processes; in this case the Translation Center was primarily used as a task-management and quality-control environment.

Appropriately tagged dates, times, and currencies were converted and formatted by WorldServer and automatically translated according to predefined formulas. This feature, also known as WorldServer Autoconvert, helped reduce the total time required to translate site content.

Translation and editing lasted approximately two weeks, including training in use of the new tool. After translation and editing, the Translation Center recorded approvals and forwarded translated content to the project manager for publishing.

Tracking and Validation

The project manager used WorldManager to track the progress of assigned translation projects and preview translated items in context. Once all translation projects had been completed and approved, the project manager conducted quality assurance. This involved reviewing and validating completed translations in Web-page context within WorldManager, from a browser pointed to the testing server.

Activating Translations

Finally, the project manager activated all validated portions of the newly translated content for publishing on the live global site. After the completed Japanese version was tested on the live server, it was connected to the English site via hyperlink. Below are the results of initial implementation.

A screen shot taken from the US-English chipshot.com home page after initial globalization

A screen shot taken from the Japanese chipshot.com home page after initial globalization

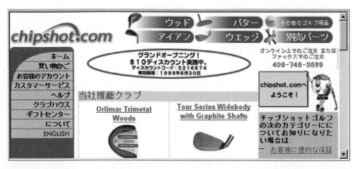

WorldManager allowed selection and control of basic content differences between the two versions. For example, site managers could specify that the Father's-Day promotion available to US-based customers be published only on the English site. A Japan-specific promotion was displayed on the Japanese site in its place. Also, recognizing the appeal of cartoon characters to Japanese customers, managers intentionally positioned Chipshot's "cartoon caddy" character more prominently on the Japanese site. A "free shipping" promotion, contests, and games available only to US customers were displayed only on the English site.

Managing Ongoing Globalization

As content or functionality is added or updated in the original-language site, the project manager uses WorldManager to detect and initiate globalization of changes for the Japanese version. The process of scanning for new or changed content, assigning items for translation, and then activating newly approved translations can be initiated as frequently as desired.

Since the English site was still the main draw and focus, Chipshot continued to make daily changes to the English site. An aggregation of these changes initially was propagated to the Japanese site approximately every two weeks, with the expectation that the revision cycle would be shortened once the marketing campaign for the Japanese site was under way.

During each synchronization or revision cycle, the project manager used WorldManager to identify new elements in need of translation into Japanese. As content was added to the original site, WorldManager registered these changes automatically and immediately prompted this content for translation the next time the project manager logged on to the system. After logging in to the Translation Center, translators received these elements as new assignments. The project manager tracked the status of assignments, validated completed assignments, and made translations go live on the Japanese site as appropriate. Here is a breakdown of the first resynchronization process (involving translation of 2,000 words), by time and staff resource:

Task	Human Resources	Time Required
Scan site and assign updated content to translators	1 project manager (using WorldManager)	1 hour
Translation and editing	1 translator (using WorldManager Translation Center)	8 hours
Review and validation	1 project manager (using management module)	1 hour
	Total: 10 hours	

COST BENEFITS

Chipshot's actual return on investment for the company's first globalization project has yet to be determined, as efforts to market the site in Japan have only just begun. However, a cost-benefit analysis is possible from an implementation standpoint.

Most other e-commerce sites that have globalized at all have employed a parallel-sites approach. These companies have built and managed foreign-language versions separately from the original native-language site. This requires manual propagation of changes during revision. Overall, the parallel-sites approach would have cost Chipshot, over a three-year period, approximately five times the resources spent to implement the maintenance system used for chipshot.com.

The estimated resource costs for initial and ongoing globalization of chipshot.com, using the parallel-sites approach, was estimated by Chipshot Web managers and developers during initial evaluation of the globalization project (see below).

Estimated work log for initial globalization

Task	Human Resources	Time Required
Reengineer database	1 developer & 1 translator	15 days
Rewrite scripts underlying Web site	1 developer & 1 translator	25 days
Extract text and graphics for translation	1 developer & 1 translator	5 days
Translation and editing	1 developer & 2 translators	20 days
Quality assurance	1 developer & 1 translator	20 days
	Total: 85 days	

Estimated work log for resynchronization

Task	Human Resources	Time Required
Identify text and graphics in need of translation	1 developer & 1 translator	1 day
Translation and editing	1 developer & 1 translator	3 days
Rebuild updated sections of Web site	1 developer & 1 translator	2 days
Quality assurance	1 developer & 1 translator	1 day
	Total:	7 days

The above estimates outline a parallel-site globalization using in-house staff throughout, except for translation. These estimates, we believe, are similar to those for a parallel-site approach that gives complete Web-site globalization responsibility to an outside vendor.

Next Steps

At the outset, Chipshot decided not to market its Japanese site in earnest until it had been running live and proved functionally successful over a three-month trial. At present writing, it has been one month since Chipshot began full-fledged marketing. The company plans to increase the frequency of revision cycles to keep product lines and site features on the Japanese site more continuously up-to-date with those on the English site.

The globalization of chipshot.com embodies the cutting-edge skills needed in communicating across cultural boundaries in the dynamic environment of the Web. Language professionals are not only required to prepare idiomatic and accurate translations of text that will appear on the Web; they must also, under the guidance of a targeted marketing strategy, tailor the message to fit the medium and purpose. Graphic designers must also provide the design framework to present this message in a culturally appropriate setting.

chipshot.com also shows how new tools are continually being developed to meet the intense language demands presented by the World Wide Web. The technology solution provided here allowed major cost and time savings, while minimizing technical difficulties inherent when multiple parties get involved in modifying a Web site.

The principles applied in globalizing this e-commerce site should help others in improving process in their own Web globalization. Given the dynamism of the Web, one can safely assume that new technologies and solutions will provide further enhancements in the years to come.

What Price Globalization?
Managing Costs at Microsoft

David Brooks
Microsoft Corporation

OVERVIEW

In fiscal 1998, over 60 percent of Microsoft's revenues came from markets outside of the United States. The majority of these revenues come from non-English-speaking markets, and a key component of Microsoft's international strategy has been to lead the industry in the delivery of localized products to these markets. In that same period, Microsoft's revenue from localized products exceeded US$5 billion. A mere five years ago, these figures were a fraction of what they are today, and as revenues have grown, so has Microsoft's investment in localization.

Localized Product Revenues at Microsoft (in Billions USD)

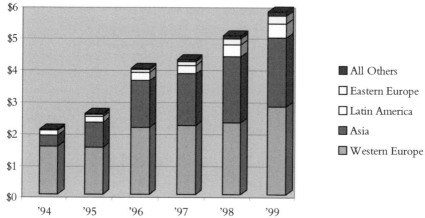

As Microsoft's product range and scope of localization grew, executives cringed at the rapidly rising cost of localization. Chairman Bill Gates characterized localization as "just a linguistic process" and expressed frustration over what appeared to him to be runaway cost increases. Worse yet, Microsoft's ability to ship localized products was being constrained: the company was having trouble delivering the breadth of localized products the market wanted and meeting customers' demands for prompt, simultaneous release of localized products.

THE PROBLEM

When Gates and Paul Maritz, then head of Microsoft's Platforms and Applications product-development group, began to look into localization in the early '90s, the situation was as follows:

- The company's ability to ship localized products was hampered by delays, bottlenecks inside and outside the company, technical barriers, and costs.

- More products and languages, combined with production bottlenecks, resulted in projects being prioritized into tiers, with the last tier delayed up to a year or more after the US product release.

- The Redmond, Washington product groups had nominal responsibility for localizing their products, but the problem fell mainly on the shoulders of the Microsoft teams in Ireland and Asia.

- With a few exceptions for secondary languages or products, most software was localized by Microsoft staff and outsourcing was limited to manuals and help files.

- Despite the lack of metrics, management believed the company's localization process was inefficient, expensive, and unable to meet market demands.

Under the sponsorship of Maritz, a campaign (or *jihad*, in Microsoft-speak) was launched to bring these problems under control. Maritz asked me to drive this initiative. I had joined his organization several years earlier as director of business operations, and had a background in management consulting and cost management. Needless to say, I faced a steep learning curve in grappling with Microsoft's localization problems.

My first step was to find knowledgeable people in the company's localization community. This led to a "localization summit" in the summer of 1994, which brought together senior localization people from around the company for two days of discussion.

Early in the game it became clear that localization is not really about translation—in fact, it is an extension of product development. Most people think "translation" when they think about localization. In a perfect world, localization would be, as Gates characterized it, "just a linguistic process," but the US-centric design of the US product, unpredictable changes in schedule, and logistical problems make localization a painful reengineering process. The chart below summarizes localization spending by discipline at the start of the *jihad*. Translation accounted for about a third of total spending, and there was a great deal of skepticism in Redmond regarding the remainder.

Globalization Spending at Microsoft by Discipline

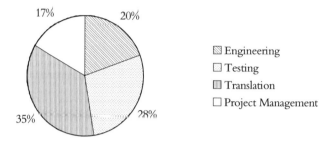

The summit resulted in a meeting with Gates later that year where a game plan for attacking localization costs was outlined. The plan was based on the following findings from the summer meeting:

- Localization is not just translation—in fact, the translation component is the more straightforward part of the job.

- The majority of localization effort goes into remedial engineering to enable the US product to work with foreign languages, and testing to assure nothing breaks during localization.

- The logistical aspects of localization—keeping track of individual files, managing changes, creating the "golden master"—require extensive project management.

- Changes in the development schedule of the US product wreak havoc on efforts to plan and execute localization projects.

- Localization costs are hard to capture; managing costs was not a priority, and there was little agreement on how to define or measure efficiency.

Maritz's Localization Directive

Maritz focused on the engineering aspects of localization, and the goals he set for the development groups reflected his assessment that US-centric design was the heart of the problem. He distilled this into a directive to the product-development teams:

- Globalize the US product so reengineering is not required during localization.

- Adopt a common set of localization tools and processes across the company.

- Reduce the level of technical skills required to localize products so that external vendors can execute many localizations in parallel.

- Maintain a single codebase across all localized versions of a single product to assure compatibility across languages.

We knew that the hardest task would be breaking through the US-centric mentality of the development community. The US is the most competitive and innovative software market in the world, and software engineers looked to the US trade press and competitive analyses as a report card on their work. Globalization and localizability were not major issues in the US, and in the minds of most developers, these chores were simply a distraction from the challenges of building new, compelling products. Nonetheless, we knew that achieving our goals required bandwidth from the development community dedicated to these issues.

Global Design

Prior to the *jihad* kickoff, localization was handled as an afterthought by downstream localization teams and vendors. Developers and engineers in the core (i.e., US) teams paid little attention to international issues, and their naïve view was that "localization equals translation." They were generally unaware of the biases and engineering limitations inherent in the US product they were building.

One example of engineering limitations is codepage support: all characters, numerals, punctuation marks, and other symbols commonly used in English (and many other Western European languages) fit on a single list of 256 characters (the codepage), each of which is addressed with one byte. Japanese uses thousands of symbols, thus the Japanese codepage numbers in the thousands and requires two bytes to enumerate each character. Thus, the protocol for addressing specific characters on the codepage must be a two-byte system (also referred to as double-byte encoding).

Codepage issues are pervasive, and double-byte enabling comprised the bulk of the Japanese localization teams' effort. Because so much source code required modification, extensive retesting was mandatory. As a result, Japanese products were shipped a year or more after the English release, and inconsistencies between the English and Japanese versions of the same product made it difficult to share files between Japanese and English users. Furthermore, there was very little available time and too few resources to add features and functions urgently needed by Japanese customers.

Maritz's directive meant building double-byte enabling into the US code, as well as adopting a variety of other practices to eliminate other engineering limitations that required reengineering prior to translation. Although this imposed a burden on US-based developers, it was obvious to Maritz that fixing the problem at the source would be a far more cost-effective and timely solution.

This initiative went under the heading of globalization, and encompassed all aspects of the development cycle, including tasks such as product-setup localization, build process, and test scenarios. Globalization was the corner-stone of the strategy to control costs, and to enable Microsoft to localize more products without a commensurate increase in staffing or costs.

Localizability

The problem proved more complex than we first thought. Even a well-glo-balized product can be difficult to localize: globalization only assures that a program can accommodate foreign-language data—it doesn't assure, for example, that nothing will break when the user-interface is translated. The majority of these problems are "simple, stupid" mistakes that should not occur in the first place, but that are almost unavoidable.

For example, a well-globalized product may fail when English commands are replaced with translated versions, because the number of spaces set aside in the code for the command (i.e., the size of the string buffer) may be insufficient to handle the translated command. These problems, which we record and report as bugs, require diagnosis and engineering to identify and solve. It is easy to automatically adjust the size of the string buffer to the size of the text, but hundreds of people may work on a piece of Microsoft soft-ware and it is inevitable that someone will forget to do this.

Another frustrating localizability problem is related to the use of hot keys. In many Microsoft products, users can change a text to bold by highlighting it and simultaneously pressing the "Alt" and the "B" keys. This makes intu-itive sense in English since "bold" begins with B, but this is not true for other languages. Localizing hot keys like this can be difficult: what do you do when there are several hot-key functions that begin with the same let-ter—change the name of one of the functions (and, of course, the help files, manual, and all other places where the function is referenced), use an arbi-trary key with no mnemonic value and force the user to learn another arbi-trary command, or simply eliminate the hot-key function?

Recognizing this class of problems was embarrassing, but resulted in devel-opment of tools and procedures to eliminate the problem at the source—i.e., in the core code. Core teams were asked to take direct ownership for German and Japanese localization in order to ferret out localization prob-lems, and developers around the company began building tools to find and eliminate localizability bugs by automatically translating user-interface (UI) elements into a worst-case "nonsense language" before shipment of the US product.

Localization Planning

The primary objective of localization is to meet consumer needs in international markets. Decisions about which products to localize, how extensively to localize them, and the delivery timeframe are driven by market considerations. We define market linguistically rather than geographically: the Spanish market is the aggregate of Spain, Mexico, Argentina, etc.—a total of 22 countries—not just Iberian Spain; "German" is similarly an aggregate of Germany, Austria, and part of Switzerland.

The primary criterion for assigning markets to categories is revenue from localized products. While there is an element of circular logic in using localized-product revenue as a basis for planning, our experience shows this is the best single indicator of sales potential. Other parameters, such as population, have little bearing on the software market, but to assess international markets we do look at the number of PCs sold into certain markets, growth rates in PC sales, and nonquantitative factors such as the degree of protection offered for intellectual property rights.

We use four major categories ("tiers") in the planning process:

- *Tier 1*. The largest international markets (Japanese, German, French) for which the majority of products are localized.

- *Tier 2*. Markets large enough to justify substantial investment in localization (Dutch, Korean, Brazilian Portuguese) but an order of magnitude smaller than Tier 1.

- *Tier 3*. Small but growing markets (Portuguese, Arabic, Hungarian) for which a subset of products with broad appeal is localized.

- *Tier 4*. Emerging markets of limited potential (Thai, Romanian, Vietnamese) for which only core products such as Windows are localized.

For planning purposes we group our products into categories that correspond to market segments—"desktop" products, such as Windows, Office, and Internet Explorer used by individuals for personal productivity; "business systems," such as NT Server and Exchange used by large organizations to run their operations; "development tools" used by engineers and developers to create software, etc.

Market tiers and product categories are arranged in a grid; based on the requirements of each tier and the product characteristics, we decide on the degree or level of localization. Localization levels, beginning with the lowest, are summarized below (each level is incremental, i.e., the localized product is both enabled and localized):

- *Enabled.* Users can compose documents in their own language, but the software user-interface and documentation remain in English.

- *Localized.* The user-interface and documentation are translated, but language-specific tools and content remain in English.

- *Adapted.* The linguistic tools, content, and functions of the software are revised or re-created for the target market.

For a tier-1 market like France, virtually all desktop products are enabled, localized, and adapted with French content. Not only are the user-interface and documentation translated into French, but linguistic, formatting, and stylistic tools like spell-checkers, business-letter wizards, and Internet links (in Internet Explorer) are redesigned to conform to and reflect the tastes and interests of French customers.

A critical dimension of localization planning is the schedule for shipping localized products. This is usually expressed as the number of days between the US-product release date and the localized-product ship date. This delay, referred to as the delta, is critical: products that ship with a small delta (under 30 days) can ride the wave of publicity surrounding the US product launch, while products with longer deltas present marketing challenges, because customers commonly stop buying existing products when new ones are announced.

Microsoft localizes key products such as Windows and Word into 25 or more languages, but when the *jihad* was launched, it was not feasible to execute all projects in parallel. Top priority was assigned to top-tier markets; emerging markets suffered from long delays (up to a year or more) before localized products were available.

Operations

Microsoft handled localization internally until the early 1990s. A single group in Redmond handled localization for all products, and was staffed with a small army of young college graduates and expatriates. The International Product Group (IPG) was far from the mainstream and had little influence on product development. Senior managers and engineers in the core teams were largely unaware of localization, how much it cost, or how it was done. Fortunately, the number of products and languages was small, and international customers were far less demanding than today.

As the scope of localization grew, managers of the product groups became concerned about growth in IPG headcount. Mike Maples, head of the product groups before Maritz, anticipated that the amount of localization work was going to grow rapidly and could not continue in "over-the-wall" mode. Maples subsequently split up IPG, divided its headcount among the product groups, assigned them responsibility for localizing their own products, and encouraged outsourcing tasks such as translation. He also established a small central group to support the product groups' localization efforts by finding suitable translation vendors, negotiating master contracts with the vendors, establishing consistent terminology, etc.

Microsoft executes over a thousand localization projects each year. (A "project" is defined as a product/language combination—e.g., French Windows 98, Polish Internet Explorer 3.0.) We do not view translation itself as a core skill for Microsoft, and based on Maples's directive we began to outsource the majority of translation work. Localization is more than translation, and even the relatively simple task of translating software can introduce problems and complexities. As a result, we adopted a mixed-sourcing model where localization of textual material like printed documentation and online-help files was virtually all outsourced, while software localization remained in-house. Most other software-related activities such as testing, compilation, build, and setup localization also remained in-house.

To handle software localization and oversee our European localization vendors, we set up a dedicated localization operation in Ireland in 1988. The decision to locate in Ireland was based on Ireland's physical proximity to continental Europe, the availability of a well-educated English-speaking workforce, a good telecommunications infrastructure, tax incentives, and Ireland's pro-business attitude. The Irish team quickly emerged as Microsoft's localization experts, and became highly skilled in fixing the many engineering glitches and localization bugs inherent in the US product, developing localization tools, and managing vendors of varying sophistication and skill. A similar process later occurred in Japan and elsewhere in Asia.

The Localization Industry

The localization-vendor industry is an essential player in the delivery of localized products. Over the past 10 years, for-hire localization has become a US$2 billion industry, and a vital link between software publishers and their international customers. Microsoft is the largest single customer for localization services.

In the early '90s the global localization community was a network of "mom-'n'-pop" shops scattered across the globe. Most were tiny, undercapitalized businesses with only a handful of permanent employees. Most work was done by freelance translators hired on a per-project basis, and the level of engineering skills was very uneven. Many of these companies started life as translation houses, and while their business skills were usually good, their software skills were often inadequate to deal with the thornier problems challenging Microsoft's localization teams.

Other firms, especially in Eastern Europe, were the opposite of the first group: highly capable software engineers utterly lacking in business skills. I still remember a visit to one firm in the former Soviet bloc. The entire staff, including many Ph.D. engineers who were refugees from the Russian space program, was jammed into a single residential apartment. Their local-area network server was located literally in the toilet, and nobody working there had ever heard of an income statement

Our ability to quickly deliver localized products to dozens of markets depends on effective utilization of the resources in the vendor base. This, in turn, requires reducing engineering and technical obstacles inherent in the product, and on the vendor's ability to supply qualified staff with the right mix of linguistic, engineering, and project-management skills.

Getting a Grip

Gates is fond of quoting Andrew Grove, former chairman of Intel: "If you can't measure it, you can't manage it." This was certainly the case with localization. Prior to the *jihad*, the little available localization-cost data were in the form of accounting records compiled at an aggregate level on a fiscal-year basis. These data failed to show how the money was being spent (e.g., how much on testing, how much on translation), neglected to address the project nature of the work, and offered no insight on the impact of increasing complexity of the company's products, shorter deltas, addition of new languages, etc.

The first step in grappling with the problem was assembling reliable, consistent cost information. Because of the mixed-sourcing model, this meant capturing internal and external costs. To get beneath the macro view, it was also necessary to define cost categories that could be used across a wide variety of products ranging from operating systems like Windows 95 to games like Monster Truck Madness.

External costs were recorded under a variety of accounts in the general ledger, and a paper trail of invoices was also available. Getting a handle on the internal costs proved much more difficult: although costs for the localization teams were recorded in aggregate at the department level, none were categorized by task or assigned to projects.

We interviewed the internal teams to establish a basis for allocating internal costs. The Irish localization teams responded to this initiative with enthusiasm (they had grown tired of having their IQ questioned). They eagerly provided the quantitative data they believed would show that the problem really was in Redmond, where the core code was developed, rather than in Dublin, where the problems surfaced. Although the allocations were approximations, they would show Maritz and Gates where their localization dollars were going and where we needed to focus in order to reduce them.

Sorting Out the Numbers

To help us understand what we were dealing with, we defined a localization cost framework based on what was being worked on, and what type of skill was being applied. The result was a matrix of skills and deliverables similar to the one below:

Framework for Localization Cost Analysis

	Software			Doc/Help
	Globalization	Adaptation	Localization	
Engineering				
Test				
Translation				
Project Mgmt				
Total				

We defined our terms as follows:

Globalization: remedial engineering the localization teams performed to make the products functional in the target languages (sometimes abbreviated to G18N).

Adaptation: the process of adding language-specific or market-specific content—e.g., spell-checkers, drivers, file converters.

Localization: translating the user-interfaceuser-interface, integrating all files into a finished product, and managing the product through the release process (abbreviated L10N).

The task categories were high-level aggregations of the many specific tasks actually required. For example, in addition to the cost for translators themselves, the Translation category also included proofreading, artwork, and other activities related to the basic task.

Once the raw cost data had been assembled and categorized, we still had to invent a way of measuring efficiency. We tried and discarded a variety of approaches, including comparisons of localization costs: a) with revenues; b) with the cost of localizing the previous version; and c) with competitors' costs as best we could estimate them. None of these indicators was especially useful because market size has little bearing on localization cost, products change enormously from release to release, quality improves with experience and turnaround time is shortened, and a multitude of other factors.

Armed with Gates's dictum that localization is "just a linguistic process," we adopted a metric based on a comparison of actual costs with a hypothetical, "pure-translation" benchmark. In response to Gates's challenge, we defined a gauge for localization efficiency based on a hypothetical cost, assuming

Microsoft products were so well engineered that nothing more than translation would be required for localization. We compared this benchmark to the actual costs, calculated the ratio between actual and benchmark costs, and used this as our measure of efficiency.

Efficiency Metric Pro Forma

Word Count		Actual Cost	
Software UI	200,000	Globalization	$50,000
Documentation	300,000	Adaptation	75,000
Online Help	500,000	S/W Localization	500,000
Total Words	1,000,000	Doc/Help	250,000
		Total Cost	$875,000

Cost Per Word	$0.25
Benchmark Cost (words x cost/word)	$250,000
Efficiency (Actual/Benchmark)	**3.5x**

What We Found

Prior to this effort, localization-cost data had not been collected in a comprehensive fashion. As a result, management found it difficult to accept what the localization teams had been saying about the amount of effort consumed in testing, building, and simply keeping track of what was going on. Instead, they wondered about the IQ of the localization teams. Once the data from our effort were in hand, the depth of the problem became apparent. As expected, actual costs exceeded the perfect-world benchmark, but how and why they exceeded the benchmark challenged the conventional wisdom about what was driving costs.

Below is an example of the data we compiled.

x-Factor Analysis of Sample Project

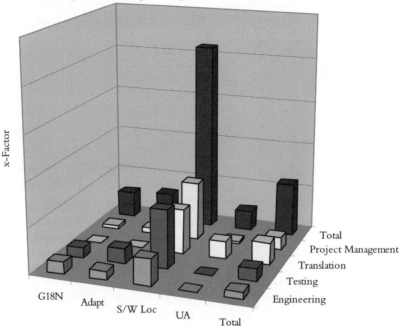

The height of the bars represents the x-factor for each activity. Within the software-localization category, for example, the tall bar at the back represents the overall x-factor, and each individual bar represents the contribution of Engineering, Testing, etc. The average x-factor for the project as a whole is a weighted average of the number of words in the software and the user-assistance (UA) material. Within the software category, for example, testing is the largest cost element and the largest contributor to the overall software x-factor.

Translation of manuals and online-help files was the most visible and easily understood component of localization. As Microsoft products grew in complexity, the size of the manuals grew. Conventional wisdom held this was a major factor behind growth of localization costs. With the cost data from the study, we discovered that, for most products, the cost of translating manuals was a relatively minor part of the total spending and was relatively efficient. As shown in the chart above, the actual cost of localizing the manuals turned out to be a low multiple of the benchmark. Taking into consideration the cost of proofreading, frequent changes, preparation of expensive artwork, and similar costs, we concluded that Microsoft's document-localization process could clearly be improved but was not seriously inefficient. The software, however, was another story altogether.

When the benchmark for software localization was calculated and compared with actual software-localization costs, the results were devastating. Software-localization costs exceeded the benchmark by a factor of 10. Software testing alone cost several times the benchmark, and the same was true for project management and other tasks. Software translation costs also exceeded the benchmark because of rework, technical review, and graphics work included in the category. The data made it clear that software was the big cost-reduction opportunity (not the ever-expanding manuals and help files, as had been believed), and substantiated the claims by the Irish teams that the cost problem was largely attributable to globalization and localizability problems in the US code.

These data were presented to Gates and Maritz early in 1996. The meeting was not easy, but we brought the heads of the Ireland teams to the meeting to explain *ad nauseam* exactly what all the reengineering and testing was about and why it was required. Maritz had already seen the data and understood the implications, but Gates hadn't. Suffice it to say he was disappointed to learn of the inefficiency of the overall process implied by the metrics. He was also disappointed by the persistence of the "simple, stupid" mistakes that contributed to extensive engineering and testing, in what should be an essentially linguistic process.

This marked the turning point in the battle to raise awareness within the development community. At a follow-up meeting with Gates and Maritz, senior engineers from each product group were invited to describe their plans for addressing engineering deficiencies. In early 1997, senior engineers were asked to explain the metrics on their latest products and agree on targets for their next products.

Impact of the *Jihad*

Microsoft's focus on globalization was initially driven by concerns about cost. When the underlying cost drivers of localization came into focus, the leaders of the development community recognized that more was at stake than costs. Microsoft's commitment to deliver localized products in dozens of global markets was threatened by the engineering hurdles that needed to be overcome and the scarcity of talent capable of doing the job. By attacking the engineering complexity and skill level required for localization, Microsoft has made considerable progress toward Gates's goal of making localization "just a linguistic process."

The data in the table below summarize efficiency gains achieved for a sample of products since the *jihad* was launched.

x-Factor Improvements

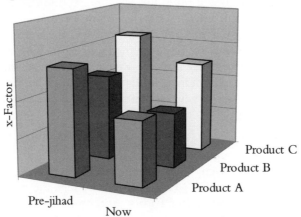

For the sample of products we have been tracking, efficiency gains range between 30–50 percent. Other insights include:

- Efficiency gains in documentation localization have been modest. The gains are attributable primarily to increased recycling of texts from previous versions, application of technologies such as translation memory, and standardization of authoring tools.

- Much of the improvement in software-localization efficiency is attributable to effective globalization of the US product and improvements in localizability as a result of "localization-sufficiency testing" of the US product.

- Testing costs remain high, but are anticipated to decline as the testing process itself is globalized. Logistics and project management continue to be significant cost elements.

- Sourcing strategies have been revised to optimize utilization of vendor resources. Outsourcing for its own sake has been abandoned, as we have found it more cost-effective to localize certain products (such as high-end operating systems) on-site. In some cases we have partnered with vendors to build dedicated capacity to meet our needs.

- Globalization has increased our ability to execute localizations in parallel, allowing deltas to continue to decline. Internet Explorer, for example, now routinely ships dozens of language versions within a matter of days following the US release.

Despite rebalancing our sourcing model, localization vendors are a critical part of our "localization machine." In many parts of the world the vendor base is very thin and is still a constraint on our ability to deliver products to these markets. The industry has undergone a wave of consolidation, increasing the possibility of sourcing multiple-language projects to a single vendor and reducing the logistical burden on Microsoft. The days of a single hand-off remain in the future, as the new generation of vendors is still in the process of assimilating recent acquisitions.

Looking Ahead: Expectations for the Future

Globalization is now a basic mission of every product group, but the hope that localization is "just a linguistic process" is threatened by changes in the nature of our products:

- Content has become a larger element of our products and, as a result, the adaptation required for localization is increasing. Products like Encarta (an interactive, multimedia encyclopedia) are an extreme example of this, while a new generation of products such as MSN, Expedia, and other online services push localization to new limits.

- The proliferation of the Internet has driven new technologies such as HTML and XML to the forefront. Documents and content authored in these languages are a mixture of code and text, and in many ways are reminiscent of the software of five years ago. These technologies are evolving rapidly and challenge our ability to build localization tools and processes to support them.

- Linguistic technologies such as speech recognition, natural-language-based search engines, and machine translation will redefine the scope of localization. These technologies are being commercialized, and will soon become mainstream utilities. Localizing these technologies really means recreating them in each target language. The effort required to create these tools is substantial and there are no shortcuts.

CLOSING THOUGHTS

The invention of the printing press eliminated the need for scribes, but created a vastly larger market for books and, consequently, countless new jobs for authors, editors, illustrators, and other specialized workers. By analogy, eliminating the engineering obstacles to translation of software and documentation will not make localization obsolete. On the contrary, the improvement in efficiency and reduction in localization cost will stimulate demand for localized products and create jobs for experts skilled in adapting linguistic tools and content to meet the tastes of local markets. Although we have a firm grip on today's localization challenges, we know our task will only become more complex and challenging in the future.

Multilingual Information Management at Schneider Automation

Cornelia Hofmann
Ovidius Gesellschaft für Technische Kommunikation GmbH

Thorsten Mehnert
Tanner Documents

MIM: THE CONCEPTUAL FRAMEWORK

Producing product documentation presents unprecedented challenges today. Corporate management increasingly understands that this part of product development is on the critical path, and thus directly affects time-to-market. But besides meeting the time requirements, document management has to cope with increasing volumes of information, needs for different formats and platforms, customer-specific information, communication in many languages, decentralized production environments, and work under strong cost pressure.

But the *real* challenges become visible once we broaden our view from documentation to the wider concept it serves: communication. Communication in turn is based on exchanging information, and the product-relevant information of tomorrow will be something quite different from what we call "documentation" today. Some examples:

- *Documentation integrated into the product.* User documentation was a separate source of information in the past, but it is becoming an ever more integrated product component. As product-based information, it appears as online help in software, as a message presented via a product-integrated display, or as a smart "wizard" that solves a user's problem or interactively guides one through one's work.

- *Information-intensive products.* Product information provides for more than just a better understanding of the product or easier interaction with it. Products require an increasing volume of information for proper performance and functioning. For example, a small pen that reads text and translates it into another language contains much linguistic data; a car equipped with a navigation system needs large amounts of geographic data. In the case of a service, the deliverable might in fact be made up entirely of information.

- *Convergence of now distinct types of documentation and means of distribution.* Traditionally, marketing, sales, and customer support each had their own type of documentation and used separate channels for communicating with the client. The Web has changed this paradigm. Information is distributed through intranets/extranets, and the content from different corporate functions has to be well synchronized and presented in a coherent fashion. David Brooks of Microsoft puts it this way: "The distinction between what is product [...], what is marketing, and what is technical material is becoming increasingly blurred."[1]

Multilingual Information Management

These challenges will inexorably alter the way multilingual product information is produced in the future. We will have to manage more interdependencies than today, due to the convergence of product and documentation and of documentation and support, and due to the need for seamless integration of the many internal and external entities participating in production. But time-to-market requirements will make the increasing number of interdependencies even more difficult to manage, since they require more concurrent processes, which in turn leads to a higher level of complexity.

To manage this complexity, we must abandon the silo perspective of product development, marketing communication, technical writing, translation, and product support. In its place, we must think in terms of a coherent environment where all entities participate in producing product-relevant information, i.e., *information objects* (IO). An IO is a collection of information which is identified as a unit. In principle, everything from a single sentence to a large information product like a manual can be modeled as an IO. Regardless of the level of abstraction, an IO always meets these criteria:

- it targets a certain information *consumer* (e.g., a user of some equipment);

- it is associated with a *business entity* (e.g., a certain product, product line, or corporate function);

- it has a *communicative goal* (e.g., it wants to warn the consumer, or helps her perform a certain procedure);

- it carries *content*, which is information coded in one or more media (e.g., text, image, or audio) and which is created for a certain locale (language/country/culture);

---

1. "Localization—The Microsoft Perspective," an interview with David Brooks, in LISA (Localisation Industry Standards Association) Newsletter, 1997.

- it might have some *publishing restrictions*, i.e., created to appear only in certain information products (e.g., in manuals but not in online help).

As an example, a typical IO in the Schneider Automation documentation environment—a fragment—is presented in the figure below.

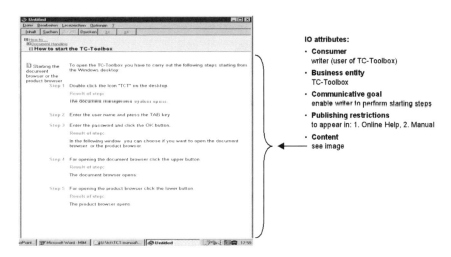

Technological developments, notably the availability of global delivery platforms like the Web, help us make such an environment reality. They even allow us to "have control over the creation, maintenance, distribution (and even the consumption) of information," as Rose Lockwood describes it with the so-called *InfoCycle*.[2] The figure below shows an extended version of the InfoCycle which we use to briefly introduce our concept of Multilingual Information Management.

---

2. Lockwood, Rose, "Are You Ahead of the Curve?", *Language International*, Vol. 10 No. 2 (1998).

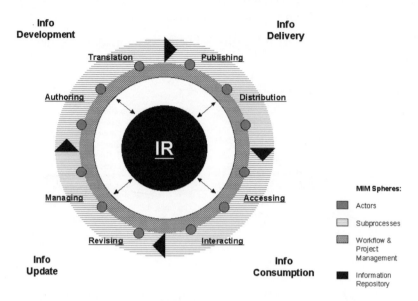

Picture the production of multilingual information as a journey: IOs are born in *Info Development*, travel their way to *Info Consumption*, and will at some point in time be reused/reauthored in *Info Update,* and reenter the InfoCycle—possibly many times. Information will not be created for, say, a manual and its next version, but systematically *engineered* to serve many purposes, and thus will have a much longer life span than today.

Derived from the marketing goals of a company, each IO can be associated with the following goal: acquire an information content, *x,* in a throughput time, *y,* moving from *Info Development* to *Info Delivery* at minimal cost. MIM is a corporate process to establish and operate an environment to meet the goal of each IO. The environment consists of the necessary processes, systems, and organizational structures.

Each individual company certainly needs a different environment to make MIM a reality, but we believe the following four spheres will always be involved:

- *Subprocesses: designing how IOs are manipulated.* The operational sequences set up to create, deliver, consume, or update information. Subprocesses include, e.g., authoring, translation, publishing, distribution.

- *Information Repository (IR): storing, managing, and retrieving IOs.* A logically central (but certainly physically distributed) database containing IOs. The information objects will be stored in a nonproprietary format (e.g., SGML, XML) that will allow reuse of IOs for different purposes and media. The IR will also provide access control, versioning, and retrieval functionality.

- *Workflow and project management: planning and scheduling IO life.* Tool support that allows integrated workflow and project management across all subprocesses. Nonintegrated workflow and project-management support (e.g., isolated functionality as part of subprocess-specific tools) will not meet tomorrow's time-to-market goals.

- *Actors: manipulating IOs.* An actor can be a system that automatically transforms IOs (e.g., a converter creating HTML documents from a number of IOs). It can also be a human transforming IOs with the appropriate support of a specialized workbench, such as a writer working with a "writer's workbench" that allows him to configure, generate, and write information products; an information manager who uses a workbench to manage and restructure the IR; or a project manager whose workbench uses functionality of the workflow and project management sphere.

MIM Rules

Successfully operating a MIM means allowing IOs to travel the InfoCycle efficiently. Before looking at how Schneider Automation approaches MIM, we will identify some general, company-independent rules that should be followed in creating and managing IOs.

Make IOs reusable. When writing or translating information, reuse existing IOs as much as possible:

- Manage their content in a nonproprietary, media-neutral way so that you can use IOs for different purposes/media/formats. Proprietary formatting tags are straitjackets and often mean less efficient production.

- Ensure that their content follows structural rules so that they can easily be assembled into larger IOs such as manuals, reference guides, and online help or even provide input for information systems (e.g., those that support product configuration).

- Automate the information production by generating their content where possible and economically sensible (e.g., by calculating values in technical specifications instead of hard-coding the numbers in cases where values change for different products or local measurement units).

- Create their content so that it can be used for as many business entities or products you have to describe as possible.

Specify IOs well and produce them accordingly. Efficient information reuse and automation is possible only if you produce correct information. Otherwise, you will multiply errors, and the resulting rework will negate the planned benefits. Some guidelines:

- Always know whom an IO should address and what effect its content should have on the consumer.

- Establish documentation standards to guide their creation, and ensure they are communicated and followed throughout the InfoCycle.

- Carefully select the people who create IO content.

- Ensure that IOs are properly validated.

Maintain IO value. IO content might be correct the day you created it, but you must set up processes that guarantee the content will still be correct tomorrow. Often IOs are not updated, and the need to maintain their value is underestimated. Therefore:

- Assign clear responsibilities for keeping IOs up-to-date. Make individuals, and not merely departments, responsible and be certain that they can oversee the entire InfoCycle.

- Change IO content only in a well-defined update process.

- Keep in close contact with IOs throughout the InfoCycle. Customer feedback must be captured and integrated. If you fail to determine customers' desired changes in IO content, IOs will reenter the InfoCycle, often repeatedly, with a content that fails to meet customer requirements.

Accelerate IO flow. Meeting time-to-market demands requires IOs to travel quickly:

- Automate workflow (e.g., establish a system that *knows* everyone in IO production, assigns predefined tasks to them, and automatically routes assignments).

- Use a project-management system that tracks production of each IO and avoids redundant project management in the different subprocesses.

- Appoint an information-logistics manager responsible for the entire InfoCycle. Setting up responsibilities for information production in the participating subprocesses like product development, marketing, technical writing, translation, etc., is insufficient.

Integrate data islands. Although you may have physically separate data collections, ensure they are connected logically and form a single *information repository.* Hiding IOs in separate data collections in your own or other subprocesses means other potentially useful IOs cannot be identified/assessed when new ones are created.

Teach everyone to think in terms of the InfoCycle. For the InfoCycle to operate successfully, everyone participating in IO production needs to consider the subsequent information-creation or consumption steps. The logistics manager should support this attitude by appropriate communication and motivational measures.

APPROACHING MIM AT SCHNEIDER

The information production at Schneider Automation is based on the MIM concept, and to date has been partly implemented. We went through three development stages, as outlined below:

Requirement	Steps Taken Regarding Production Environment
Provide technical information in more than one language	Introduction of translation-memory tool
Represent the same technical information in help files and in manuals Come as close as possible to simultaneous publication in four languages	Single-source publishing by enhancing desktop-publishing tool already in use
Represent the same technical information on various media in many languages Create coherent information at remote locations	Development of an SGML-based cross-media publishing system

This case study describes the final two development stages:

* Enhancing the Interleaf desktop-publishing tool to create a single-source publishing tool (which has now been in use for three years).

* Developing an SGML-based cross-media publishing system called TC-Toolbox, implemented in late 1998.

The Transit translation-memory tool (Star) was part of both approaches.

Schneider's Technical Communications Team

Schneider Automation, a global provider of automation systems, is a Strategic Business Unit of the French Groupe Schneider. Schneider Automation was created by combining AEG Modicon (Germany/US) and Télémécanique (France) under the parent organization Groupe Schneider. Today, Schneider Automation has R&D and production sites in the US, France, and Germany. R&D projects are carried out by joint international teams, which results in individual parts of one product often being developed at different sites.

Technical Communications, such as R&D, is spread over three sites in three countries. Technical information on individual parts of a product is always created at the engineering site. In the case of large systems, the corresponding documentation is created at three sites, in three countries, in three languages, by writers separated by thousands of miles.

This particular situation of the Technical Communications Team—now commonplace in international business—led to development of the TC-Toolbox. The first steps were taken under slightly easier circumstances: fewer output media were required and information was created mainly at a single site.

First Approach: Documentation and Help from a Single Source

The problem. The project that raised the issue of single-source publishing was the documentation for new programming software under Windows, which required localization into four languages. We were tasked with creating help files and manuals, and translating them and the software user-interface into three languages. A further challenge: the software was created in English and the first released language version was to be English, while most documentation was to be written in Germany in German.

Three main challenges were clear from the beginning:

- We had to publish the first translated version of the documentation before the source-language version.

- We had to create help files and manuals simultaneously, although we had resources for only one medium.

- We had to translate into more languages than before—and the language versions had to be published in quick succession.

The solution. We pursued two basic ideas to achieve our goal:

- Create help files and manuals from one single source.

• Make the translation process as quick and efficient as possible.

Let us examine the realization of both ideas in detail.

Create help files and manuals from a single source.

This idea was realized by developing an enhancement to Interleaf that enables creation of help files from the Interleaf source. With this enhancement, a writer using Interleaf can key in "meta" information for help files, such as topic titles, topic IDs, keywords, etc. While writing a classical manual with chapters and subchapters, the writer can also define a topic in the help file, define information that will appear in the help file and not the manual (or vice versa) or both, and also create help hyperlinks (jumps) beyond the manual's traditional cross-references ("see page ..."). While editing, the writer can see only one layout on her screen, one that approximates the appearance of the manuals. Layout of the online help, however, differs completely and is adapted to the common help style.

Not all information would appear in the online help and the manuals:

• Software installation instructions are not included in online help, since the software is already installed when the online help is used.

• The detailed menu and dialog descriptions are not part of a manual, since they are mainly required when the software is used.

With our Interleaf enhancement, the single source contains all information, including meta information. We gained two advantages with this tool:

• Information must be created only once.

• Translating one Interleaf file represents translating a help and a manual file in a single step.

The latter advantage also contributed to achieving our second goal.

Make the translation process as quick and efficient as possible.

This goal was met by applying a translation-memory tool.[3] Since Transit from Star allowed customization to our needs, we introduced this tool and incorporated it into our documentation process as shown in the figure below.

---

3. We will not describe this type of tool here; refer to the LCC KnowledgeBase at www.lcc-online.com for detailed information.

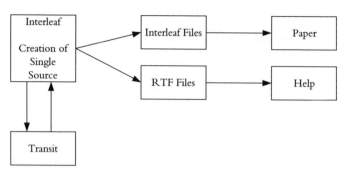

This resulted in the following advantages:

- Translation of a new version of a text used *all* the translated text of the previous version. Nothing had to be translated more than once, and changes did not have to be filtered out. This saved time and money.

- Terminology was better maintained, which increased translation consistency and quality.

- Reformatting of translated documents was almost no longer necessary, which resulted in major time savings.

With Transit, we could create and translate in parallel. Even at times when many changes were still being made to the software, translating did not represent a waste of time or money, since we knew the exact location of the changes and could focus any rework on those passages. In this way, we translated some thousand pages from German into English, while still creating in German. When the software was released, the English manuals and help files were ready, along with their German counterparts.

We also used Transit to translate the user-interface of the software. The main advantage was the ability to create a terminology database containing only menu and dialog terms, which could then be used for translation of all IOs in the project. The terminology database ensured consistency between all these IOs, regardless of whether they belonged to the user-interface, help files, or manuals.

The results. We published the first translation before the source-language version, and the other language versions shortly thereafter. With our method, we managed to achieve intervals of only one month between the language releases, and the first translation (English) was ready simultaneously with the English software version.

We overcame the challenge of scarce resources as well. Although the writers had to learn to write manuals and help files simultaneously, in the end they mastered this technique. Of course, creating manual and help files simultaneously took longer than one of those tasks alone. But the time needed was far shorter than that required for writing one after the other, even taking into account that large parts of the text can be copied. We could thus complete the project using only existing resources.

Second Approach: Cross-Media Publishing from a Single Source

The problem. The impending need to place our technical information on the Internet, and an increasing number of projects handled at an international level, led to the decision to convert to an SGML-based cross-media publishing system.

The project we now faced was again documenting new programming software under Windows, with localization into four languages. We were tasked with creating help files, HTML collections, and manuals, and translating each of these and the software user–interface into three languages.

The main challenges we knew from our first approach were still present, with several new ones added:

* We still had to publish the first translated version of the documentation (English) before the source-language version. But this time, we had two source languages, since some parts of the documentation were written in German, others in French.

* We still had to create help files and manuals simultaneously. But this time, we also had to deliver HTML collections, and we still only had resources for creating information products in one medium.

* Again, the language versions had to be published in quick succession.

The solution. The TC-Toolbox controls the following types of IOs (see the figures below):

* *Fragment*: a physical file containing information of a certain revision, version, and language.

* *Information Unit (IU)*: the totality of all revisions, versions, and translations of *a single* fragment.

* *Collection*: a logical assembly of several IUs.

* *Information product*: an assembly of fragments, selected and laid out for a certain destination medium (e.g., a manual) and language. From each IU of a certain collection, exactly one fragment of a defined revision,

version, and language is selected to participate in a certain information product.

Traditional chapters are split into small fragments. This allows several writers (at different sites) to work together on one chapter and reuse the fragments. The fragments are created by the writers independently of the destination medium. Splitting into fragments is not done at the level of SGML elements, but at a level that can be compared with the traditional subchapter level, as illustrated below:

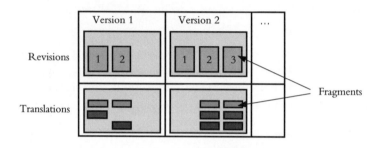

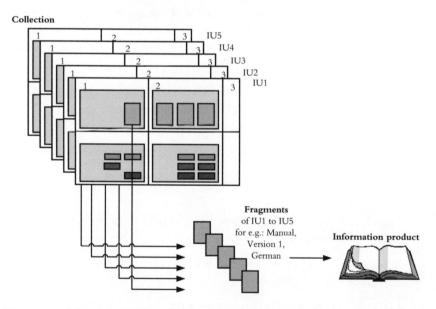

The core of the TC-Toolbox is the document-management system (DMS). The DMS controls all IOs and is the starting point for all user actions. An SGML database is unnecessary since our fragments more or less represent subchapters.

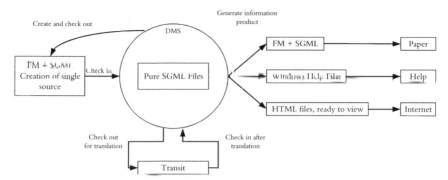

How writers work with the TC-Toolbox. The writers' main activities are:

- *Editing fragments.* We use Adobe FrameMaker+SGML as an editor. The editing application contains a DTD which allows editing all destination media in parallel. The layout presented to the writer on screen resembles the layout of the final manual, but is not identical.

- *Translating fragments.* Translation is assisted by the Transit tool (as in our first approach). Translation memories and terminology databases are controlled by the DMS.

Building information products. To build an information product, the writer must create a list of fragments that should be included in the information product. Creation of information-product files in formats such as FrameMaker for paper + PDF, RTF for Windows help, and HTML for Internet or CD-Rom is done by filtering processes or conversion (metamorphosis) into DTDs that are adapted to the medium. In addition, the FrameMaker application for paper output differs from the editing application.

Advantages of TC-Toolbox architecture. Separating editing and production applications provides maximum flexibility in the tools used and the ability to integrate other output formats into the TC-Toolbox. This separation also allows optimal adaptation of the resulting information products to the destination medium.

Field data. The TC-Toolbox was implemented at three sites and used in the project mentioned above. Our initial experience shows:

- Cross-media writing requires advanced training and experience. It requires a change of thinking achieved only through practice.

- Cross-site writing needs a strictly defined style guide. Style naturally differs from writer to writer even at a single site, and all the more so from culture to culture and language to language. To create information products in a consistent style is nontrivial, and requires substantial work beforehand.

The question whether cross-media publishing is worth the investment is considered in the "Quantitative Assessment" section below.

Creating Correct Information and Maintaining Its Value

Reusing information and automating its production can only be done efficiently if: a) correct information is produced; and b) production setup guarantees that this information will still be correct tomorrow. Otherwise, errors are multiplied, and the resulting rework might offset all the benefits one hoped to achieve through reuse.

Maintaining the value of information is not a single task, but requires that the whole InfoCycle be designed to manage information accordingly, as highlighted below.

Problem-focused information. Since there is no point in creating and managing information that has little benefit to the client, every IO we create has a clear definition of: a) the information consumer it must target; and b) the IO's communicative goal.

This approach is currently being refined and expanded throughout the entire product lifecycle. We have also observed how customers' information needs vary in different phases (e.g., presales, sales, installation, operation, and migration to another product). We intend to meet these changing needs by structuring the information so that each IO will be attributed to a certain lifecycle phase and will satisfy the customers' information need. Associating IOs to lifecycle phases will allow us to retrieve information with high accuracy.

Uniform production environment. Schneider's documentation production is decentralized and must cope with the additional challenge of integrating people from companies that had formerly been separate entities. Efficient production requires a uniform environment with standardized processes. The TC-Toolbox assists in this effort, but in itself is insufficient to synchronize our activities. Therefore we are currently developing a Writers' Manual that will ensure consistent treatment of the following at all production sites:

- Writing and translation processes
- TC-Toolbox usage

- Layout styles

- Writing styles

Qualification of content providers. To reuse information efficiently, our product information needs to be of high quality, the cornerstone of which is clearly well-qualified talent to produce it. Our skill profile for translators includes:

- Technical expertise in automation technology

- Demonstrated understanding of our products

- Track record as a professional translator

- Native speaker of the target language

- Familiarity with PCs

Such individuals are rare, and we often must compromise. Lack of expert knowledge about automation technology must often be compensated for by close interaction between translator and writer.

Review process. A well-defined and functional review is essential to the MIM concept. Reviewing source fragments and translations consists of two distinct phases, a technical review and a language review.

The technical review verifies correct content:

- The procedures which the user is to follow are correct, understandable and complete without misleading information.

- The specifications are correct and complete.

Although a first review should be done locally with the source file, the complete international review can only be done by reviewing translations. Clearly, changes demanded by the technical review must be made in the source fragment first, and then in the translations.

The language review verifies correctness of the translation itself. Does the translation express the same content as the source? Has defined terminology been used? These are the main issues apart from formal checks like spelling and grammar. One remark concerning the reviewers' comments: in general it may be necessary to translate the comments, since a writer may not be able to understand the comments in another language. We have not found this necessary to date, since the writers involved in these projects were bilingual.

Roles and Responsibilities in MIM

Our production environment comprises the following roles:

Role	Responsibility
Writer/Project Manager	Create IOs for an information product in one language. Plan, prepare, and manage translation work of this product for all other language versions.
Translator	Translate information products and participate in terminology work. For qualifications, see above.
Reviewer	Check source fragments and translations (reviewers are mainly engineers and marketers; a language reviewer must be a native speaker of the target language).
Administrative Support	Select translators, verify their availability for a project, and handle quotes, orders, and invoices.
Technical MIM Expert	Monitor use of TC-Toolbox and manage its ongoing development.
Logistics Manager	Plan and design information flow through the InfoCycle along with representatives from product development, marketing, support, etc.

Given their key role in our MIM, writers take on additional tasks at Schneider, primarily in the project-management area:

- A writer leads a team to define and maintain terminology for the systems she controls.

- The writer partners with the translator throughout the translation. She qualifies the translator's product knowledge, and is the first contact for the translator in case of questions.

- The writer prepares the fragment translation because she is the only one who knows when it is ready for translation.

- The writer initiates and follows up the review processes.

MIM Evolution

Which MIM rules have we implemented and how? The following table shows implementation in the first approach, the progress made in the second, and an outlook on TC-Toolbox Version 2.

MIM Rules (detailed above)	1st Approach (Interleaf enhancement)	2nd Approach (TC-Toolbox V1)	Outlook for TC-Toolbox V2
Make IOs reusable.			
Manage their content in a non-proprietary, media-neutral way.	One Interleaf source for help files and paper, but Interleaf is still proprietary. Content and format are combined in Interleaf.	One SGML-source for all media; SGML is nonproprietary. Content and format are strictly separated in SGML.	
Ensure their content follows structural rules.	To a very low degree.	Fragments are created according to structural rules as implemented by the DTD. Fragments are smaller units than traditional subchapters. They are stored in the database and may be linked to form many different collections.	
Create their content so it can be used for many business entities.	For similar Schneider Automation products, the respective information products are created using attribute control, i.e., product names and special features can be hidden according to the actual contents.		
Specify IOs well and produce them accordingly.			
Always know whom an IO should address.	Our documentation is structured according to the information goal and the target-user groups.		IOs are assigned clearly defined attributes according to the actions the user carries out with the product. This improves the user's ability to search for special IOs supporting individual activities.
Have documentation standards set up to guide their creation.	A writers' manual described the following: Creation and translation processes Layout styles Writing style was not described. The writers tried to achieve a common style via close communication.	A writers' manual will be created, as outlined above.	
Carefully select those who create IO content.	Our writers specialize in Programmable Logical Controller (PLC) technology. The writer's first priority, however, is to specialize in documenting information and using information technology. We aim at long-term relationships with translators to improve their knowledge of PLC technology.		

MIM Rules (detailed above)	1st Approach (Interleaf enhancement)	2nd Approach (TC-Toolbox V1)	Outlook for TC-Toolbox V2
Ensure that IOs are properly validated.	IOs pass through technical and language reviews. The review process described above is not yet controlled by the system. However, the 2nd approach allows validation based on the SGML DTD.		The review process itself will be controlled by the system to a certain extent.
Maintain IO value.			
Assign clear responsibilities for keeping IOs up-to-date.	There are clear responsibilities: • for authoring each fragment: writer • for translating each fragment: translator • for collections and information products: project manager (writer)		Responsibility for creation of information will also be given to people outside Technical Communications.
Change IO content only in a well-defined update process.	Writers work under a defined update process, with only little administration taken on by the system.	Revisions and versions are administrated by the DMS.	
Keep in close contact with IOs throughout the InfoCycle.	Reply forms asking for customer feedback are attached to the manuals. Technical Communications stays in close contact with the Product Support Department which receives most of the customer feedback.		Closer integration with Customer Support will increase feedback. Through use of the Internet, we expect more and more direct customer feedback.
Accelerate IO flow.			
Automate workflow.			Parts of the workflow may be integrated into TC-Toolbox.

MIM Rules (detailed above)	1st Approach (Interleaf enhancement)	2nd Approach (TC-Toolbox V1)	Outlook for TC-Toolbox V2
Appoint an information logistics manager.			Our future realization will merge our data collections with those of other parts of the organization, building a single, logical technical information repository. A logistics manager will be given responsibility for the data repository and the complete InfoCycle.
Integrate data islands. In both approaches, data collections are created and managed fairly independently from each other.			
Make everyone think in terms of the InfoCycle. One individual from Technical Communications is responsible for a given international documentation project. This includes responsibility for all IOs involved.			

Quantitative Assessment

Brief economic analysis of our cross-media publishing system. Does cross-media publishing save money? Without it, parallel creation/translation of documents for several media would be necessary, resulting in redundant, avoidable activities. The following tables shows a comparative calculation of the estimated costs (10,000 pages) per year and for 15 writers:

Per 10,000 Pages	Costs without Cross-Media Publishing	Costs with Cross-Media Publishing	Savings through Cross-Media Publishing
Creation			
1 target format	DM 3,000,000	DM 3,000,000	—
2 target formats	DM 4,000,000	DM 3,300,000	DM 700,000
3 target formats	DM 5,000,000	DM 3,600,000	DM 1,400,000
Translation			
1 lang., 1 target format	DM 500,000	DM 500,000	—
1 lang., 2 target formats	DM 900,000	DM 500,000	DM 400,000
1 lang., 3 target formats	DM 1,300,000	DM 500,000	DM 800,000
3 lang., 2 target formats	DM 2,700,000	DM 1,500,000	DM 1,200,000
3 lang., 3 target formats	DM 3,900,000	DM 1,500,000	DM 2,400,000
Total (4 lang. incl. source, 2 target formats)	DM 6,700,000	DM 4,800,000	DM 1,900,000
Total (4 lang. incl. source, 3 target formats)	DM 8,900,000	DM 5,100,000	DM 3,800,000

Within one year, cross-media publishing for two destination formats will save DM 1.9 million based on a conservative calculation. The calculation is based on the assumption that the creation costs with cross-media publishing for two destination formats is 10 percent higher compared to one destination format. The costs for the case without cross-media publishing, however, have been calculated at a very low level, since updating the content to a new product version in two destination formats very often costs nearly twice as much as updating similar information in just one destination format. During initial creation of information, the cost difference is not as dramatic, but we experience updates more often than first-time creation.

Quantitative assessments of our approaches. The following table shows the cost and time savings of our two approaches, along with expected savings of the next MIM development phase. These aspects characterize TC-Toolbox V2:

- Better IO reuse

- Higher integration in managing translation memories and terminology

- Intuitive user-interface offers better support for writers during editing

	1st Approach (Interleaf enhancement)	2nd Approach (TC-Toolbox V1)	In preparation (TC-Toolbox V2)
cost savings	DM 1.9 million in one year	> DM 3 million in one year	> DM 3 million in one year
costs of system development & implementation	DM 0.2 million	DM 0.9 million	ca. DM 0.4 million
costs of conversion of legacy data	DM 0.5 million	DM 1.1 million	none
time saving	20% of creation time 45% of translation time	30% of creation time 60% of translation time	40% of creation time (est.) 65% of translation time (est.)

Glossary

Term	Definition
Collection	A logical assembly of a number of IUs.
Cross-Media Publishing	Publishing information for several media from a single source.
Document Management System (DMS)	A DMS organizes and manages IOs.
Document Type Description (DTD)	Expression of SGML-based structural and semantic rules which IOs must obey.
Fragment	A physical file containing information of a certain revision, version, and language.
FrameMaker+SGML	Desktop-publishing tool by Adobe.
Information Object (IO)	A collection of information identified as a unit. In principle, everything from a single sentence to a large information product like a manual can be modeled as an IO. Typical IOs at Schneider Automation are fragments, information units, collections, and information products.
Information Product	An assembly of fragments, selected and laid out for a certain destination medium (e.g., a manual), version, and language.
Information Unit (IU)	The totality of all revisions, versions, and translations of one fragment.
Interleaf	Desktop-publishing tool by Interleaf Inc.
PLC	Programmable Logical Controllers.
Revision	A fragment in a draft or intermediate status. A revision will not be published.
Standard Generalized Markup Language (SGML)	The international standard (ISO 8879) defines SGML as a language for document representation that formalizes markup and frees it of system and processing dependencies.
TC-Toolbox	SGML-based cross-media publishing system, owned by Schneider Automation, developed by Ovidius GmbH, Berlin.
Translation Memory System	Focuses on increasing the translator's productivity and typically offers features for reuse of already produced translations, preservation of a document's format during translation, automatic search for terminology, etc. Synonym: translator workbench.
Version	A fragment ready for publishing. Fragments will only be published as part of an information product.

The Role of Translation in an International Organization

Andrew Joscelyne
Equipe Consortium Ltd.

In a rapidly changing, globalizing world, you might think that the translation departments in the world's international organizations would adopt the same cost-cutting and technology-driven solutions as their private-sector counterparts.

You would be partly right. The European Commission's *Service de Traduction* is a prime example. They recently deployed an "information-gisting service," which provides machine translation (Systran-based) for Commission staff who need rapid raw translation delivered over an in-house network. It is called "gisting," since the computer-generated translation generally provides enough substance that the reader gets the "gist" of what is being said. It is also no secret that in 1998, a team from the United Nations translation department commissioned a report on the use and viability of the machine and machine-assisted translation service at the EC, presumably to examine the applicability of such technology to its own needs.

Similarly, calls for tenders are regularly issued by large international organizations for external translation suppliers. They often require assistance in specific language combinations, or in machine-translation post-editing, to offset pressure on in-house teams. In line with the general trend, translation volume has grown exponentially across the spectrum of international organizations.

Despite these shared features of the translation landscape, there are specific aspects of language-transfer management in international organizations that are not echoed in private-sector practice. This is largely because of the role translation plays in these organizations, a translation ethos that quite often differs from market-driven private-sector translation departments.

By focusing on the Organization for Economic Cooperation and Development (OECD),[1] this case study attempts to show that the specific nature of language, and *a fortiori* translation, in these organizations determines the options available for translation management.

A Multilingual Mandate

Most larger and older international organizations differ from corporate users of language services in one way: built into their founding charters is a clause enumerating the organization's official languages. The United Nations, for example, has six working languages; the World Bank, the IMF, NATO, and OECD each work in two official languages. We call this property *foundational multilinguality.*

Many global organizations (as opposed to regional international organizations in Africa, Asia, and Latin America) were created in the aftermath of World War II, following the creation of the United Nations and the 1944 Bretton Woods conference. Their foundational multilinguality tends to reflect the linguistic configuration of diplomacy at that time, with French and English chosen as the major working languages, rather than the German or Japanese of the recently vanquished nations.

This is not the place to analyze the historical and political sources of language choice in such international organizations, or to survey the range of possible forms of foundational multilinguality (or, possibly its replacement by *de facto* rather than *de jure* multilinguality in more recently founded organizations). For the purposes of this study, we shall assume that foundational multilinguality is valid for the specific case of language management we shall examine—that of the OECD.

Foundational multilinguality as we define it is rarely, if ever, found in the bylaws of a private company, although many multinational corporations encourage multilingual practice by staff in order to pursue their business goals. Since corporate ownership, geographies, market range, and business lines are in near-permanent flux, any decision to stipulate linguistic practice as constitutive of a corporation would be tantamount to business suicide.

---

1. René Prioux, Head of the Translation Division at the OECD in Paris, provided me with a comprehensive tutorial about translation at the OECD and international organizations in general. His willingness to share and explain these procedures allowed me to write this account. Any shortcomings and inaccuracies are my own.

Translation Preserves

The continued identity and existence of international organizations, however, is largely predicated on balancing the interests of nation-state members. This means that explicit foundational multilinguality—what is written into the organization's founding charter—will rarely be questioned or modified in response to market or other external pressures. Any translation practice set up under such foundational multilinguality therefore tends to endure, whatever the changes in the external balance of linguistic power.

A possible threat to the linguistic status quo of international organizations is a voted decision at the UN allowing Japan and Germany to sit on the Security Council, due to their clout on the world economic stage. If accepted, the language range of the UN would have to expand to accept German and Japanese, and possibly European and Brazilian Portuguese.

Similarly, some may claim that the diplomatic, political, and economic role of the French language has declined since 1945; hence there would be no overriding statistical or strategic reason for French to be a consistent core member of the family of foundational languages.

The evidence so far suggests, however, that foundational multilinguality is highly resistant if not immune to such changes. As a result, the translation departments of these organizations form a unique "translation preserve" which operates with significant autonomy compared with the rest of the world's translation activities.

INSIDE THE OECD

The OECD has been described as a rich-man's club of like-minded members—part think-tank, part monitoring agency, and part nonacademic university. It groups 29 of the world's most developed countries in an organization that provides governments with a platform to discuss, develop, and refine economic and social policy.

Founded in 1961, it replaced the Organization for European Economic Cooperation (OEEC), which was formed to administer US and Canadian aid under the Marshall Plan for the reconstruction of Europe after World War II. The member countries each send an ambassador to the OECD, and each contributes to the ca. US$200 million annual budget.

The OECD's purpose is to build strong economic policies in its member countries, improve efficiency, hone market systems, expand free trade, and contribute to the development of industrialized and developing countries. It functions through a cascade of committees, the preeminent one being the

Council, which has decision-making power and works at the ministerial level with member countries. Some 200 other specialist committees, working groups, and expert groups deal with specific issues of policy, with each producing a steady stream of knowledge in the form of documents.

The OECD is run by the Paris-based Secretariat, which fields 1,850 staff members to directly or indirectly support committee activities. Seven hundred economists, scientists, lawyers, and other professional staff, mainly based in a dozen major directorates, provide research and analysis. An additional six general secretariat units and a half-dozen semi-autonomous bodies produce knowledge eventually translated by the Translation Division, as we shall refer to it.

Knowledge: Instrumental vs. Discursive

Knowledge production is used here as a catch-all to cover the OECD's core activities. However, it has sufficient resonance to capture a significant feature of such organizations, and shed light on how they differ fundamentally from many private-sector organizations.

Today, knowledge management is a key operational feature of any organization: companies, governments, associations, even families, produce knowledge of one sort or another, or can be engineered to produce such knowledge by configuring information-technology systems to capture it. Information from your credit-card transactions can be transformed into knowledge about you as a desiring, buying, preferring customer by a computer system. The result, *instrumental knowledge*, serves some further purpose of the knowledge producer.

At the OECD, however, the production of knowledge (almost totally embodied in documents) is the organization's end purpose, and it takes a discursive form, packaged for human (rather than, for example, machine) understanding. In this sense it operates like a consulting or market-research firm rather than a manufacturing company. Like any other organization, it will inevitably publish knowledge about itself (instrumental knowledge) to achieve some other end, though its primary task is to produce knowledge as the end product of its own processes.

This knowledge is delivered to its clients in the form of reports on areas of concern, sets of statistics, and reasoned conclusions about the relative significance of this quantitative and qualitative information. Thus, the OECD is, for our purposes, a discursive knowledge-producing organization.

Where discursive knowledge is embodied in figures, words, statistics, and reports, the organization's knowledge-producing function intersects with its foundational multilinguality. At the point of intersection stands the Translation Division.

Translation at Center-Stage

In a very real sense, the Translation Division stands at the center of the organization's activities, acting as a quality filter through which the organization's bilingual discourse passes. Four key aspects of knowledge production at OECD effectively empower translators and endow them with a status they rarely enjoy in private-sector work:

- *L2 Authoring.*[2] Many authors of the source material, i.e., the knowledge producers, write in a non-native language—mainly English, one of the foundational languages of the organization. In other words, the linguistic expression of the knowledge produced is often nonstandard.

- *Committee-Authored Documents.* This does not refer simply to multiple-author documents, which are increasingly frequent in cooperative work environments. Rather, it refers to documents which have been serially, rather than synchronously, edited, often by hand, by a cascade of different committees, each with their red-penning habits and linguistic (often L2-authoring) quirks.

- *Multiculturalism.* The organization produces knowledge based on material that is itself the product of other traditions of knowledge production, in particular knowledge produced by client members of the organization. As the OECD has 29 members, its products allude to, draw on, and exploit extremely culturally heterogeneous information. Unlike companies that might have a single corporate idiom disseminated to end-readers in a broad array of languages, the OECD must occasionally incorporate a broad array of idioms into a document which is then translated into just one other language.

- *High Referentiality Index.* This is a typical property of the way knowledge is distributed within documents. Since part of the knowledge produced by the OECD involves legally binding resolutions, international conventions, and the like, it inevitably refers to previous OECD documents and those of other international organizations.

---

2. René Prioux uses the French term *allophonie*. However, an English borrowing might cause confusion with the linguistic term "allophone," which refers to the phonetic variants of a single phoneme.

The Translation Division thus does not simply translate all relevant documents into its two official languages, but serves as a quality-assurance filter in delivering the organization's major products.

Translation-Division Structure

The OECD's Translation Division was founded concurrently with the organization in 1961. In 1996 it was integrated into a more general Language and Conference Services Division. The Conference Services department takes charge of all interpretation requirements within the organization, but there is no direct operational association between the two departments.

The Translation Division is expected to supply specific linguistic services to any of the 20 or so in-house units (often called Directorates) which cover the following subject areas: food, agriculture and fisheries, money laundering, social policy, public management, science, technology and industry, statistics, regions, cities and countryside, relations with nonmembers, economics and long-term analysis, sustainable development, energy (the OECD includes the International Energy Agency and the Nuclear Energy Agency), environment, finance, investment, taxation and competition, regulatory reform, and electronic commerce.

The Translation Division consists of four language sections and a relatively well-staffed Reference and Terminology Unit (RTU), which provides comprehensive translation support. The workforce breaks down as follows:

Section	Staff Members
French	53
English	11
German	13
Reference/Terminology	8
Management	2

At the OECD, and at most other international organizations, translators are recruited as knowledge workers with a similar civil-service ranking within the hierarchy to that of engineers and lawyers. They are viewed as skilled professionals rather than subordinates to the more "important" work of knowledge producers.

The translators act as an intermediary in the knowledge value chain, as the following diagram shows. The two-way arrows indicate that the translator will be involved in various cognitively rich feedback loops—checking with the authors, inventing neologisms as new concepts emerge,[3] establishing official usage, and reusing finalized knowledge products to decode new knowledge:

Consider, as a point of contrast, the translator's role in an organization with no foundational multilinguality. In such organizations, translation will be subordinate to rather than coordinate with the knowledge-producing chain: documents will by and large be finalized before translation, and language transfer may be relatively mechanical, cognitively independent of the knowledge-production chain:

Recruitment. To recruit the best staff, the Translation Division uses a fairly elaborate and time-consuming vetting procedure. Candidates must pass written and oral examinations, given in a number of separate centers (including Washington, DC) where the organization has satellite offices. The 1998 recruitment drive attracted 400 candidates, of whom eight were shortlisted and four finally chosen. This is fairly standard for international organizations, where about one percent of candidates are hired.

The Translation Division looks for people able to analyze a document and convey the information clearly and accurately. The existence of L2, committee-driven authorship means that source documents must first be understood, and then translated into an adequate target version. Ancillary skills—e.g., word processing, Web wizardry, DTP—are far less relevant criteria.

This means that graduates fresh from translation schools or universities are unsuitable candidates. The typical profile of a new recruit is a professional translator with several years' experience either in other organizations or in

---

3. For example, *PECO*, a term currently used in official international discourse to refer to the Eastern and Central European countries (based on a French acronym), was invented by the OECD Translation Division.

the private sector. However, OECD records suggest that mature translators with translation-school training usually make better candidates than mature translators with only university training in modern languages.

Qualifying External Suppliers. The Translation Division outsources work to some 100 external suppliers in a typical year. These translators are qualified on the basis of their personal profiles; there is no qualification examination. The main purpose of outsourcing translation is to benefit from either specific language-pair skills (e.g., Thai to English), or specific subject-area expertise (e.g., nuclear-waste management).

Languages Covered. The fundamental mission of the OECD translation service is to translate between French and English, the two official languages, producing a bilingual version of the knowledge produced by the organization. At the request of the national members, German and Italian are also provided as target languages. There have also been requests on occasion for Japanese target translations.

There are no official source languages apart from English and French, but there may be requests for documents to be translated from any number of source languages. In a typical year, the Translation Division provides translations into English or French from the standard West European languages (Spanish, German, Italian), strategic East and Central European languages (Czech, Hungarian, Polish), strategic Asian languages (Chinese, Japanese, Korean), and any number of other languages on an ad-hoc basis (e.g., Bulgarian, Macedonian, Turkish).

Since 1985, the relative proportion of French and English target translations has changed dramatically. Fifteen years ago, 70 percent of all documents were authored in French for translation into English. By 1999, this relative apportionment had radically changed: today over 80 percent of all source documents are in English, and only 20 percent are authored in French.

Target Language	Share of Volume
French	80%
English	17%
German	1%
Italian	1%
Other	1%

These figures clearly show that the L2-authorship phenomenon primarily affects French translators.

Total Annual Translation Volume. The Translation Division translated some 80,000 pages (24 million words) of material in 1998 (all languages combined). This represents a 100 percent increase over 1985, or a manageable 10-percent annual increase.

Document Types and Content

A translation department in any international organization (or for that matter in any standard in-house translation service, private or public) is expected to handle almost any kind of document, from half-page memoranda to an occasional 900-page report. The choice as to how a document translation is handled is a matter of local negotiation with the requesting service.

The OECD produces a steady stream of knowledge embodied in documents, including:

* reports on various issues of interest to its members—for example, on social affairs, corporate governance, nuclear-waste disposal, and fishing rights—ranging from 200 to 900 pages and involving a broad range of technical material;

* economic reviews for about 20 of its 29 member countries per year, as well as twice-a-year forecasts in most economic and business sectors;

* official treaties, agreements, and other legally binding documents such as the Convention on Double Taxation;

* conference papers, reports, and summaries of conferences, and other material associated with international communications on issues of interest to OECD members.

Documents often include graphs, tabular information, and other formats depicting quantitative information.

The Translation Process

In terms of basic workflow, there appears to be nothing specific to the OECD translation process. A request is received, translated by the person(s) management assigns, revised, and the target document is returned to the requesting unit in the appropriate form.

In-House vs. Outsourcing Translation. More significant is the decision procedure whereby a given translation task is assigned either to an in-house translator or is outsourced. The following type of documents point to in-house translation:

- *Confidential.* Confidential documents are always translated in-house, thereby fulfilling one of the key roles of the translation function.

- *High-Profile.* Documents involving the organization's image are also translated in-house for confidentiality reasons.

- *Urgent.* Speeches from senior offices must be translated rapidly in keeping with OECD terminology standards.

- *Committee-Authored.* These tend to be hard to read due to the multiple commentaries and edits that have been added to print documents. They are often hard to invoice, since they invariably consist of an already translated version of a previous document scattered with updates.

Outsourced translation tends to be:

- long, nonurgent, lower-priority documents;

- meeting reports, where there is a low OECD image quotient and which are often circulated among insiders;

- highly technical documents, where in-house skills do not exist;

- more obscure language pairs;

- emergency jobs due to in-house sickness, etc.

Revision and Rereading. There are two levels of revision at OECD—instructional revision and rereading.

- *Instructional Revision.* This refers to the work that a senior translator (i.e., one who has been with the Division for some time), might supply to a junior (i.e., new) translator who requires aid in learning how to read through L2-authored or other parameters of OECD documents.

- *Rereading.* A more systematic work-through of the text. This process is performed either by a member of the Translation Division, or by one of the requester authors.

In general, the Translation Division is not sufficiently resourced to carry out a comprehensive revision of all texts. This means that key strategic texts where the organization's image is at stake are revised, but that other material, of lower priority, is not. This in turn has an impact on whether or not a document is outsourced for translation. Only translators considered capable of delivering a target document that does not need significant revision will be chosen.

Translation Tools and Resources

Because the Translation Division plays a role in controlling quality of the knowledge produced in the OECD, terminology and document reference management is critical to the life cycle of any translation. There are a number of reasons for this:

- the high referentiality index: many documents refer to and contain citations of other documents produced within the same or similar organization;

- multiculturalism of content;

- the current lack of a comprehensive translation-memory system;

- the relatively wide range of subjects treated in documents.

The Translation Division therefore works closely with the RTU to respond to these constraints.

Terminology Resources. RTU members are not terminologists in the strict sense of the word. A certain amount of terminology management (the extraction, maintenance, and access to terms) is integrated into the overall workload of the translator.

Translators are expected to use the services of the reference staff when possible to check on documents and validate wording. A translator who spends an hour on the Internet seeking terms and checking in and out of terminology forums and the like is not rewarded for her/his initiative. On the contrary, this is considered a waste of resources, since there are staff available to make more efficient searches for them.

In other words, translation management is organized to ensure that translators work *in tandem with* reference staff to carry out their special role of mastering document meaning. The driving idea is for all translators to be able to choose the most effective tools to meet their needs. The RTU team provides translators with documents from a number of text bases, computerized or print. They also manage the aligned bilingual versions of key resolutions and regulatory documents available online to translators.

Translators themselves have created and maintain a set of about 20 specialist glossaries on recurring subjects (e.g., nuclear safety, macroeconomics, e-commerce, agriculture) developed out of their own terminological consultation work based on documents provided them by the RTU staff. These glossaries are formatted as simple two-column Microsoft Word files and are available both online and as hard copy.

The Translation Division has successfully marketed a few of these glossaries as printed volumes (the first editions of the economics and agriculture glossaries have sold out and revised editions are in the pipeline). The department also makes use of the Microisis bibliographic database system developed by Unesco as a tool for ensuring that document titles and acronyms are systematically available to translators.

Cooperation Among Internal Organizations. The OECD translation resources are not limited to in-house material. Unlike most corporate terminology users, intent on protecting their proprietary terminology, international organizations have an unwritten policy of coordinating and sharing their terminology and translation resources. This is because the documents produced by these organizations often cite each other, or deal with similar concepts and usage, and therefore benefit from the extension of terminology validation to any future translation of such documents.

The directors of the translation departments of international organizations meet regularly to discuss such collaboration, and there is even a project under way to make all international-organization terminology available electronically via an intranet for direct access by translators with access rights.

In addition, there appears to be a relatively significant flow of staff translators between international organizations. One of the effects of this community of international-organization translators is to call on one another for terminological and other aid when translating, and thereby benefit from a hotline to insider knowledge.

This informal dimension of professional translator behavior also exists in other sectors (for example, all translators who work on medical documents between certain languages) and has been largely enabled by the emergence of translator and terminology networks on the Internet. But the critical dimension in international-organization resource management appears to be at the level of lengthier citations as much as term strings. If a translator in one organization has easy access to a document, a translator in a second organization has easy access as well.

Improving Resource Availability. Despite the available manpower and existing access to a range of terminology in the semi-informal international organization network, the Translation Division is planning to reengineer its terminology access methods. The current plan is to simplify access to glossaries by porting them into a Microsoft Access database and designing a single interface. The user will be able to rank the relevance of the various glossaries when searching for a term and benefit from other functions.

Interestingly, the department has decided to develop its own terminology database based on off-the-shelf software packages, rather than purchase one of the dedicated terminology-management systems now on the market. Translation-Division managers usually explain this decision by expressing doubts about sustainable support services from dedicated terminology-system developers. They are also expected to purchase software solutions that are multi- rather than mono-functional.

Translation Tools and Translator Status. We have seen that translators are valued within the organization as coordinate (as opposed to subordinate) knowledge workers. Much of their relationship with translation tools is colored by this status.

Until 1988, translation at the OECD was mostly handled in pre-PC mode by a two-person team: the translator would dictate and a transcriber would type and format. The PC is now *de rigueur* in the department and is systematically used for urgent translation work. But translators may still choose to translate longer reports by dictation and then have them typed up and formatted separately by transcribers.

Translation-Division management does not feel that the PC has significantly reduced the cost of in-house translation, nor has it radically affected productivity. Since they see their staff as translation professionals, and not a mix of secretarial worker, data-input operator, and language professional, they are concerned with optimizing the conditions under which quality translation is produced, not minimizing the staff or unnecessarily overloading translators with non-core tasks.

This means, for example, that it is more productive for translators exclusively to translate, and have transcribers produce the numerous tables and graphs that appear in a report. OECD translators are not paid to master a graphics package, but they are encouraged to be flexible in their use of tools—using a PC or resorting to dictation where appropriate.

Machine Translation and Translation Memory. The OECD Translation Division does not use machine translation (MT) in any form. There is apparently fairly strong agreement among the heads of translation divisions at the major international organizations that MT does not yet offer the required reliability and quality. This is despite (or because of) systematic use of Systran as a language-support tool at the EC, and a certain interest by the UN Translation Division in its possible impact on productivity.

A number of organizations produced internal reports during the late 1980s when the availability of MT technology first reached public awareness. The

World Bank actually licensed the Tovna MT system, but apparently decided it was not a suitable translation tool and never fully deployed it. The general consensus is that MT will not provide a solution to the foundational translation needs of international organizations for at least the next 10 years.

Translation memory, however, is being actively examined and in certain cases (e.g., at the EC), deployed in the same organizations. On the agenda at the OECD is a project to introduce Trados Translator's Workbench, a translation-memory system fed by Multiterm, its terminology-management component. The goal is to ensure that new translations can automatically draw on validated terminology, thereby harmonizing terminology across all documents in the organization.

The Translation Division can also benefit from this validation system by outsourcing terminology-ready source texts to translators, without having to spend time preparing extensive terminology sheets to accompany the documents. If this proves feasible, translation memory will offer the OECD a tool to address one constraint on its translation—the high referentiality index.

S U M M A R Y

We can briefly pull together the key points developed in this profile, by listing the ways in which the four constraints on knowledge production in a context of foundational multilinguality impact decisions in translation management.

Constraint	Impact on Translation	Impact on Management
L2 authoring	Requires trained readers Contact with authors	In-house capacity Careful recruitment MT unusable
Committee-authored documents	Requires trained readers Access to in-house document cascades	In-house capacity Reference support MT unusable
Multiculturalism	Requires trained readers Controlled terminology	In-house capacity Reference support
High referentiality index	Access to in-house document cascades	In-house capacity Reference support TM usable

This brief profile leaves many questions unanswered: for example, can editors be employed to standardize the L2-authored texts that are currently filtered by the Translation Division? Or indeed, what happens to these source documents when the translated targets have improved on them? In particular, it would be interesting to have more comprehensive statistics on the nature and source of these L2-authored documents.

This wish will be partly answered in due course; the OECD Translation Division is to start implementing a new translation workflow-management system in 1999. This will streamline the translation request and production process and simultaneously provide a rich stream of data about the who, what, where, when, how much, and how often of the Division's translation productivity. Which means that, like other organizations, public and private, it too will be producing instrumental knowledge about its own behavior.

Localization at Hewlett-Packard's LaserJet Solutions Group

Karen Combe

SUMMARY

Hewlett-Packard (HP) is a large, diverse corporation in which each business function operates with considerable autonomy. This case study addresses how a single group, the LaserJet Solutions Group (LSG), has reengineered its language processes.

The Information Engineering (IE) department in LSG functions as an internal service bureau, providing English-documentation development and localization services for LSG products. IE selects suppliers, designs deliverables, manages projects, and delivers final output to its clients. IE must demonstrate its value to LSG during periodic reevaluations. It is therefore critical for IE's survival that its supplier program be successful, and be seen as successful.

In this case study, we examine IE's change from exclusively using an HP-internal localization group in Europe to establishing a viable, US-based, localization supplier program. We also look at the benefits derived from extending the "HP Way"—management principles typically applied only internally within HP—to its supplier program.

BACKGROUND

For its initial entry into localization, IE went to an internal HP group in Europe that provided localization into nine European languages. Contracting to small translation agencies and individual translators throughout Europe, the group could not be considered a full-service localization agency that offered complete project-management services. One person within IE, the localization project manager, supported and coordinated the effort on the US side.

It was hardly a "black-box" approach, as the US engineers were quick to discover. In the normal course of localization, translators need access to subject-matter experts to clarify text. Translators contacted the US-based IE localization project manager directly, who answered their questions with help from the engineers or the technical writers within IE. This coordination required considerable effort from IE.

IE recognized several additional shortcomings in this model:

- Because the number of projects and languages was slated to increase, using a single localization supplier, even an internal one, posed a risk.

- The eight-hour time difference restricted real-time communication.

- In the early '90s, knowledge of internationalization and localization was not widespread in the LSG labs or among the content developers. IE managers felt that a more team-oriented approach to localization projects between HP and a nearby supplier would facilitate sharing of knowledge and yield better global products.

- The translation coordination effort noted above would soon have required IE to add staff, as the number of languages and products needing localization multiplied. The table below shows how staff would have to be added under the old model as projects increased, as compared to fewer coordinators needed under the new model of adopting a local partner.

Old Model		New Model	
up to 2 projects	1 coordinator	up to 4 projects	1 coordinator
2–4 projects	2 coordinators	4–8 projects	2 coordinators
4–6 projects	3 coordinators		

REQUIREMENTS

These reasons were sufficiently compelling for the company to adopt a new model, and IE decided to change to a US-based, full-service localization supplier. HP managers faced two challenges: 1) choosing the right supplier; and 2) setting up a program that would get the best performance from the combined efforts of the supplier and HP teams. The supplier would have to meet multiple criteria:

- financial stability, including a sufficiently large customer base so that HP would not constitute too much of the supplier's business;

- proven multilanguage localization capability, with systems in place to ramp up new languages quickly;

- substantial production capacity in translation, desktop publishing, and engineering;

- project-management systems sufficient to handle very large projects;

- strong software-engineering skills;

- quality orientation and procedures;

- compatible corporate culture.

IMPLEMENTATION

Choosing a supplier proved simple compared with the actual implementation. After a several-month search, IE chose International Language
Engineering (ILE) of Boulder, Colorado (USA).

The supplier program benefited immensely from application of HP's core
management philosophy. This is particularly significant given the nature of
the translation and localization industry. Although localization is complex
and is in the critical path to launching a new product, language companies
have rarely been considered as real partners in the success of new products.
HP's approach to localization represents, in my view, pioneering work in
the application of real partnering with a language-services provider.

In his book, *The HP Way*, David Packard explained his approach to management: "No policy has contributed more to Hewlett-Packard's success
than the policy of 'management by objective.' [...] Management by objective [...] refers to a system in which overall objectives are clearly stated and
agreed upon, and which gives people the flexibility to work toward those
goals in ways they determine best for their own areas of responsibility."[1]

According to management guru Peter Drucker, "in the traditional organization—the organization of the last 100 years—the skeleton, or internal
structure, was a combination of rank and power. In the emerging organization, it has to be mutual understanding and responsibility." Packard notes
that, "though Hewlett-Packard is hardly an emerging organization, mutual
understanding and responsibility have been, for many years, key characteristics of the HP style of management."[2]

IE chose its first and subsequent localization partners very carefully and
then invested time and training in the relationships. Having selected what
IE considered to be the best available partners, those companies were then
empowered to do the best job. HP makes its expectations clear and then
gives the suppliers the freedom and responsibility to reach those objectives;
client and supplier are intended to act as colleagues rather than masters and
vendors.

---

1. Packard, David. *The HP Way*. HarperCollins Publisher, Inc., New York, pp. 152–153.
2. Packard, p. 154. Drucker's quote comes from an interview in the spring 1993 issue of the
Harvard Business Review.

For its part, IE shoulders its own responsibilities in localization: defining the project, specifying reasonable turnaround for issue clarification, attending to internal problems, and providing its share to any mutual process improvements. By working in partnership with its suppliers, IE has determined that it gets more for its money—suppliers start thinking on HP's behalf, continuously looking for improvements in systems and processes.

Below are two examples of how this supplier program has worked.

Example 1: Establishing Engineering Confidence

The first stumbling block in the IE-ILE relationship occurred over engineering issues. In a project that we will call Kinley (not the real code name), part of the printer software was supplied by a third party. During localization into nine languages, ILE engineers discovered that the localized context-sensitive help was broken, although the English version functioned properly. ILE asked HP what could be causing the problem, and HP in turn referred ILE to the third-party developer. Meanwhile, because of tight deadlines, the project was advancing through its normal process. In the end, ILE and HP engineers together determined the problem and its solution. However, the delay in resolution resulted in a considerable list of content issues to be taken care of by translators at the final verification (linguistic QA) stage, which meant that, because of an immutable deadline, normal QA tasks got short shrift.

The localized software first delivered to HP contained mistakes such as duplicate hot keys. Although ILE had helped solve online-help problems, HP engineers saw only the rudimentary errors and questioned ILE's engineering competence. Although the HP and ILE engineers worked together quickly to eliminate these low-level mistakes and HP delivered a defect-free localized product, the confidence problem remained.

Rather than simply casting aspersions, HP was able to apply its empowering management philosophy. IE managers realized that since ILE had clearly demonstrated engineering expertise in other ways, there must be some other forces at work here. Instead of blaming the supplier for sloppy work, HP worked with ILE to understand the root cause.

The root-cause analysis yielded several important conclusions:

- HP gained a greater understanding of the importance of process in large, multilanguage localization projects. If the designated tasks cannot be accomplished during the appropriate phase, and therefore extra tasks accumulate for completion in the final phase, then that final stage will produce quality problems unless that phase is lengthened.

- Failure to resolve serious issues had constituted a threat to quality and delivery. Project managers at ILE accepted their responsibility to clarify issues sufficiently to HP so that correct decisions could be made.

- HP recognized the importance of getting questions answered and issues resolved promptly.

- The software had basic internationalization errors which the HP lab did not recognize. Conclusions:

  - The HP labs needed training in software internationalization.

  - The labs would need to monitor the internationalization status of third-party software.

  - HP engineers had little understanding of the localization process and the relevance of the QA steps involved. This would be problematic for future working relationships with ILE or any other localization supplier.

ILE and IE instituted the following process improvements:

- An engineer-exchange program was instituted.

  - At project kick-off meetings, ILE project engineers would visit HP and review the software with HP developers. This provided a platform for feedback to the HP engineer on localization issues, along with the opportunity to resolve issues early in the project. ILE engineers would become familiar with the software, learn to build the product, and discover any idiosyncrasies from a language-engineering perspective.

  - HP engineers would visit ILE once the project was under way to observe the localization process. ILE would provide structured training on localization to the engineers.

  - Over the course of several projects and through mutual feedback from HP and ILE engineers, a localization kit, called a Localization Instruction Worksheet (LIW), was developed and refined. This LIW contained all the information needed for the localization supplier to complete the software portion of a project.

This exchange program, started in 1994, still continues today.

- Based on their increased understanding of localization process, IE project managers agreed to respond to project-related questions within 24 hours. Although complete answers were not always available in that time, HP worked towards the fastest-possible resolution. They understand that if issues are unresolved within times they agree on with their supplier contacts, schedules may need to be adjusted or QA steps added to ensure quality.

- ILE provided internationalization training to HP software and firmware labs. HP developed internationalization standards in their labs, and provided further training in their own teams. This training, which began in 1994, continues today for new engineers.

- ILE modified its standard process by adding a translator QA for projects with substantial translation during the verification stage.

IE mustered internal support for these initiatives. The manager of the localization group within IE set up meetings with lab managers to discuss internationalization requirements, and sponsored training sessions for lab engineers. Lab managers were invited when ILE presented new internationalization or localization technologies at HP. IE localization managers included engineers in project "post-mortems." The figure below illustrates the integration of localization project management with internal engineering staff.

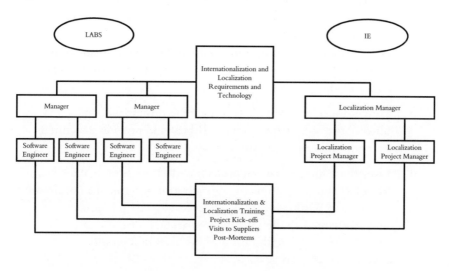

Example 2: Outsourcing English Development

In 1995, IE determined that HP would be best served by outsourcing development of learning products—the term it uses for the help and documentation accompanying its hardware and software products. Technical writers and graphic designers who created learning products had until then resided within IE. The technical writers also served as project managers on the cross-functional teams that included software labs, marketing, HP's localization project manager, and the printing/distribution specialist.

Through closer involvement with localization, IE now understood that the way English learning products were developed directly affected how easily they were subsequently localized. For example, if writers index an English manual by inserting markers and using the index-generation feature in their desktop-publishing software, translated indexes could be generated with minimal manual intervention. But if writers used manual techniques on the English, such as post-editing the generated index, that manual work would have to be repeated in each localized version—up to 30 languages for HP. Every error or inefficiency in the original English is magnified many times over by the time localization is completed.

IE saw the value of combining English development and localization services. HP's suppliers added development resources to accommodate the new need, and opened local offices for proximity to HP's subject-matter experts. HP gained the benefits of one-stop-shopping for English and localized languages, as well as the improved service resulting from having local suppliers.

Once localization and development were combined, other synergies came to light. English writers could now serve as subject-matter experts for translators and localizers, and could also formulate text more clearly for that purpose. Writers could provide information for translators before translation began, and answer questions quickly once a project was in flight. Similarly, translators would provide feedback to writers on the localizability of the text they were creating, and help raise the level of internationalization in HP products. In addition to outsourcing English development, HP in effect outsourced localization support.

Within HP, outsourcing English development of learning products evoked a certain unease, since the help and documentation were viewed as integral to the products. IE worked to alleviate this response:

- For unusual project needs, such as instant response in a time-sensitive situation, IE implemented special processes to ensure that a supplier's writer or graphic designer would be available immediately to rectify any problem.

- The supplier's writers and project managers were drawn into HP's planning process (detailed below).

- HP project teams were involved in evaluating bids and awarding projects, giving them a sense of comfort with a supplier's capabilities.

- HP employees worked with suppliers on special projects, such as stylesheet design.

The figure below shows the organizational structure at IE before and after outsourcing English development.

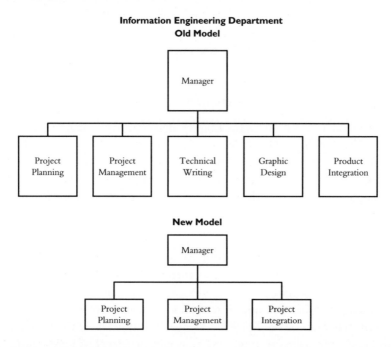

Expanding the Model

Integrating English development and localization in a single company or partnership outside HP, compounded with increasingly complex projects, compelled HP to involve suppliers earlier in project planning—in some cases two to three months before English documentation development begins, versus the prior norm of two to three weeks. The supplier's writers and designers give feedback on the technical feasibility of desired options, serve as experts and consultants to HP project teams, and harness new technologies for information delivery.

Since HP continues to expand into new languages, the supplier's localization experts must validate the English information strategy. For example, a particular strategy for online information delivery may work well with tools available for English and even European languages, but not for Asian languages, Arabic, or Hebrew.

Earlier involvement also lets suppliers estimate costs and schedules earlier. IE project managers may also ask suppliers for cost and schedule scenarios earlier on, thus broadening their options. HP and its supplier can debate the pros and cons of various approaches. HP recognized that the stakes were significant: localization budgets may be four to five times larger than the cost of English development, and time-to-market for localized products was all-important.

Research on Early Supplier Involvement (ESI)

In evaluating early supplier involvement (ESI) initiatives in high-tech firms, researchers at Michigan State University found the following 12 success factors (ranked in order of importance):[3]

1. The supplier's employees were members of, or participated in, the buyer's project team.

2. There was direct cross-functional, intercompany communication.

3. The two companies shared education and training.

4. The two companies set up common and linked information systems (e.g., electronic data interchange, CAD/CAM, email).

5. Some of the buyer's and seller's personnel were located in the same place.

6. Technology was shared.

7. Formal trust-development processes were established.

8. Information about customer requirements was exchanged.

9. Information about technology was shared.

10. The two companies shared physical assets (plant and equipment).

11. There were formalized agreements on sharing risks and rewards.

---

3. Discussed in Jukka Nihtilä and Francis Bidault (of the Theseus International Management Institute of France), "Sensitivities of Shared Product Development," *Financial Times*, Mastering Information Management series, 22 February 1999.

12. There were commonly agreed performance measures.

Establishing trust is a *sine qua non* of a successful supplier/client relationship:

> Trust is one of the most important factors in successful technological collaborations between companies. Fundamentally it is a belief that another person (or organisation) will behave in ways that will not be detrimental to us even if unforeseen circumstances should arise. Yet in this day and age, when technology is so pervasive, trust may look like a throwback to a time when ignorance prevailed, a time when traders had to "believe" in the honesty and competence of the other party because they did not have enough information about them. But now parties to a transaction have a wealth of information on one another's capabilities and reputations (and on alternative partners); surely information makes trust unnecessary because it can replace faith with knowledge.
>
> On the contrary, many pieces of research—including the Michigan State University survey mentioned earlier—point to the renewed importance of trust. And this is quite consistent with what we know of ESI partnerships. These relationships are quite complex from an organizational standpoint, let alone a technological one.
>
> As companies enter ever more ambitious relationships, which involve a great number of competencies, to address markets with innovative, immature technologies, they expose themselves to a very high level of risk. And trust is vital in risky situations. Consequently, companies are treating trustworthy partners as assets of enormous value because the development of trust between companies is a lengthy, risky, and thus very expensive, process.[4]

Although it did not explicitly reference such research in adopting its supplier policies, HP embodied many of these principles in ESI and, as we attempt to quantify below, was able to reap the benefits in terms of improved cost-management and faster time-to-market.

---

4. Ibid.

TOOLS TO MANAGE THE RELATIONSHIP

Relationships as complex as those between IE and its suppliers cannot be managed without tools and well-defined processes. Two tools proved particularly useful in keeping the companies in alignment.

"TQRDCE": A Critical Acronym

HP's most important tool in supplier management is the TQRDCE evaluation, which has the following components: Technology, Quality, Responsiveness, Delivery, Cost, and Environment.

Although combined HP/supplier teams meet for project post-mortems, the annual TQRDCE allows IE management to identify trends and summarize performance. Suppliers are rated on a scale of one (lowest) to five (highest) in each area, with three defined as meeting expectations. The IE Supplier Manager receives feedback from each team that has worked with the supplier, and formulates a summary report including areas of excellence and areas for improvement.

Suppliers generally know how their projects have gone in the course of a year. But though they may be aware of missed delivery dates or substandard deliverables, they may not be aware of the overall impact on their HP counterparts. The TQRDCE evaluation is as much a measure of perception as fact, and perception counts for a lot in relationships. If the delivery of one project with software problems creates a perception in the HP labs of supplier quality problems, the supplier will understand it must work to change that perception.

Conversely, if the supplier has discovered areas of innovation that benefit HP, the TQRDCE offers a medium to call out those successes. If a supplier can deliver certain languages on an accelerated schedule, for example, IE may encourage the supplier to institutionalize the process so that HP can take advantage of early availability of those languages, or extend the innovation to other related areas.

Regular Business Meetings

HP's IE team meets twice a year with each supplier's management team. Each company updates the other on its strategic direction, accomplishments, and plans for the upcoming period. This information allows the suppliers to prepare for new requirements, whether they be more micro issues such as the need to add Lithuanian translation capability, or more macro issues such as the need to cut project cycle time. HP is made aware of its suppliers' emerging areas of expertise or expanded service offerings. The contact between management teams helps to keep the partners in strategic alignment and enhance the relationship.

In addition to the management-level meetings, HP or the suppliers may initiate meetings to address more tactical issues such as refining project estimating or streamlining the review of translations by HP's in-country representatives.

BENCHMARKING

In the critical early years following the change to US-based suppliers, IE measured program success in three key areas: quality, cost, and on-time delivery.

- During that period IE did not submit localized products for in-country review on a per-project basis. Instead, the "product champions" in each country were polled annually. The positive feedback from these experts assured IE that suppliers' translation quality was good.

- Cost comparisons over several years and across multiple projects indicated no increases in unit costs for translation/localization, while volume of work increased and cycle times were shortened.

- Careful tracking of projects showed improved on-time delivery with the new program.

IE continues to benchmark its program internally based on the hard criteria of cost, on-time delivery, and quality. Suppliers generally have lowered prices with heightened efficiency, and time-to-market pressures have also forced shorter turnaround times. In-country reviews are now performed more frequently, particularly for the recently added languages, so that HP gets regular project-level feedback on terminology and translation quality.

IE has also added some softer, less tangible measures:

- *Supplier Evolution.* Client requirements are continually changing; suppliers are expected to design and implement improvements across the whole range of 30 languages covered.

- *Productivity Trend Data.* With time, project budgets should decrease comparatively, as more text is reused and processes are improved. IE is finding its own headcount is staying relatively flat although it is handling more projects.

- *Perceived Value.* IE gets regular feedback from its internal customers on the value of the services they provide to LSG.

CONCLUSION

By becoming students of the localization industry, IE managers have been able to assure that their translation program is competitive. They attend industry conferences, such as STC, LISA, and Seybold, and monitor industry watchers such as The Gartner Group.

HP's IE group has implemented an English development and localization program that responds effectively to the needs of internal customers and ensures IE's value to the LSG organization. By applying HP's internal management philosophy to the supplier program, IE has developed partners that work on their own and on HP's behalf to continuously improve process, increase value, cut costs, and decrease time-to-market. This case, from both HP's and its supplier's perspective, has all the earmarks of a success story.

Shortening the Translation Cycle at Eastman Kodak

Suzanne Topping

OVERVIEW

The worldwide market for digital cameras is among the most competitive. The hottest sales period for new models typically comes in the first weeks following product introduction. And although Kodak tried to strategically schedule announcements around the world, once a product appeared in the US, news spread quickly. Kodak needed to get the cameras into other regions sooner to take advantage of the initial buying flurry.

Translation of product literature and software is, by definition, in the critical path for shipment of these products: no translation, no product. Marketing staff, not familiar with translation and localization complexities, saw the typical timetable for language work and asked, predictably, "Why does localization take so long?"

Typical Timeframe for Release of Localized Products

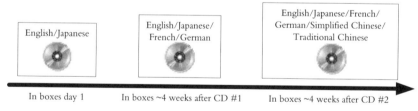

English/Japanese	English/Japanese/French/German	English/Japanese/French/German/Simplified Chinese/Traditional Chinese
In boxes day 1	In boxes ~4 weeks after CD #1	In boxes ~4 weeks after CD #2

The marketing department was intent on cutting localization time, and targeted simultaneous availability of the product in all languages (not the current scenario of the foreign-language versions lagging the English). While the lack of understanding on the part of the marketing managers was frustrating, we in the localization group understood that their need to get localized products sooner was based on hard market drivers.

Process improvement and cycle-time reduction had been an ongoing initiative of the localization group. Marketing's request for simultaneous launch without English delay simply escalated the need for change. The original request for simultaneous shipment came in September, 1998, and the first successful simultaneous launch occurred in April, 1999. While many of the product-development changes and evaluation of QA process alternatives were already underway, the bulk of the research and the actual changes all took place within a seven-month period.

WORKLOAD STATISTICS

The Digital and Applied Imaging localization team handled a variety of project types and sizes throughout the course of the year.

Small Projects

Type. Project types ranged from a few strings to small packages or flyers.

Size. Up to a few hundred English words. Vendor costs were generally less than US$1,000. Localization-management time was between one and five hours.

Volume. About four small projects per month.

Language sets. Language requirements could be as simple as a single language (like Japanese), a few languages, or a wide range of languages (e.g., French, Italian, German, Spanish, Japanese, Simplified Chinese, Traditional Chinese, Russian, and Netherlands Dutch).

Turnaround times. Generally quite short. Very little advance notice about the project was given to the team (under a week), and clients usually needed them within a few days. Project timelines were determined by clients. Elapsed project time was consistently under two weeks, and usually less than one week.

Resources involved. Resources required for small projects were limited. Typically, the jobs were for a single person (e.g., a package designer). One localization team member managed the project, using a multilingual vendor to get the translation done. Sometimes a second vendor was used for linguistic quality assurance (QA).

Mid-Size Projects

Type. These ranged from individual user's guides to product maintenance releases. Maintenance releases could involve:

- changes to software only (in all languages);

- addition of a single language to the existing product language set (impacting all components);

- changes to a product name (impacting all languages and all components).

Size. From several hundred to 50,000 English words. Vendor costs were generally between US$1,000 and US$20,000. Localization-management time was between five and 20 hours, over the course of four to six weeks.

Volume. Ca. six per year.

Language sets. As few as two languages or as many as five (typically French, German, Japanese, Simplified Chinese, and Traditional Chinese).

Turnaround times. More advance notice was typically given for mid-size projects. Planning might begin up to a month before localization activity started. Turnaround times were usually short, however. Software changes were frequently completed within two weeks. User's-guide revisions could take up to four weeks. Turnaround times were negotiated between the client and vendor. Elapsed time for entire projects was between four and six weeks.

Resources involved. This depended on the project. For software changes, players were the localization project manager, a software lead, up to five software engineers, an installer developer, a QA lead, a few software testers, and a help-system developer. Multilingual vendors did the translation, and occasionally a second vendor provided linguistic QA. Regional QA reviewers, print production staff, and logistics personnel were also involved.

A typical project of this type involved approximately 13 Kodak product-team members, along with vendor resources.

Large Projects

Type. Typically localization efforts for entirely new products. Required localization of all components including: camera or scanner hardware LCDs, multiple pieces of software, help files, readme files, documentation, and packaging.

Size. From 50,000 to 100,000 English words. Vendor costs were generally between US$20,000 and US$200,000. Localization-management time was close to 200 hours, over the course of about four months. The percentage of time spent in various project stages is listed below.

Stage	Month	Percentage of Localization Management Time
Planning	1	5%
	2	10%
Project Execution	3	80%
Wrap-Up	4	30%

Volume. Ca. five large projects per year.

Language sets. Same as for mid-size jobs.

Turnaround times. Extensive advance planning took place for large projects. Planning would begin three months before localization started. Turnaround times remained aggressive. Software localization took place in several iterations over the course of about three weeks. User's-guide localization was scheduled to take six weeks, but usually took closer to eight.

Resources involved. Many internal resources were required for large projects. In addition to the typical players in mid-size projects, large projects required a package designer, a user-document author, and a product-marketing manager. One localization staff member managed each project, with support from the team's manager. Multilingual vendors were used to do the work, and occasionally a second vendor provided linguistic QA. Regional reviewers, print-production staff, and logistics personnel were also involved.

A project of this type might involve some 27 Kodak product-team members, along with vendor resources.

Detailed Camera-Product Description

Digital cameras were the most complex large projects needing localization. Since they were consumer-oriented, the products included substantial software elements, and packaging and presentation were glossy and rich in text. Typical components included:

- Camera user-interface (fewer than 200 words)
- Packaging (1,261 words)
- User's guide (22,415 words)
- Quick-start card (856 words)
- Miscellaneous printed pieces (3,000 words)
- Software (3,370 words)

- Help systems (30,705 words)

- Readme files (16,801 words)

- Installers (2,920 words)

- CD sleeves (96 words)

- CD silkscreens (10 words)

The software itself consisted of multiple Windows applications and two or three Macintosh applications. Additional prelocalized applications were also included on the CD, and installed by the same installer. All software for both platforms was presented on a single multilingual, multiplatform CD.

Simplified Version of a Typical Camera Offering

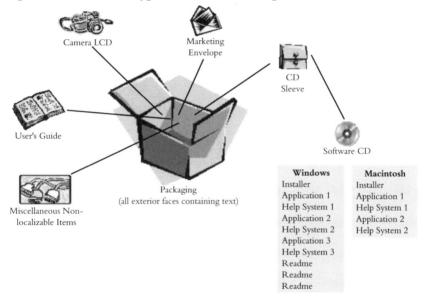

Geographically Diverse Teams

As the product itself was complex, so was the development-team structure to manage it. Kodak's digital-camera teams were geographically diverse, with team members in Rochester (New York), Boston, Yokohama (Japan), and Harrow (UK). For some teams, even project management was divided, with co-project managers in Rochester and Yokohama (where the cameras were manufactured).

Localization was primarily managed from Rochester, but most Japanese items were created by Kodak Japan, and some of the software was handled in Harrow.

Breakdown by Site of Localization Product Development

	Rochester					Boston					Japan			U.K.				
	E	J	F	G	C	E	J	F	G	C	E	J	C	E	J	F	G	C
Project Management	✓										✓							
Localization Management	✓	✓	✓	✓	✓						✓			✓	✓	✓	✓	
Software Development	✓					✓					✓			✓				
Help System Development						✓												
Installer Development	✓	✓	✓	✓	✓													
Software QA	✓	✓	✓	✓	✓	✓	✓	✓	✓	✓								
CD Builds	✓	✓	✓	✓	✓													
User Document Development	✓																	
User Document Printing	✓		✓	✓								✓	✓					
Packaging Design	✓										✓							
Packaging Printing	✓		✓	✓								✓	✓					
CD Sleeve Printing	✓	✓	✓	✓	✓													
Product Pack-out	✓		✓	✓								✓	✓					

As the figure above shows, packaging design and user's-guide writing took place in Rochester; help systems were developed in Boston; software was developed by a variety of engineers in each location.

Both the Rochester and Boston teams conducted software and CD testing. While the Rochester site also managed the production of CDs for all countries, the CDs themselves were sent to Yokohama for packaging with Japanese products. Rochester also managed the printing of English, French, and German documents, while Yokohama printed the Japanese and Chinese materials.

Having a distributed team meant that information and files came from diverse locations to be localized centrally, and were returned again once localization was complete. Tracking each item throughout localization and production cycles was crucial.

Team Communication

The physical distance between team members complicated communications, which were vital on projects with such tight deadlines. Weekly product-team, software, localization, and logistics meetings were held in Rochester, with team members calling in from remote locations. Video-conferencing was used for periodic reviews. Because of time differences, meetings were frequently held either evenings or early mornings US Eastern time. Email remained the primary method of communication; it was used to broadcast messages to team members, verify status of action items, address or raise issues, distribute status reports, and create a "paper trail" for various events.

DIAGNOSING THE PROBLEM

In reality, translation and localization itself actually took only a very small fraction of the total time. The figure below illustrates the activities and approximate duration for each task associated with producing localized CDs. Only a few days were spent updating localized versions, and most of the time was spent on testing and production.

Breakdown by Task of Localization Process

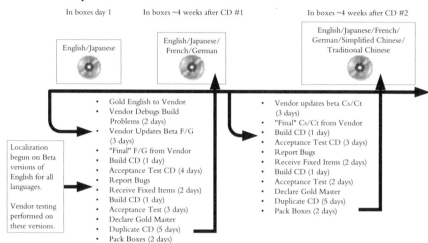

In boxes day 1   In boxes ~4 weeks after CD #1   In boxes ~4 weeks after CD #2

English/Japanese

English/Japanese/French/German

English/Japanese/French/German/Simplified Chinese/Traditional Chinese

Localization begun on Beta versions of English for all languages.

Vendor testing performed on these versions.

- Gold English to Vendor
- Vendor Debugs Build Problems (2 days)
- Vendor Updates Beta F/G (3 days)
- "Final" F/G from Vendor
- Build CD (1 day)
- Acceptance Test CD (4 days)
- Report Bugs
- Receive Fixed Items (2 days)
- Build CD (1 day)
- Acceptance Test (3 days)
- Declare Gold Master
- Duplicate CD (5 days)
- Pack Boxes (2 days)

- Vendor updates beta Cs/Ct (3 days)
- "Final" Cs/Ct from Vendor
- Build CD (1 day)
- Acceptance Test CD (3 days)
- Report Bugs
- Receive Fixed Items (2 days)
- Build CD (1 day)
- Acceptance Test (2 days)
- Declare Gold Master
- Duplicate CD (5 days)
- Pack Boxes (2 days)

The people in the trenches—project managers, software developers, QA testers, and documentation specialists—understood that the entire *product-development process itself* needed to be restructured to achieve simultaneous worldwide launch without English delay.

Various digital cameras had been localized several times already, and the team had made impressive strides in cutting cycle time for printed documentation. Packaging, user's guides, and other printed materials were already on an accelerated track (frequently underway even before the actual software-user interfaces or camera LCDs were finalized)—and the translation time saved proved invaluable in accommodating long print lead times.

With the process for printed material in reasonably good shape, the biggest challenges were related to translating and localizing the CD-based software.

In the end, the entire software-development process was examined and refined. It was broken down into three stages:

- Software development

- Translation and localization

- Multilingual software QA and testing

Since translation and localization time was already quite short, the greatest savings would eventually come in development and testing.

Problem Area I—Software Development

Software-Handoff Problems

Since the digital cameras included so much software and other "soft" files, the absence of a strong procedural link between developers and localizers caused numerous difficulties in creating multilingual CDs. Further accentuating the problem, software came from a variety of locales and sources. And while some developers structured their applications well and handed off complete packages for localization, many did not.

For each project, the localization team gave blank specification forms to the software developers, hoping that these checklists would remind developers to provide all required files, graphics, environment information, and build instructions along with the resource files. The team provided the completed checklists to the localization vendors, along with the files. In most cases, however, the vendors still did not receive everything they needed; build instructions were incomplete, header files were missing, or tool versions were listed incorrectly.

Tracking down answers to vendor questions became a seemingly infinite loop. Once one question was answered, it frequently opened the door to another problem. For example, the localization vendor might try to run a build, only to find that a header file was missing. Once the header file was sent to them, they would run the build again. The compiler would go one step further, but stop to report that another header file was needed.

Working through these issues frequently delayed the start of localization by several days. When dealing with timelines as tight as those for the digital cameras, these delays are enough to derail a schedule.

No Identification of Strings

Kodak commonly received software back from vendors which contained strings (such as registry entries) that were translated when they shouldn't have been, and other strings left in English when they should have been translated. This occurred because no instructions were given about which strings to translate. The vendor had to sift through resource files, trying to figure out which strings in the code were translatable.

Complex Build Processes

The process of building software tended to be complex, requiring shared files and structures provided by other software developers. For example, one application needed a COM .dll to run, and that .dll was being built with the rest of the application, and not merely provided for the application's use. Handing off such a complicated build process to a vendor was inefficient.

Undocumented Build Processes

For several years, software developers had been working under tight deadlines, leveraging applications over and over again. This meant that they did not tend to document how they built their applications. Unfortunately, localization vendors were "flying blind," and the developers were not very thorough when it came to passing along instructions at localization time.

Readme File Formatting

A surprising number of problems came from an unexpected source: readme files. Part of the problem was that there were so many of them, covering a wide range of issues. For one camera project, there were a total of six English readme files. When five new languages were added, the result was 36 opportunities for something to go wrong. The most common problem found when receiving translated readme files from vendors was corrupt format. This was caused either by using a tool other than the one the English author had used, or by using tabs and soft returns rather than spaces and hard returns. The group also found that opening a file in various text editors yielded different formatting results, even when the same formatting approach had been applied.

Solutions

The localization team held brainstorming sessions with software developers. One outcome of these sessions was a key procedural document, "Development Guidelines for Easy Software Localization." The information in these guidelines seemed merely common sense to the localizers, but writing it down seemed to formalize and legitimize it. And since the developers themselves suggested the solutions, there was immediate buy-in from them.

Some of the most significant changes were to:

- *Isolate localizable strings.* For each application, all translatable text would be pulled from the various resource files and placed in a single, text-string-only .rc file.
  Handling the text in this way made instructions completely clear for the vendor. Everything needing translation was in one file, and no

other files should be touched. It also helped prevent accidental changes to functionality, since the translated file did not contain code.

- *Make all font information modifiable.* For some applications, font information was defined in code rather than in editable resource files. This prevented the localization vendor from making adjustments to increase legibility or to fix font-related bugs. The developers agreed to ensure that all font definitions were editable during localization.

- *Simplify build processes.* The developers agreed to review their build processes and pare them down to a more elegant form.

- *Document build processes.* The development community agreed to start documenting how builds were run. Explicit instructions would be written so that *anyone* could sit down at a PC and build the application. Not only did this help localization, but it also made it easier to transition work between developers.

- *Pre-build before handoff to the vendor.* As a final precaution, someone other than the developer would build the software before it was sent to the vendor. This meant that missing files or other problems were identified *before* localization actually began.

- *Deliver readme files as PDF files.* English readme-file authors would use word-processing or desktop-publishing applications rather than a text editor, and use all of the formatting tools available (tables, bolding, etc.). Once files were completed, they would save them as PDF files, and translated readme files would be delivered in PDF format as well. This precluded format changes that arose depending on the text editor in use.

Most of these principles were included as requirements in software-specification documents, to help ensure that the guidelines were followed.

Problem Area 2—QA/Testing

Back-End Problems

Once the front end of the process had been addressed, it was time to look at the back end.

The QA process faced far more significant challenges than development. As in most software communities, QA always pays the price for schedule slips and feature "creep" (changes in features while the project is being finalized). No matter how significant the changes to plan, QA had to struggle to somehow make up for the lost time. In addition, QA groups were often strapped for resources, and frequently had to rely on inexperienced contract labor. (Total number of testers was between eight and 10, depending on the project.) Engineering releases for existing products tended to keep the QA leads busy between peak camera-project timelines. Because of these factors, test plans and cases were frequently not kept up-to-date, and by the end of a project, they often did not match the features of the product. The QA leads were aware of this problem and worked around it with the testers, since they didn't have time to update the documents.

Test labs were also a problem. While language versions of the various operating systems were available, there were not sufficient systems to run several languages under the same configuration. This created troubleshooting slowdowns, because developers reading bug reports frequently did not know if the bug occurred in all languages, each operating system, or in more than one camera model.

The development of the DC220/260 digital camera in early 1998 illustrates the challenges that these products presented. The cameras were launched at the same time, and used the same software CD and user's guide. They had slightly different feature sets, however, and the full suite of test cases had to be run on both camera models. The figure below illustrates the test scenario for one of the cameras. Before shipping the multilingual CD, this testing had to be run on both cameras.

Test Scenario for DC220/260 Camera

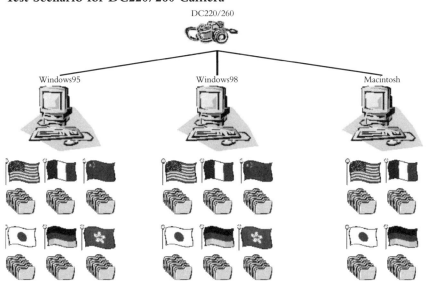

For Windows systems, each set of file folders in the figure represents an installer, several applications, matching help files, and four readme files. For the Macintosh, the folders represent a slightly smaller set of files. (Cameras after the DC220/260 would also support Windows NT, and would include more applications for the Macintosh.)

Given the large number of camera/application/platform/language combinations, testing all languages simultaneously would require a huge lab and many test engineers. Since testing occurred only at project end, or roughly every six months, it was hard for Kodak to justify investing in these resources.

Solutions

Changing the Model—Outsourced vs. Internal Testing

As described earlier, testing was handled in a distributed fashion. Functionality testing was conducted by groups in Boston and Rochester, and interoperability testing (of English software only) was conducted by a separate group in Rochester. The first task, therefore, was to evaluate whether or not these internal organizations could manage simultaneous testing of all languages.

It was fairly quickly determined that this approach was not feasible due to the following issues:

- *Camera Availability.* If testing were distributed between several Kodak sites, each would need a minimum number of cameras. But there were insufficient preproduction cameras for each site; centralized testing would require fewer cameras.

- *Lack of Linguistic Resources.* Test engineers within Kodak were primarily in the US. Some might have a passing familiarity with another language, but this was inadequate.

- *Difficulty in Obtaining Localized Third-Party Applications.* One of the advantages of using a localization company for testing was the availability of localized versions of operating systems and applications (e.g., Simplified Chinese versions of the graphic software Adobe Photoshop). Further, copies of localized software are expensive and often difficult to obtain in the US.

- *Testing Inefficiencies.* Distributing testing by language within Kodak would prevent the simultaneous comparison of bugs. However, if testing were split up so that each site tested a few applications in all languages, there would be no efficiencies in minimizing the number of languages/systems that would need to be maintained in each site. Neither option was attractive.

Once the team determined that outsourcing was the only viable alternative, the next step was to evaluate vendor options. Throughout the previous year, many localization companies had begun offering testing as a separate service in light of perceived market need. To ensure a thorough evaluation, the localization team involved QA and software development in qualifying vendors.

Flow Chart of Vendor Selection Process

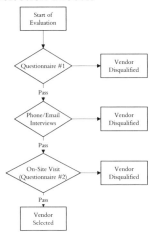

To gather information quickly and objectively, a series of questionnaires was developed. The first requested information on quality and process metrics, processes, and sample documents. A second was designed for use during on-site visits to the vendor. The goal of this questionnaire was to investigate issues of particular concern, and to ask for demonstrations of technologies and evidence of required resources.

After the list of potential vendors was narrowed, on-site visits were made to five promising companies. The primary goal was to find a company offering testing services in the United States, but companies in Ireland were also investigated.

Managing the Change

The team realized that for outsourcing to work, the entire testing paradigm would have to change. Some of the most significant issues identified are listed below.

• Software specifications had to be thorough, and finalized early.

- QA plans and dozens of test cases had to be updated throughout the life of the project, to ensure that changing functionality was accurately represented.

- Kodak, the localization vendor, and the testing vendor had to agree on terminology before testing could begin. Therefore, glossaries had to be developed, reviewed, and approved early.

- Clear delineation of responsibility had to be established between what the localization and testing vendors would do. The localization vendor would only perform basic user–interface testing, and the test vendor would only perform functionality testing.

- Localized-software testing would begin on beta localized versions, rather than on the versions built from the final English software.

- Localized-software testing would run in parallel with the English testing, rather than wait until English testing was complete.

- Kodak QA staff had to evolve from "doers" to managers of vendor activities.

- Kodak's localization project management and its two vendors had to develop a communication process for bug reporting so that information would flow smoothly.

Given the short timeline and the distributed development group, accurate identification of who owned each bug was crucial. Determining whether a bug was caused by localization or by development had to happen very quickly. Communication was critical.

Communication Flow During the Localization Process

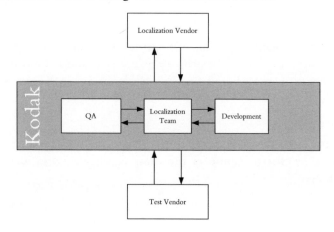

RESULTS

The efforts of the team eventually paid off. The DC240 launched in spring, 1999, with all foreign-language versions shipping concurrently with the English.

One problematic area remains, related to version control during localized-software testing. The team found some confusion when managing software versions being tested by the testing vendor. Occasionally, bugs were reported that had already been corrected. For future projects, version control and communication related to version levels need to be addressed.

SUMMARY

Short time-to-market cycles for innovative products are critical for success in today's competitive business environment. For Kodak's digital cameras, shortening localization time has meant revamping product development.

As long as the time spent on localization is greater than zero, there will always be pressure to do it faster, better, and more cost-effectively. We who have been instrumental in translation and localization at Kodak are prepared to meet these daunting yet exciting challenges in the new millennium.

Making a Global Product at MapInfo Corporation

Ricky P. Thibodeau
MapInfo Corporation

In recent years, software sales outside the US have outpaced domestic growth. US software companies often report international revenues exceeding 50 percent of total sales. One contributor to this growth is software localization.

Creating a version of a program that is appropriate for a group of users in a particular part of the world entails not only translating text into the target group's language, but also recognizing relevant aspects of the local culture. Since "localize" means to adapt for a specific locale, it is more accurate than "translate." Localization entails the linguistic and cultural adaptation of the software and user-interface (UI), documentation (books, online help, tutorial), and packaging to accommodate requirements in foreign markets.

In this case study, we examine how MapInfo, a fast-growing US company, developed a successful localization strategy for worldwide distribution.

LOCALIZATION OVERVIEW

A major reason for localizing software is economic. Initially, software localization may increase a company's sales by at least 25 percent. A product that is barely making a profit domestically can be a highly profitable venture overseas. All else being equal, a software product that is not localized is less likely to survive over the long term.

A localized product will help spread R&D dollars over a wider base, as a localized version can extend a product's life cycle. If the domestic market is declining, an international market may be emerging or still growing, and sales abroad will help finance the next generation of products. In addition, most products can be more profitable overseas, since these markets often support a higher price level.

A localization strategy outlines the goals for product localization and helps determine which products to localize and which markets to enter. The strategy should fit into the company's overall sales and marketing plan to ensure that products planned for localization will enable the sales organization to penetrate the desired markets. Decisions can then be made about what languages to choose and when to release each language edition. Based on this strategy, some products may not be localized at all. At MapInfo, we use business models and do careful analysis for each language to determine if localization is warranted.

Value of Communication

Successful localization requires an entire organization to embrace the idea that its products are being designed for international markets, and to set up the appropriate procedures and channels of communication.

From the very beginning of the product-development cycle, communication channels need to be established with key people in each department. Product managers must bear in mind that each proposed product may also be marketed internationally. Developers should both understand and observe internationalization requirements while writing code. Documentation material must also be developed accordingly. Quality Assurance (QA) testing needs to include an international plan. Finally, shipping must be well coordinated with the overseas operations. When all key team members of product development proceed with international considerations in mind, localization can be successful.

Models

There are a variety of models that a company can use to implement a localization strategy, and it is imperative that a company choose a model that fits within its long-term goals. Below we outline the most common models used in our industry.

Distribution Network

The distribution-network model is often used for new and emerging markets, but serves equally well as a main global strategy. In this scenario, a company already has a worldwide distribution network in place. These distributors are then enlisted to participate in the actual localization of the product. The main advantages are that distributors already have a strong product knowledge base and an understanding of corporate plans, as well as low overall localization costs. Conversely, the distributor may not have the resources in place to meet schedules for deliverables, thereby prolonging ship dates.

Single Language Vendor (SLV)

With the single-language vendor (SLV) model, localization is usually done "in-country" with native translators who can naturally observe the cultural requirements of the target language. This model can be used when testing markets and is more targeted than the distributor model. SLVs are more likely to meet localization schedules for deliverables, thereby allowing international product shipments to occur shortly after English product shipments. In the long run, the SLV approach may be more economical than the multiple-language vendor (MLV) approach discussed below.

Multiple Language Vendor

The multiple-language vendor model may be a good alternative, particularly if the goal is simultaneous release in multiple languages. In this approach, each project is supervised by a team leader who assembles a team of project managers, translators, editors, and proofreaders to coordinate and ensure a quality translation for each project. Centralization of product management can lower costs and raise consistency and leveraging. This model may not be cost-effective for smaller companies.

Mixed In-House/Outsourcing

The mixed in-house/outsourcing model is probably the most popular and flexible, since the publisher decides the strategy for each project. However, localization activities scheduled in-house may not be a viable model for smaller companies since they would need to secure in-house resources to do the localization during product development.

LOCALIZATION AT MAPINFO

MapInfo provides Internet-enabled products and solutions for business-intelligence applications. By detecting and charting patterns in corporate databases, MapInfo products provide greater overall corporate efficiency. Over 300,000 users in a wide range of industries use MapInfo solutions to streamline business activity. Its products are deployed on the desktop, on enterprise servers, on the Internet, and as embeddable mapping objects in decision-support and enterprise-wide applications.

Headquartered in Troy, New York, MapInfo has over 450 employees worldwide (295 in North America). MapInfo products are available in 21 languages and are distributed in 58 countries by more than 1,000 partners.

The business has grown anywhere from 10 percent in the more mature markets of Australia and New Zealand to 31 percent in Southeast Asia and Europe. Direct sales versus indirect sales varies geographically, except for

Southeast Asia, where all business is conducted through channel partners and local distributors.

MapInfo's main European office is located in the United Kingdom, with Asia/Pacific support offices in Australia and Japan. We also have offices in Germany and Sweden, as well as a strong distribution network worldwide. The operations manager in the UK office is a key figure in overseeing the success of our European localization activities. Similarly, our corporate Asia/Pacific team and our Australian office are critical for our success in Asia/Pacific.

Upon deciding to implement localization at MapInfo in 1995, we concentrated our efforts on MapInfo Professional, our main desktop product, localizing it into 13 languages worldwide. This product is now available in 21 languages, including English, generating over 50 percent of our revenue in foreign markets. We have also started to localize many of our other products, including MapX (developer product), MapXtreme (Internet/intranet product), and SpatialWare (enterprise/client-server product).

Localization Roles

Role	Responsibility
Localization Director	Manages the entire localization process (includes localization agreements, finalizing localization schedules for each product release, coordinating activities with international offices, and overseeing staff to meet corporate goals and objectives)
Software Engineer (Speaks Fluent Japanese)	Internationalization–related activities (includes automating localization-kit builds, verifying localization kits, developing international Localization Automated Testing System [LATS], managing localization schedule, project managing for Japan, fixing localization bugs)
Localization Engineer (Understands French, Spanish)	Builds of each language, Notes administration, installer issues, assisting with localization-kit builds, coordinating documentation, testing language builds, debugging, beta program
Localization Engineer (Speaks Fluent Mandarin)	QA lead, assisting with ATS, project managing for China/Korea, providing technical support for Asia/Pacific, testing of each language edition, fixing localization bugs
International Team	Europe and Asia/Pacific support (includes production, shipping, selecting vendors/localizers, localization agreements, budgets)
Engineers	Internationalization requirements, fixing bugs
QA Team	Running automated localization-kit builds, international testing plans, investigating bugs related to English products
Localizers	Localization, local testing, overseeing local beta program

MapInfo's Model

Localizing MapInfo Professional primarily entails the localization of books, online help, and software—but there are dozens of additional elements to manage, from sample data to media-label art. The NY-based R&D localization department distributes the English resource files (menu items, error strings, dialogs, bitmaps, etc.), books, and online help electronically to our international localizers, who are largely our international distributors. The localizer performs the translations and returns the localized files back to us via the Internet translated, compiled, and tested. These files are then substituted for the equivalent English files to produce the local-language editions of MapInfo Professional. We then return complete, installable image files to each localizer for final testing. We work with the distributor, our production department, and our international offices to coordinate duplication, assembly, and fulfillment of the full products. A sample localization-kit directory is as follows.

Notice that we distinguish the user-interface (UI) resources from other resources. This helps localizers identify which components are needed to compile the resources from other support files such as documentation and installer resources. We separate our localization of 20 languages into the following two groups:

- *Full localization (14 languages).* This includes the UI, books, online help, online tutorial, and third-party applications. Full production of the language-specific product is done. Full localization is necessary in the large European and Asia/Pacific markets.

- *Partial localization (6 languages).* The UI is localized and occasionally online help is as well. Distributors ship our standard English version and include a diskette containing the localized resource DLLs and support files—a cost-effective plan when a company wants to enter a smaller market without incurring high localization costs associated with documentation. For MapInfo, these language markets include Arabic, Hebrew, Czech, Slovak, Dutch, and Turkish.

Prior Model

Early on, our strategy was to use MapInfo distributors as localizers. Our country managers from Europe and Asia first identified which distributors had adequate resources. MapInfo would then initiate a localization agreement, compensating them with sales credits. Very rarely did a distributor that we approached turn down the opportunity to participate, since they wanted to ensure product quality. Also, this model provided them access to corporate staff such as engineering, technical support, and quality assurance, via the localization department.

All 13 languages that we shipped in 1995 were localized by our distributors, with the exception of Japanese. Using the distributor model, MapInfo saved hundreds of thousands of dollars. The Japanese language was done by a very large MLV, costing six times more. This first foray into the MLV process has deterred us from using MLVs, although we do not rule out future work with them.

Current Model

Such cost-effective localization requires strong project management and communication with distributors and localization vendors. We use Lotus Notes, further explained below, as our main tool of communication with all localizers.

Currently, we still rely heavily on our distributors. We use 14 MapInfo distributors and six localization vendors, all of whom are SLVs doing the localization in-country. This hybrid model (distributor/SLV) works well. SLV companies tend to be better than distributors at meeting deadlines.

As our core product now includes multiple features from third parties, increasing the localization work, we have implemented a model with three of the languages whereby some distributors only localize the UI, given their strong product knowledge. Documentation (books, help, tutorial) is outsourced to an SLV, freeing up the distributor for marketing and sales, thereby increasing revenue while still meeting delivery dates.

Product Development with Emphasis on Internationalization

The localization team is very much involved with product development from the beginning of a project, and globalization is at its core. Although developers may realize that the product being built will be localized, it is still necessary to continually reemphasize internationalization standards. Some of the major standards we emphasize at the software-architecture stage include:

- writing software with localization in mind: dialogs, menus, text, and other localizable components should be stored in separate resource files (resource DLLs), not hard-coded into the source files for the executable;

- sort order and searching differences (e.g., Danish and Swedish alphabetize differently than English);

- double-byte enabling the code;

- testing source versions' internationalization features;

- requiring that third-party components be internationalized.

We usually assign a project manager to each product being built to ensure that all localization requirements are met. At MapInfo, product development and internationalization are so tightly integrated that they can be considered a single process.

Managing Third Parties

With the high costs of development, it is not surprising that third-party products are making their way into a company's core product line. When bundling an application with a core product, the product manager must address internationalization/localization needs. Clear communication between the product managers, development, and the localization department is crucial.

Internationalization and Localization Requirements

During a release of our core product, MapInfo decided to include a new feature developed by a prominent third-party software company. Corporate Engineering and Product Management were aware that the third-party product would be localized and shipped worldwide—but initially, many issues regarding localization were not clearly identified. These included:

- Is the product internationalized? Is it localized?

- Is a localization kit available?

- Are documentation resources for book, tutorial, and online help available?

- Does the product support all character sets, including double-byte languages such as Japanese and Chinese?

- Are bugs directly related to localization easily identified and fixed?

Fortunately, midway through the project, our localization department was able to open communication lines with the third party and identify and resolve these problems.

MapInfo's Third-Party Strategy

MapInfo has created a Third Party Technical Group (TPTG), which is part of QA, to address these scenarios. The TPTG joins the MapInfo/third-party discussions at the contract-negotiation stage. The TPTG submits a list of questions to the third party to learn about their development practices, differences in terminology, etc.

Once development begins, the TPTG is responsible for monitoring the progress of the project and making sure that designated milestones are met. MapInfo TPTG conducts basic stability testing of the third-party deliverables and provides feedback as needed. If at any stage MapInfo TPTG feels that the proposed deadlines may not be met, it notifies the involved parties and a joint decision is made on how to proceed. This kind of technical involvement as early as the contract-negotiations stage helps MapInfo and the third party develop joint products in a shorter time frame while maintaining quality.

Quality Assurance/Worldwide Beta Program

For our English products, MapInfo has an extensive beta program that includes some international partners. Beta programs are crucial in helping QA ensure that a product meets corporate quality-assurance standards.

For each international release, we incorporate a similar program on a much smaller scale. For obvious reasons, we cannot rely on the company doing the localization to also perform QA. Our strategy is to enlist strong users in each country to participate in the beta program. We usually allow a few weeks of extensive testing and then collect feedback from the beta sites. This information is then analyzed to determine if any problems are localization- or core-code-related, and take appropriate corrective action.

Worldwide Strategy

Schedules

If MapInfo is to be successful overseas, our international release schedule must be coordinated with our overseas offices. The localization department prepares a detailed analysis to determine when localization kits can be assembled, including availability of documentation resources. We then determine an overall localization schedule, including the timeframe for actual deliverables of translated resources from the localizers. All of this information is communicated to our UK and Australian offices to ensure that schedules can be met according to quarterly product-delivery goals.

Vendor Selection

The localization department works closely with the operations manager in the UK and with our corporate Asia/Pacific team to determine which vendors and distributors will be used for the next localization project. Our plan is simple: select a distributor/SLV that we have either used in the past and know can deliver quality products on time, or follow recommendations from our industry peers. Once we have agreed on a localizer, we set up an agreement, establish communications (via Lotus Notes), and conduct proper training. For first-time localizers, we usually visit the site to make sure proper resources are available, and also to conduct detailed training on localizing our products.

Country Manager's Role

Our international country managers are essential to maintaining a strong distribution network. They also have the task of creating a business plan to support the introduction of new languages to be localized. Contrary to popular belief, at least at MapInfo, the localization department does not decide which market to penetrate next. Rather, the country manager's business plan helps identify the potential profitability for that untapped market. Cost/benefit analysis needs to encompass any engineering and localization costs incurred by introducing a new language.

Production Issues

MapInfo's general production manager works with the manager of each product to determine the bill of material (BOM). Every product is issued a unique part number, and each component of the BOM is considered to be raw material. The raw materials are each issued a part number that may be included in many products. Examples of raw materials would be the program CD, manuals, serial-number stickers, registration cards, product boxes, and license agreements. By keeping a generic registration card or product box that is suitable for multiple products, we can order a higher volume at lower costs. In our accounting system we take the orderable item–part number or "parent number" and build the raw material part numbers underneath it, thus creating the BOM. The accounting system takes all costs associated with a specific raw material and creates an average cost, which is then "rolled up" into the cost of goods sold for the parent number.

Determining print quantities is a particularly difficult task for a production manager. When a new manual is being written, the product manager must work with the international offices to forecast the number of manuals needed for the current quarter and anticipate for subsequent quarters. From corporate headquarters in Troy, New York, our production department ships directly to all customers in the US and Canada. Internationally, we ship to our foreign MapInfo offices, distributors, and resellers.

Our previous model required all production and fulfillment to be done from our corporate headquarters. With our current production model, production (media duplication, printing) and fulfillment for all European languages is handled in the UK. Production for Japanese and Korean is currently done in the United States, Simplified and Traditional Chinese in Beijing. Our future plan is to centralize all Asia/Pacific languages in Asia.

MapInfo Localization Development Cycle

To achieve simultaneous language releases, a company must develop localized versions in sync with original product development. This is often unfeasible, particularly for smaller companies, due to the additional resources required. MapInfo's goal is to consistently release the major languages as close to the English release as possible. In the past, for a major point release with new documentation, this could take eight to 12 weeks. Smaller maintenance releases without documentation rewrites would usually occur six to eight weeks after English shipments. We have instituted a strategy in which we use the product-development schedule as our main tool for producing deliverables. We call this the localization-development cycle. We can now ship major releases in six to eight weeks, and maintenance releases in four to six weeks.

Defining the Process

Product development is a documented process with specific schedule requirements and associated target timeframes. The outline gives us an overview of the entire localization process, in a form that is easily communicated to our international offices and localizers. To get a head start on UI localization, we release a beta localization kit three weeks before UI freeze.

We then give the localizers the delta kit a few days later. By the time localizers receive documentation resources, the UI component and initial builds of the product should be complete and testing should be under way. Below is a schematic of our localization development cycle.

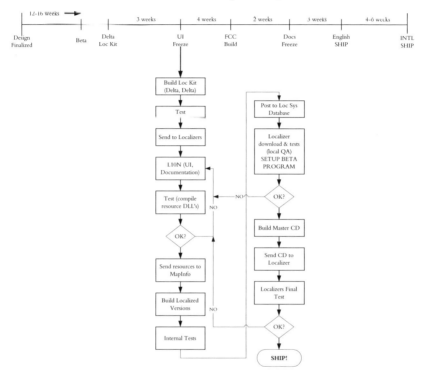

Tools: Lotus Notes and the Internet

Thanks to Lotus Notes, we now have a communications model that enables us to distribute localization-related resources (localization kits, installable images, etc.) to localizers worldwide. Notes enables the team to download localization files and updates, and saves us weeks compared with our previous model of shipping resources on diskette. In the past (1995), the only communication between localizers and Corporate was fax or mail. Now we can have "live" discussions and respond to problems the same day, as the following illustration shows.

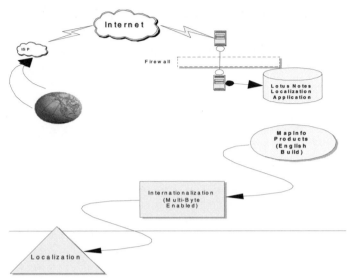

Since 1995, we have been using Notes as our main source of communication with our worldwide distributors and localization vendors. If they have access to the Internet, our systems can be configured to allow them access to our Localization System and Discussion databases (described below).

Notes was selected as our main communication tool with localizers for these reasons:

- It is a document database system that communicates over the Internet.

- It allows database replication to client machines (important because our localizers cannot be expected to install servers).

- Since the database is large, scheduled replication can happen overnight, while Web pages must be downloaded manually, document by document.

Localization System Database

A Notes database was specifically designed for posting our installable image files and localization-kit resources. With access to our databases, a localizer can download the latest localization kits and start work immediately. Also, once we have built a specific language version for them, they can download the images immediately after we post them. They can then conduct internal testing and make changes as needed. This process continues until we are ready to produce a CD master.

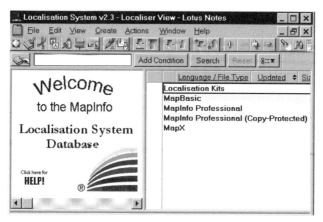

Our Notes administrator is responsible for content and assigning access and security rights. For example, when we post the Japanese MapInfo Professional installable images, only MapInfo Corporate and our Japanese localizer would see this posting.

The following screen shows the layout for posting files to the database. We determine the options for the language, product, file type, version, and build number, as well as a checkbox if the software is copy-protected.

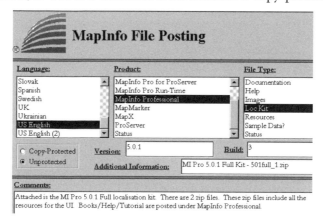

The following figure shows the layout of the localization-kit posting screen. This is the view localizers have when they are ready to download specific localization resources.

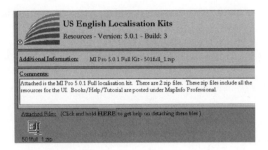

Localization Discussion Database

A discussion database was also developed which enables open communication among localizers throughout the world. Due to our relatively small staff, this database became critical in resolving issues. To be an effective tool, the database must be monitored daily and localizers encouraged to participate. Someone must be designated as the database owner to ensure active participation.

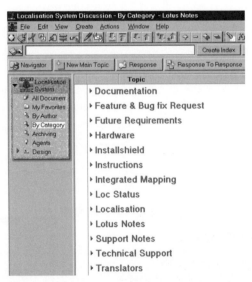

One can display topics by category, author, or favorites. Access and security rights for each database are set at the field level. With the discussion database, we grant localizers rights to post and edit their own documents and respond to all documents.

Below is an example of the thread of communication, and how localizers can help each other resolve problems. In this example, a Chinese localizer posts a problem communicating with other localizers. A Russian localizer responds with a solution.

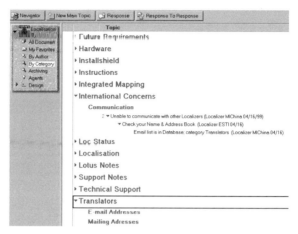

Quantitative Analysis

A quantitative analysis of each localization model requires a separate examination of costs associated with each language and then an overall compilation for each model. Each table shows the cost of the model as a percentage of actual translation cost of the full localization budget. First is a breakdown prior to 1996:

Model	Languages	% of Actual Translation Cost	% of Full Localization Budget
Distributor	12	55%	30%
SLV	0	0%	0%
MLV	1 (Japanese)	45%	25%
Total	**13**	**100%**	**55%**

Analysis: Fifty-five percent of the full localization budget was used for direct localization cost associated with translating 13 languages. Twenty-five percent of that budget was for one language. The actual cost of the single language done by an MLV was about 80 percent of the entire amount for the 12 languages done by the distributors. For 1996 to present, the breakdown is as follows:

Model	Languages	% of Actual Translation Cost	% of Full Localization Budget
Distributor★	14	60%	40%
SLV	6	40%	25%
MLV	0	0%	0%
Total	**20**	**100%**	**65%**

★Documentation resources outsourced for three of these languages.

Analysis: Sixty-five percent of the localization budget was used for direct localization cost associated with translating 20 languages. There is much better balance in our current model. The actual cost of the six languages done by the SLVs was about 60 percent of the entire amount for the 14 languages done by the distributors. Cost per language as compared to the previous model was reduced by 25 percent.

Note that had we not used distributors in our model, the cost of exclusively using the SLV/MLV model would have been 55 percent more for actual translation expenses, a savings of over US$300,000. Additional savings have been realized by implementing Lotus Notes our primary mode of data transmission.

Internationalization/Localization Problems and Issues

Updates: Trying to release the international versions shortly after the English version requires us to provide several localization-kit updates to our localizers. In the past we have sent updates to the localizers as soon as we received them. Depending on the stability of the English software, this could amount to several updates. Now we gather them and send them as needed. Our goal is to release a delta localization kit usually three weeks before UI freeze and then release a final delta one week after UI freeze, resulting in minimal disruption to the localization process. We maintain a public database with all the changes and the associated files.

Bug fixing: After release of a product, bugs will inevitably be found. Whenever we get bug reports from our localizers, the localization department is responsible for duplicating the bug and determining if it is localization-related or also part of the English build. There are now plans to start posting corrections for international builds on our US Web site.

Schedule nonadherence: At the beginning of the localization process we set up a schedule and then check with the localizers to see if they have the resources to meet this schedule. Generally, they agree and sign a localization agreement. If not, we work around them to find another satisfactory release date.

Ongoing scheduling problems: Once the schedule is agreed, we still have localizers that do not adhere to dates for resource deliverables. Since distributors are performing localization for sales credits, their sense of urgency is not high. We have moved large-market languages to SLVs where there is much higher success in getting projects done on time.

QA issues: We have initiated an international beta-testing procedure for localized versions. We plan on investigating public betas for international versions.

QA testing process: The small size of the localization department coupled with so many language-specific releases forces MapInfo to rely heavily on outside localizers and distributors to perform most testing. However, as products become more complex, localization bugs are being discovered more frequently, requiring localization engineers to spend a significant amount of time manually testing the product. With 20 language versions, this can be extremely time-consuming and is often unreliable. In response to this, a prototype Localization Automated Testing System (LATS) has been developed internally. It is designed to maximize efficiency and reliability and minimize manual testing. LATS test script can work with all 20 languages that we support. There are pros and cons for writing universal test scripts, as outlined below:

Pros:

- Single test script can run on all 20 languages, therefore it does not require us to rewrite for each language.

- When we modify the test script due to a feature and/or version change, we need only update one test script.

Cons:

- Since test scripts must work on all 20 languages, you can only test very common operations. Therefore, LATS is a very powerful tool for "smoke testing."

- Writing a universal test code is very tricky. A condition may work for some language but not for others. The test script must be fully tested to make sure it will work in all 20 language environments, which can be very time-consuming.

Hardware issues: We used to keep multiple operating systems on a single machine but now we create "images" that allow us to clean the machine before doing installations. We create these for about 16 languages under Windows NT.

Estimating project-localization time: We estimate the time we think that it should take someone to localize any given project by doing a detailed analysis of the delta localization kit as well as the full localization kit, usually based on number of words and number of files, dialogs, etc. required for modification. This estimate works for about half of the localizers. It seems that skills and productivity vary greatly. We generally use one of our better SLV's quotations as a benchmark.

Internationalization (I18N) and Localization (L10N) Problems

Below are some typical problems we have encountered.

I18N Problems:

Third-party products: In a 3D graphics dialog, items in the "Type" field shown below as "Tyyppi" are hard-coded in English. This may be due to an internationalization error, or might be localization-related if localizers forget to translate the strings.

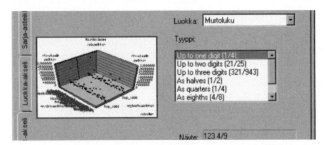

In the MapInfo "Preference" dialog, there is no scroll bar in the directory list. Therefore some items are not accessible using the mouse. In the English dialog, all items are shown. However, some languages require more spaces to show all items. This can be remedied in two ways.

1. Localizers can adjust the list to show all items. This method requires localizers to make this adjustment each time there is a new version, since we usually add more items in each version. This is our current approach.

2. If development adds the scroll bar, then localizers need not adjust the dialog each time. We hope to move to this solution.

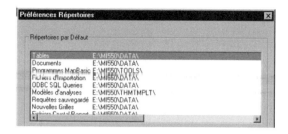

LI On Problems:

Localizers do not always update the resources we send them. This shows up in many places such as a missing "Installer" string in the Russian example below.

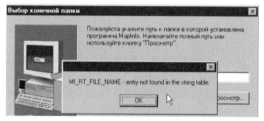

Localizers must convert any characters above an ASCII value of 128 into their own character or use some other representations. For example, "half" can be written as ½ in Latin1. Internally this representation is 189 in the Windows Latin1 code page. But in Latin2, like Polish, 189 is the "double acute accent" illustrated in the dialog below. There is no ½ in Latin2, and localizers will need an alternate representation such as "0,5".

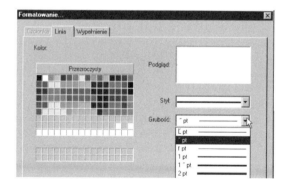

Summary

In this case study, we have attempted to show the importance of a centralized localization strategy. Even a smaller company attempting to tackle international markets can, with some ingenuity and discipline, develop the systems and procedures needed to deal with localization and translation in a proactive, strategic manner.

We have also found that the latest technology, most notably the Internet and workgroup solutions such as Lotus Notes, can prove invaluable in speeding the localization process and ultimately time-to-market.

Finally, we at MapInfo have taken important first steps in attempting to develop quantitative models for gauging price and quality. Though much remains to be done, as of the present writing, we have turned localization and internationalization to a largely predictable process with predictable—and profitable—outcomes.

A Quality-Assurance Model for Language Projects

Siu Ling Koo
L&L Gebruikersinformatie B. V.

Harold Kinds
Van Zwol Wijntjes

Translation quality is difficult to judge, let alone quantify, and the question of how to measure it has long been subject to debate. Not only are conflicts between clients and translators common, but translators themselves also regularly fail to agree on basic principles. What is needed is a rigorous yet real-world approach, one that can be used easily, reliably, and consistently, often under intense time pressure.

This article documents an attempt to meet these requirements. L&L, a Netherlands-based translation and localization services provider, has applied the Quality Assurance Model of the Localisation Industry Standards Association (LISA), and a translation sampling method developed for use with it. The tools used to grade both translators and translations have led to a more explicit, objective, and uniform understanding of quality among translators and reviewers. In addition, early sampling has allowed early feedback and error rectification—critical in the fast-moving localization business.

THE LISA QA MODEL

The QA Model used was developed by a LISA Special Interest Group (SIG). LISA, a nonprofit association, is a global trade organization for localization, internationalization, and multilingual publishing. In addition to holding four forums a year throughout the world and publishing a regular newsletter and other industry information, LISA promotes the development of processes, tools, and technologies that support the localization business.

The first version of the LISA QA Model was published in 1995, and grew out of real-life quality metrics provided by companies such as Microsoft, Digital Equipment, Rank Xerox, IDOC Europe, DLS, and IBM. Work on version 1.0 was coordinated by Teddy Bengtsson of Oracle. The metrics were adapted to produce checklists for formatting QA, functional QA, and language QA, along with a reference manual and QA form templates. Version 2.0, released in August 1999, has been expanded to cover all aspects of localization, from documentation, help, and software to packaging and CBT (computer-based training) tutorials, as well as including Asian-language support and a Microsoft case study. Companies involved in the work included Bellcore Learning Support, Hieronymous, International Communications, Language Management International, Microsoft, Nokia, One World, Oracle, Prolangs, SDL, Augur, and Compuware, with the coordinator being Siu Ling Koo of L&L.

The basic ideas driving the QA Model's approach are *repeatability* (one person doing the same work twice should obtain the same result) and *reproducibility* (two people doing the same work should also obtain the same result). In addition, the Model makes a fundamental distinction between quality assurance (QA), with checks based on sampling, and quality control (QC), which entails a 100-percent review. Thus, in the LISA QA Model, quality assurance is performed twice during projects: on the translations when first submitted, and on the final product (i.e., following QC and implementation of the resulting changes):

The LISA QA Model Workflow

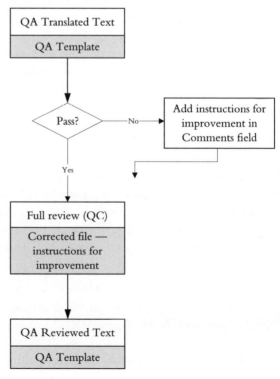

In sampling, texts corresponding to a predefined percentage of the total volume are collected and tested for specific categories of errors. The share of texts selected is often 10 percent, although the figure can be customized to individual needs.

L&L has chosen to enhance the LISA QA Model with more rigorous sampling methodology, and has developed its own statistically based sampling approach. Errors are broken down into a number of categories and classified according to severity. They are recorded on special Excel templates supplied with the Model (see figures below).

The presence of even one critical error means that the work is rejected (i.e., returned to the supplier for rework with details of the error); otherwise, major and minor errors are weighted and counted towards a maximum permissible number. This total is then translated into a final Pass or Fail for the sample (and, where applicable, for the entire job).

PASS OR FAIL CRITERIA

Error levels are defined as follows:

Critical error

- an error in a particularly visible part of a document or software (first screen, document title, etc.);
- a major error repeated in several locations;
- a localization error causing an application to crash, negatively modify/misrepresent functionality of the software;
- weighting: maximum number of error points allowed plus one (+1).

Major error

- an error in a highly visible part of a document or software (header, TOC, menu command, help/CBT topic);
- an error resulting in a misleading statement;
- a minor error repeated in several locations;
- a case where previous QA feedback was not applied;
- an error resulting in a potentially offensive statement;
- weighting: five error points.

Minor error

- any error of a lesser severity than major;
- weight: one error point.

The default for the maximum number of error points allowed for the sample to pass is set at one percent of the total number of words in the sample. However, the client and/or service provider may customize the maximum error points allowed, how these allowed points are distributed among the error categories, how the error types are defined, and how the templates themselves are configured. This ensures the necessary flexibility across different types of projects, languages, and cultural environments.

LISA QA Model Error Categories

Mistranslation	• Punctuation
Accuracy	• Spelling
• Omissions	**Style**
• Additions	• General style
• Cross-references	• Register/tone
• Headers/footers	• Language variants/spelling
Terminology	**Country**
• Glossary adherence	• Country-specific standards
• Context	• Local suitability
Language	• Company standards
• Grammar	**Consistency**
• Semantics	

Sample LISA QA Model Template

Quality Assurance Form							
Language:	QA'ed by:		Date:	Result: *Pass*		Comments:	

Client Name					
Project Name					
Project Number					
Project Manager					
			Critical	max. error points + 1	
Number of words	0		Major	5 points	
Max error points allowed	0		Minor	1 point	

Error Category	Minor	Major	Critical	total	max. allowed
Mistranslation	0	0	0	0	0
Accuracy	0	0	0	0	0
Terminology	0	0	0	0	0
Language	0	0	0	0	0
Style	0	0	0	0	0
Country	0	0	0	0	0
Consistency	0	0	0	0	0
			Total	0	0

More elaborate descriptions of the error criteria can be found in the LISA QA model version 1.0 Reference Manual.

USE OF THE LISA QA MODEL AT L&L

L&L mainly works for businesses in the IT industry. The firm provides translation, desktop publishing, engineering services, and localization, the adjustment of a product to cultural and local circumstances.

Time pressure is always high and the need for reliable quality vital. These circumstances have made it necessary to develop a system that speeds up review and delivers a level of quality that can be guaranteed within predictable limits. Two years ago, the company introduced the LISA QA Model, developing its own sampling methodology to streamline the review process. With sampling, a translation can be evaluated quickly and the level of confidence that the acceptable quality level has been achieved is known. Beyond cutting review time, sampling also results in a classification of the errors found by the reviewer along with error trends. These can help the producer prevent repetition of these errors in their implementation of corrections and in future jobs.

L&L found it rather difficult at first to get reviewers to work with the model, especially those used to doing complete reviews. It is of great importance that taste is not an issue and that only those errors that are justifiable are actually recorded. Introducing such subjective judgements renders a sampling method of little use or difficult to implement. However, experience showed that after reviewers had used the model for some time, they came to appreciate it. In fact, in judging a text they preferred to have the quantification that the model provides them, something they could not achieve without this approach, even if they were to read the entire text rather than a sample.

One of the problems often mentioned by reviewers was that it was very difficult to distinguish between a major and a critical error, or a major and a minor error. For the model to work properly, critical errors must be carefully defined before a project starts. To avoid confusion, errors should also be defined similarly for projects involving similar types of materials. For example, errors in titles, phone numbers, addresses, and index entries in user manuals should be consistently defined as critical errors. The difficulty in distinguishing between major and minor errors is more common and more difficult to resolve. The choice of defining an error as major or minor may become significant in the overall evaluation, and only consensus between the producer and the receiver will resolve to which category a particular type of error belongs.

Furthermore, although the LISA QA Model is based on sampling, a reliable sampling method is not available for it at the moment. Reviews are mostly performed on samples selected at random by the reviewer. After a quick browse through the materials, the reviewer will generally have a feeling of what to select for the sample, based on which section is the most difficult or representative of the whole. However, in order to have a truly reliable QA model, a more systematic sampling method must be developed. With a reliable sampling method, a higher confidence level in the accuracy of the Pass or Fail score, and ultimately in the quality of the final product, can be achieved. For this reason, L&L has augmented the LISA Model with its own sampling methodology, outlined below.

L & L S A M P L I N G M E T H O D O L O G Y
Illustration of the Sampling Concept

The idea behind sampling can be illustrated as follows:

A manufacturer of bolts wants to guarantee the quality of the bolts he sells. This means that he has to perform a quality check. He has two options:

1. check all bolts that are produced; or

2. devise a plan with which he can guarantee to a certain extent that his bolts will pass his customer's requirements.

Option 1 is clearly impractical, expensive, and time-consuming.

Option 2 requires a sampling plan. He must first agree with his customer on the number of bolts that can fail and then determine his confidence level that the bolts he delivers comply with his customer's requirements. In other words, he must determine how large the sample should be and which particular bolts are to be quality-tested.

If the bolts are to be delivered in boxes (clusters of bolts) he can also determine which boxes to check and then proceed accordingly.

Methodology Developed at L&L

In a similar manner, a tool was developed by Harold Kinds, statistical consultant to L&L, to determine the acceptability of a text based on a sampling plan in conjunction with the error definitions, weights, and criteria as outlined in the LISA QA Model.

A sampling plan should consist of these two components:

1. determination of a sample size;

2. determination of a procedure to select a sample.

These steps can be approached in a variety of ways. We chose to base our sampling plan on a technique for monetary-unit sampling.[1] At L&L this sampling plan has been in use for a several months, and the method will continue to be monitored and adjusted as necessary. A brief overview of the method and the results to date are described below.

---

1. J.H.G. Kinds, "Virtual Sampling Techniques for Monetary Unit Sampling in Statistical Auditing," Statistical Auditing Conference, The Hague, 1995.

Sampling Plan

The L&L sampling plan is derived as follows:

1. The translated text to be reviewed consists of x words.

2. Each word has the same importance, and all words can be regarded as equivalent units. This is not strictly true in actual language usage, but it is nearly impossible, if not impractical, to assign varying importance to word categories.

3. The sample will be based on the original document, which has a one-to-one relationship with the translated text. Again, this is not completely true for each individual word but will be true for the selected group of words.

Sample Size

Sample size is determined by the level of confidence with which the producer can assume that an acceptable error limit will not be exceeded. Both the confidence level and the acceptable error limit are set at the beginning of the project by customer and producer. (Determination of the size is based on Poisson distribution as an acceptable, even somewhat conservative, approximation of the binomial sampling distribution.) If the level of confidence and the acceptable error limit are changed, the size of the sample changes accordingly.

For example, if the level of confidence is set at 95 percent and the acceptable error limit (inaccuracy) for accepting the translation is set at 2.5 percent, this would lead to a sample size of 120 words.

Real Sampling Design

After determining the number of words in the sample, the question is how to select these words from the text in such a way that the reviewer can have a reasonable opinion about the quality of the translated word. In translation, it is impossible to check on correctness per word. This would mean that a sample of a number of random, individual words would be taken and checked as to their correct translation, as was done in the illustration with the bolts.

However, a word always occurs in a context, and cannot be checked on its own. A statement on the quality of the document arrived at by checking 120 separate *words* would therefore be meaningless.

Virtual Sampling

Virtual sampling does not look at random words, as would be the case in a *real* sampling design, but rather at clusters of words. Based on the same probability distribution, we can compute the probability that one or more words of a particular cluster are within the selected words of the sample. If one or more words in the cluster are selected, this cluster must be reviewed. The size of the cluster is not important and can vary within the project.

The words are not checked individually but are in the context of a page, for example. The number of words on each page is counted and regarded as the cluster. Since clusters can vary in size, pages can be used as a means of clustering. The same goes for paragraphs, or other units that seem reasonable.

Virtual sampling can be refined to more inspection levels, which can be regarded as different sampling plans. If a page contains one or more selected words, it will be inspected for at least one or more critical errors. The probability can now be determined that one major error which, according to the LISA Model, is the equivalent of five minor errors, or a minor error, which is equivalent to one word, will be selected. The determination of this probability is computed using the same method as described above. For each page the probability is determined that:

- a critical error occurs on a page, which results in a minor inspection of that page;
- a major error occurs on a page, which results in an average inspection of that page;
- a minor error occurs on a page, which results in a tight inspection of that page.

Example

A sampling plan for a 21-page document based on a 95-percent confidence level and an inaccuracy level of 2.5 percent appears as follows:

Page	No. of Words	Critical Error	Major Error	Minor Error	Inspection Plan
1	12	0	0	0	no inspection
2	120	1	0	0	minor inspection on critical errors
3	129	1	0	0	minor inspection on critical errors
4	104	1	0	0	minor inspection on critical errors
5	43	1	0	0	minor inspection on critical errors
6	228	1	1	0	average inspection on major errors

Page	No. of Words	Critical Error	Major Error	Minor Error	Inspection Plan
7	180	1	0	0	minor inspection on critical errors
8	199	1	0	0	minor inspection on critical errors
9	222	1	0	0	minor inspection on critical errors
10	96	1	1	0	average inspection on major errors
11	165	1	0	0	minor inspection on critical errors
12	171	1	0	0	minor inspection on critical errors
13	53	1	0	0	minor inspection on critical errors
14	168	1	0	0	minor inspection on critical errors
15	23	1	0	0	minor inspection on critical errors
16	114	1	1	0	average inspection on major errors
17	214	1	0	0	minor inspection on critical errors
18	124	1	1	1	tight inspection
19	236	1	0	0	minor inspection on critical errors
20	37	0	0	0	no inspection
21	0	0	0	0	no inspection

In this example, 18 out of 21 pages, or 86 percent of all pages, must be inspected for critical errors (entailing minor inspections). This means that these 18 pages must be scanned quickly, since critical errors are mostly very obvious errors. If a critical error is found, the document is rejected and returned to the producer.

If no critical errors are found, the document is inspected for major errors. In this particular example 3 out of 21 pages, or 14 percent of all pages, require average inspection. Thus, the pages where major errors may occur are reviewed with more care than in a minor inspection. The pages inspected for major errors have already been inspected for critical errors. Thus, a page requiring an average inspection has always been inspected at a minor inspection level. If a major error is found, the document is rejected.

If no major errors are found, the document is inspected for minor errors. In this example, only one of 21 pages (ca. five percent) requires tight inspection. A tight inspection always includes a major and a minor inspection. A tight inspection means that the page where the minor error may occur is subjected to careful and detailed reviews. If a minor error is found, the document is rejected. If no minor error is found, the document is accepted.

The following is an outline of actual results when this system was applied. L&L was contracted to review translations for a particular customer. The contract duration was for one year and translations produced by several vendors ("producers") were to be reviewed. Turnaround time was critical. It was of great importance that translation quality was assessed quickly so that decisions could be made as rapidly as possible as to whether or not to send a problematic translation back to the producer or have the reviewer implement corrections.

The first problem encountered was that the customer wanted quality but then failed to clearly define what quality meant to them. In other words, definitions for critical, major, and minor errors could not be given. In this case, L&L used its own standards and hoped that this definition suited the customer as well. At the beginning of each review cycle, certain information was routinely checked independent of the sample. This included article numbers, phone numbers, addresses, etc. If such information was incorrect, a Fail (according to the LISA QA Model) was given and the producer received a warning. If the review of the sample received a Fail, the translation was returned to the producer.

L&L is using the sampling model in two stages of translation. First, it is used to sample translations at the start of a project. After about 5,000 words have been translated, the text is reviewed to assess whether or not instructions given at the start of the project have been followed. On pages where a tight inspection has to be performed, errors are categorized to give feedback to the translator. The following categories are used:

- Grammatical and typing quality
- Mistranslation
- Style
- Country-specific standards

If necessary, instructions are given to improve the translation. In extreme cases, translators have been pulled off the job. This has proven to save time for the reviewer. When several translators work on the same project, this check helps to establish consistency, apart from the other advantages mentioned earlier.

Sampling is again employed when review of the total project starts. All words per page are counted and a sample is taken. The levels of inspection per page in the sample are computed and review starts accordingly. It will be necessary to randomly perform a complete review to see if the method remains valid under varying circumstances.

NEXT STEPS

L&L started using the sampling method recently. In the beginning, projects that had already been reviewed were tested against the results of a traditional review. The results were very encouraging. The next stage is to use the sampling plan and then use the traditional method to compare results. This will be done for several months, in order to have confirmation that the method is valid and for the reviewers to gain confidence in the method. After this stage has been satisfactorily completed, customers will be introduced to the method. The model can then be customized for each customer.

The time in which a review is performed can be greatly improved by using valid sampling methods and valid quantifiable criteria to check the sample. Greater certainty about the level of the quality received will also be a natural result. The application of quantitative methods to the language business will, we are confident, greatly help project throughput and quality.

Part of this case study is based on an article by Deborah Fry in Language International, *October 1999.*

Terminology Management at Ericsson

Gary Jaekel
Ericsson Language Services

A glance at any business newspaper reveals the impressive strides in telecom technology in recent years. Behind the headlines, a silent revolution has accompanied these developments: consumers are placing ever more stringent demands on the quality of the information that accompanies these products. Further, as sluggish national monopolies have been displaced by private telecom operators, the new ventures can ill afford downtime and delays in time-to-market. Telecoms are increasingly dependent on product information that is clear, concise, and accurate—both for subscribers and internal staff. Miscommunication is something providers feel on the bottom line.

One key to clear communication is effective management of terminology. Terminology databases can help ensure greater consistency in documentation, which can not only make documentation easier to read and understand, but also avoid miscommunications that might result in customer dissatisfaction or give rise to potential product liability.

Recent years have also seen the rise of more sophisticated tools in managing terminology, including translation memory, a technology that allows users to leverage or reuse existing translations. Effective terminology management cuts costs, improves consistency and hence linguistic quality, and—most important in this era of intense time-to-market pressures—reduces turnaround times for translation.

In this case study, we examine the implementation, over a span of years, of terminology management at telecom giant Ericsson.

BACKGROUND

Ericsson's commitment to terminology management is hardly a recent development. From about 1980 to 1985, a group of translators at Ericsson worked to publish a telecommunications glossary in five languages called Eriterm. Eriterm was published in book form in 1985, and featured 13,000 Swedish terms and their equivalents in English, French, and Spanish (the original goal of including German was not met at the time). Each of some 13,000 term records contained a domain, but no definitions. Eriterm gradually became well established within the Ericsson world, although it was not afforded the status of a standard. At the same time, a database called Term resided on a mainframe, and was administered by what was then the Standards Department. This database included most of Eriterm, as well as many other terms submitted by various units within Ericsson at their own discretion.

In the late '80s under my management a new project set out to republish Eriterm in five volumes: each proceeding from one of the five languages, this time with the inclusion of German. Around this time, responsibility for Term was transferred from the Standards Department to Ericsson Language Services. Aside from the need to update the material in Eriterm, the idea of using any language in the original data as a source language created problems of which we were originally unaware. Since the original Eriterm used Swedish as a source, alternate terms in other languages were given that did not necessarily result when the records were reversed. We also initiated further development of the database so that we could get print-ready copy directly. This project continued until the publication of the new Eriterm in late 1992, which contained about 15,000 terms. Besides a broader array of terms, the new edition included better domain information, but still lacked definitions.

Once Ericsson Language Services had been assigned responsibility for the Term database, we felt that the next step would be to make the database more accessible to our in-house operations, making it easier to upgrade future releases of Eriterm in whatever form. To this end, we began looking at the various terminology-management products on the market, while not completely disregarding the idea that we might develop our own application in cooperation with Oracle, for example. In the end we opted for Trados's Multiterm as the tool which most closely met our needs. On this platform we began development of Termelsa, our in-house database.

Sample Trados MultiTerm Record

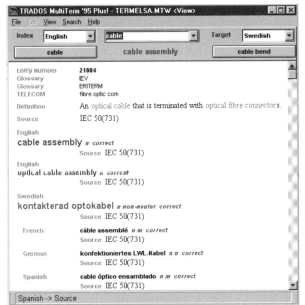

A new edition of Eriterm in book form has not been released since the 1992 edition, and it is extremely unlikely that any new book versions will be published in the future. On the other hand, Eriterm-PC was developed in the mid-nineties, first in DOS and then in Windows. Eriterm PC includes definitions or context for most term records.

Once the dust had settled after the release of the new Eriterm in 1992, we began to take a more structured look at how we intended to build up and maintain our terminology competence, as well as keep our product as up-to-date as possible. We found we had to:

- clearly define who was responsible for terminology for each language and who would manage both strategy and operations;

- establish routines for database management and input of new terms, both from customer-based and in-house perspectives;

- ensure that all aspects of terminology operations were well documented;

- establish plans for further competence development for all involved;

- plan for future development, including resource availability.

Terminology Management at Ericsson: Overview

Stage	Year	Content	Scope
Original terminological material compiled in pamphlet form in five languages	1980	general telephony terms	5,000 terms
Eriterm in one volume, from Swedish, and lacking German	1985	Eriterm	12,500 terms
Eriterm in five volumes from each of the languages and greatly restructured	1992	Eriterm vol. 1-5	13,500 terms
First DOS, then Windows version, including definitions Reorganized domain structure	1995-1998	Eriterm PC	14,000 terms
On CD for PC and Unix with considerably updated terminological content	1999	Techniterm	16,500 terms

RESPONSIBILITY AND MANAGEMENT

As we had five languages in which to maintain terminology competence, one person was named terminologist in each: Swedish, English, French, Spanish, and German. One team member took responsibility for database management, and another for terminology management as such. Initially terminology was treated as a separate unit within the organization, but was later merged with translation operations.

Interestingly, none of those involved in terminology projects at Ericsson Language Services were terminologists, either by training or previous experience. This *tabula rasa* allowed us interesting insights into how a terminology operation can be established.

In addition, our approach to terminology was always more practical than theoretical. And because Ericsson Language Services was a member of the Swedish Centre for Technical Terminology (TNC), we were entitled to a number of hours per year for terminology seminars and the like. We also attended various conferences and seminars organized, for example, by Termnet, and made trips to TNC's counterparts in various countries. We also maintained collaborative relations with other companies and organizations with terminology operations resembling our own. We invested in training in the various tools we used, including database management, translation memory, and machine translation.

The responsibilities and authority of the terminologists were documented in individual role descriptions.

Routines

Well-documented work procedures for all involved are absolutely necessary to maintain an in-house database of value to the user and, in our case, to ensure that our product would remain up-to-date and attractive to our customers.

Term Selection

Naturally, terms from new technology were particularly interesting, as were those which were in vogue with our customers at any given time. As we have all experienced, certain topics and their accompanying terminology tend to flow in waves through any large company, even if the flow at first seems sluggish. Typically, an area such as corporate training generates an increasing demand for writing and translating documents, as the subject gains visibility. This results in a universal attempt to develop new ideas and approaches, and one fine day, without warning, a flood-tide of consciousness breaks over the company, washing up terminology that may be excellent or questionable by turns, but is nevertheless in common use. At Ericsson Language Services, we realized early on that these "beachcomber" terms would not only enrich the database, but would provide the raw material that we could later refine into new releases of Eriterm. In addition, these terms and their equivalents in other languages would clearly assist other translators with similar projects, even if the terms had not been formally approved or fully specified.

The Translator/Terminologist

Our first responsibility was to identify and establish work routines for those who would collect raw terminological input—the translators. This was no easy task, considering its hit-and-miss nature, which involved scanning individual card indexes, hard-copy lists in binders, the odd flat file on our PCs, and the brains of people whose expertise we trusted. The next step was to see that new terms were entered into the database with reasonable regularity. For translators, this involved two jobs in parallel: handling translation projects that came in, and extracting from each project terms they felt warranted inclusion in Termelsa.

The terminology group—consisting of the translators, the database administrator and the manager—met once a month to review terms added to the database in the preceding period. The group extracted the terms deemed to be of interest, and tried to find equivalents in the languages not already represented, as well as applicable definitions or contexts.

The database administrator would compile a log of terms that had been queried in the database in that month (a function available in Multiterm). This log was then examined for terms of particular interest, a judgment based partially on the number of searches related to it. Any terms that met the criteria were handled according to the same routines as above.

Any term records that included at least two languages other than the source-term language as well as a definition or context would then be assigned a domain, and possibly subdomain, according to an established list. The term record could then be formally approved and the necessary administrative data assigned.

At the outset of large translation projects, terminology lists were compiled and used as input to the database. We were further able to apply our inside knowledge of new product developments at Ericsson and the telecom sector in general, making our terminology decisions particularly informed and relevant.

Each translator/terminologist was expected to devote four hours a week to this work, not counting the monthly terminology group meetings, which might last half a day.

The Database Administrator

Besides the tasks mentioned above, the database administrator was expected to follow tool and software developments, manage a test database, maintain a log of any database modifications, keep all documentation current, and ensure that data were always backed up. As the person with the most in-depth knowledge of Multiterm and Termelsa, the database administrator was also very influential in troubleshooting the overall system and devising more efficient work methods.

Term Record Classification and Access Authority

Multiterm has eight levels of term-record classification, of which we used three.

- *Class 1.* This is the standard classification for new term records. All records receive this designation before they can be developed further.

- *Class 2.* This designation is used once a term's content and English equivalent are approved. Equivalents in other languages that have not been verified are labeled "to be verified" under the attribute "Acceptability."

- *Class 3.* When a term record is approved by the terminology group, it is "fixed" at classification 3, which means it may be altered only by the database administrator. All classification-3 terms are also set aside in a separate database copy for the production of future glossaries.

We have also established four levels of access authority:

- *Guest.* A guest user has read-only access to all term records.

- *Translator.* A translator can input classification-1 term records, but has read-only access to classifications 2 and 3.

- *Terminologist.* A terminologist can input or update classification-1 and -2 term records, but has read-only access to classification 3.

- *Database Administrator.* The database administrator can update all three classifications, fix terms at classification 3, and temporarily upgrade any user's access authority.

Documentation

As an Ericsson company, Ericsson Language Services was required to be ISO-certified. This meant, among other things, that clear rules governed the documentation of our processes, products, and routines. Specifications, descriptions, user manuals and reference guides were drafted, discussed, and evaluated by everyone working in the terminology team. In particular, it was important to document how we adapted Multiterm to suit our needs. This documentation was, of course, updated several times as new ideas and requirements arose.

Record Structure
Domains and Subdomains

In the original Eriterm, we specified such a plethora of domains that we found the database difficult to administer in the long run. We therefore decided to group many of the earlier domains into subdomains under more general major domains. The following is the current domain structure with a breakdown of term totals.

BUSINESS & ADMINISTRAT.
business
administration
commerce
dependability
finance
insurance
law
office management
personnel management
project management
quality
safety
security
standardization
training

DATA PROCESSING
character recognition
computers
computer graphics
computer security
logic elements
printers
word processing

DESIGN & DOCUMENTS
design technology
documentation
flowcharts
printing
signs & symbols
R & D
technical drawing

GENERAL TERMS

MATERIALS
paints and varnishes
plastics
product form
strength
surface properties

MECHANICS
equipment practice
fasteners & threads
mechanical
engineering

MISCELLANEOUS TECHNOLOGIES
automatic control
buildings & construction
climate control
environmental engineering
general tech.

PRODUCTION
maintenance
manufacturing
engineering
marking
metallurgy
product management
soldering
supply & distribution
surface treatment
tools
welding
wire–wrapping
wires & wiring

SCIENCES
chemistry
economics
ergonomics
geography
geometry
geophysics
mathematics
mineralogy
optics
physics
linguistics
meteorology
statistics

TELECOM
AXE
antennas
audio & video
broadband
cables
charging
cryptology
datacom
digital transm
fibre optic com
IN
ISDN
manual switching
military
mobicom
network management
O & M
OSI
outside plant eng
PBX
plant eng
radar
radio

radiowavepropag
space
signalling
switching
switching (code)
switching (crossbar)
switching (rotary)
SDH
telecom networks
telecom services
telephone
setstelephony
traffic engineering
transmission
waveguides

TESTING & MEASURING
telephonometry

Most terms in the product are related to telecommunications, though they are likely to be found in other areas of business and technology as well. Aside from the telecom domain, the obvious growth area is data processing, which we expect to eventually outgrow and even incorporate telecom to some extent.

New Techniterm: Terms Per Domain and Share of Total

Domain	No. of Terms	% of Total
Business & Administration	730	4.5
Design & Documents	353	2.1
Data Processing	2493	15.2
Electricity	1195	7.2
Electronics	981	5.9
General Terms	333	2.0
Materials	279	1.6
Mechanics	466	2.8
Misc. Technologies	683	4.1
Production	734	4.5
Sciences	648	3.9
Telecom	7096	43
Testing & Measuring	327	2.0
Total	**16,318**	

Term Record Structure

The following table shows a term record structure. Though fixed, the structure can be modified based on reasonable user feedback. Not all fields are required.

Heading	Value	Content/Comment
The following applies to the entire term record:		
Creation Date		Applies to entire record
Created by	logged user-id	Applies to entire record
Change Date		Shows the latest change in any field
Changed by	logged user-id	Can be changed at input
Entry class	1, 2, or 3	Shows access authority
Entry number		Number series
[DOMAIN]		Main headings in the Domain List
Subdomain	see Domain List	Subheadings in the Domain List
System	MD110, IDF, etc.	To more closely specify a term
Method	PROPS, MQR etc.	To more closely specify a term

Heading	Value	Content/Comment
Glossary	ELS, ERITERM, Ericsson Standard, etc.	Indicates collection of terms the record comes from
Definition		English definition is placed before the English term. Can also contain a translation of a non–English definition
Source		Indicates where a term or definition has been found (e.g., dictionary, standard, magazine)
Definition note		Connected to the definition or other terms in the record
Technical note	(very concise)	Technical information about the concept other than what can be found in the definition syntax
The following headings apply per language:		
English		English term or abbreviation
French		French term or abbreviation
etc. for each language...		
Grammar	n; n m; n f; n n; n non–neuter; n pl; n mpl; n fpl; n npl; n non–neuter pl; n inv; n f, n m; n m, n n; nf, n; n; adj; adj inv; adv; v; vt; vi; vt ind; phrase	Additional grammatical information Even applies to English and Swedish terms
Usage	UK; USA; AUSTRALIA; CAN; FRANCE; BELG; SWITZ; GERMANY; AUSTRIA; SPAIN; LATIN AMER; ERICSSON	Used for regional differences and can also be used to indicate that the term is Ericsson-specific
Source		Where a term or definition has been found (e.g., dictionary, standard, magazine)
Customer	ERA, EBC, etc.	
Acceptability	• correct • avoid • to be verified • preferred	*correct*=term is approved *avoid*=not to be used (an alternative or another reference is given) *to be verified*= term is not fully approved, but can be used *preferred*= term should be used before another correct term in the record

Heading	Value	Content/Comment
abbr.		An abbreviation is written as a normal term (with an index) and abbr is added (this attribute has no field value)
Note	(certain standard formulations may apply)	1) Indicates limits to the term's use: - "The /French/ term does not apply to /metalworking/" - "applies to keyboards" 2) See records: - "See: ^...^" (automatic text link) 3) Indicates a variant much like the term: -"Also, logical", for the main term "logic" 4) Clarifies a term whose context is not clear from the term itself, e.g., <English>equivalent noise voltage <Note>of a one-port device
Linguistic note		
Miscellaneous		Contains information that cannot be put into another field, e.g., information may later be used to create a definition or "Technical note" Contents not intended for publication
Context		Shows the term in context

Every record also has a "Type" field, which may contain one of the following values:

- A: attribute field
- I: index field
- P: picklist
- S: system field
- T: text field

Aside from German terms and proper names, terms are always written in lower case. Abbreviations are always written in all-caps. The field "Linguistic note" may be used to indicate that the first letter of the term is normally a capital letter.

FUTURE DEVELOPMENT

After operating as an Ericsson unit for many years, and as a company within Ericsson Group for three years, Ericsson Language Services was bought by Interverbum in late 1997. The prime purpose of the merger was to access a larger pool of language resources, and to secure competence in language-related technology.

Aside from our established method of working with terminology, Ericsson Language Services brought with it considerable experience of working with tools for machine translation. Interverbum, on the other hand, has worked for several years with a number of translation-memory tools. Because we are aware that the key to successful use of these tools is a systematic approach to terminology, we are initiating plans to implement the Termelsa database as a standard terminology platform throughout Interverbum. Further, we are examining how we can structure our work with the database and its content to conform to the needs and routines of a large organization.

We have decided to change the name Eriterm (due to its strong Ericsson associations) to Techniterm, reflecting our goal of including terminology from other areas, embracing, for example, the automotive, IT, and pharmaceutical industries. We have also discontinued the Eriterm-PC product, and are moving its contents to a new platform, Multiterm Dictionary. We have found this product easy to use and upgrade, and very cost-effective. Apart from the new platform, we have two to three thousand new term records ready for import into the database. The new Techniterm has been slated for release on CD during the autumn of 1999.

Sample Record from Trados MultiTerm

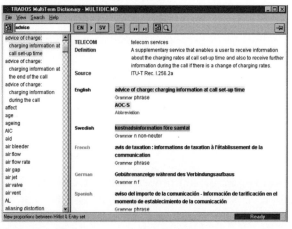

A Unix interface to Techniterm is under development. Many of our customers, particularly engineers, designers, and documentation professionals, work in a Unix environment. Work is slated for completion in 1999.

We are constantly being asked when Techniterm will be Web-enabled. While this presents no major technical problems, we need to carefully examine how we can be compensated for its use. Several possible solutions are in use in other service or product areas, but further cost-justification is needed before making this major investment.

Quantifying the Results

Below is a breakdown of the income and expenses from terminology management at Ericsson. Monetary figures are in millions of Swedish crowns.

In-House Person-Hours	Cash-Out Development	Sales
9,200	1.6 MSEK	3.8 MSEK
The above figure is based on hours reported from the beginning of the 90s, and does not include marketing and other similar efforts.	The largest cost here is the printing of Eriterm in 1992. Other costs, such as mainframe database maintenance, were not necessarily booked as such by Ericsson at the time.	Includes the sales of the 1992 Eriterm and licensing agreements to date. The first versions of the glossary were available free within Ericsson.

The Rocky Road and the Superhighway

While the rocky road of implementing effective terminology management has now become passably paved, a true terminological superhighway is still well in the future. Awareness has grown and tools are available, but with each new positive development, new problems also arise.

One seemingly thorny issue is copyright. A company that pays for development of a glossary pertaining to its area of business is loath to see that terminology used by a competitor. I do not claim to have a ready solution to this problem, but find it most gratifying that terminology is now considered something of real value. A similar problem has appeared concerning the ownership of translation memories. I would maintain that, in the end, the terms you make are equal to the terms you take.

From my perspective, the greatest problem and the greatest opportunity before us rest in the transfer of terminology across language-technology tools. Though this may pose great challenges, the amount of structured terminology in existence as separate islands of competence and reference is unsupportable in the long run. Admirable work has been done to create standards, and projects are in progress to facilitate terminology exchange, so perhaps we are beginning to see the light at the end of the tunnel.

Terminology is gaining visibility as a discipline in its own right, in response to the heightened importance of user documentation, maintenance manuals, and technical specifications that accompany the vast array of services and products we encounter in our daily lives.

Mission-Critical:
Translating for Regulated Industries

Robert C. Sprung
Harvard Translations, Inc.

INTRODUCTION [1]

Translation presents acute challenges to companies in regulated industries—those which are subject to domestic or international oversight, and which must closely tie their processes to larger industrial or governmental standards. Examples include medical-device manufacturers, pharmaceutical companies, law firms, financial institutions, auto makers, and many businesses where user-safety or legal-liability concerns loom large. The stakes are high: in the medical-device industry, for example, problems with labeling (which includes translation) are a major cause of recalls.

Much of the translation produced for regulated industries is required by law. Examples range from the label text found on a medical device or pharmaceutical, to the SEC filing for an initial stock offering, to the emissions manual for a new car. Many firms are quickly learning that translation is a subtle task requiring strategic thinking in order to cut cycle time and assure quality that will pass muster with regulatory authorities. Though translation usually represents a small proportion of total product-development expense, glitches in translation quality and turnaround time can create problems out of all proportion to the cost of such services.

In this case study, we examine the foreign-language solutions developed and implemented by Harvard Translations over some seven years for two leading Johnson & Johnson companies—Johnson & Johnson Professional (JJPI) and Ethicon Endo-Surgery (EES).

JJPI is an old-line medical-device manufacturer. Although a recently created corporate entity, it grew out of Codman and Shurtleff, one of the oldest New England medical-device firms. EES is more entrepreneurial, specializing in the latest technology for endoscopic surgery. Many EES

---

1. This case study is an adaptation of presentations, some given jointly with J&J personnel, at conferences sponsored by Canon Communications and *Pharmaceutical and Medical Packaging News* magazine, in which the author publishes a regular column on language issues.

products have a short life in the marketplace, and every week of translation time that could have been spared represents significant lost revenues.

Both companies began with little coordinated effort to release their products with labeling in multiple languages. Their main challenges included:

- how to *organize and proceduralize translation*;

- how to create a *scalable multilingual effort* to meet rapidly rising demand;

- how to *cut translation time* to improve time-to-market;

- how to *measure and control translation quality* in the face of a complex regulatory framework.

The solutions they implemented, together with Harvard Translations, offer valuable insights for many companies—large or small—in other highly regulated industries.

CASE STUDY I:
JOHNSON AND JOHNSON PROFESSIONAL (JJPI)

Baseline Situation (1992)

JJPI's situation was similar to that of most large firms exporting in the early '90s: translation was *ad-hoc*, an afterthought tacked on to the technical-writing and packaging process.

The Medical Device Directive (MDD) changed all that. In the early 1990s, this European Community legislation required companies marketing in Europe to include labeling in local languages ("labeling" includes all text associated with a product, whether the printing on the box or the instructional insert inside it). The MDD fueled large-scale translation efforts—many manufacturers erred on the conservative side and translated into languages of countries where they had small current sales, but did not want to be denied entry in the future (e.g., Finnish and Greek are official languages of EC countries, and it was not uncommon for even a small medical-device manufacturer to include these languages).

The MDD—and similar legislation in other industries—forced many companies to take translation seriously, as a *strategic* issue.

Challenge I: Time-to-Market

Lacking an organized framework for discussing and analyzing translation, the language challenge that JJPI first noticed lay in clear sight—*Why does translation take so long?* In some cases, it had taken six to eight months to produce a single instructional insert in seven languages.

The root of the problem was the company's patchwork approach, with varying sources of translation (some outsourced to local vendors, some done by individual country distributors) and multiple points of contact within its own organization for approving translations. J&J had to approve translations once they were completed, but this approval was not procedur alized—it might be done by a marketing manager in Italy, a regulatory-affairs expert in Spain, and a packaging engineer in Japan. Many of these affiliates within J&J performed the approvals in addition to their already crowded job description. Since this was perceived as an added duty, quality and timing of approvals were unpredictable.

Translation approvals suffered from what we may call the Rule of the Least Common Denominator. Since most of these medical devices were designed for the entire world and required *all languages to be complete* before shipment, a single late affiliate reviewer could delay shipment of a product. JJPI discovered that the "dog ate my homework" defense was hardly limited to American schoolchildren: claims of faxes never being received or labels never sent for approval were not uncommon. Such clerical errors could add weeks or months to the translation process, causing major shipment delays and lost revenue.

The company also discovered that affiliates celebrated holidays and took vacations at different times of the year. When producing a label in 12 lan-guages, one could count on a given day being a bank holiday or saint's day in one affiliate country, or at least one affiliate disappearing for a four-week vacation. Resolving even a simple question across all languages (e.g., adding a new caution statement) could easily add two weeks to the process.

Finally, J&J realized it had little *political clout* over reviewers. An affiliate might resent marching to the beat of a foreign drummer when reviewing foreign-language text, and might doubt a US firm's ability to speak his or her language accurately. Though late delivery of a review might have pro-found repercussions on a product's ship date and revenue picture, headquar-ters had little recourse in such cases.

Solution: Centralization

The first key to reining in the problem was centralizing the process. Together with this J&J company, we created:

* *a single* set of procedures;

* *a single* hub for project management/trafficking;

* *a single* contact point for assessing project status and coordination.

The first step in creating a standardized process was to *batch translations*. In the past, small installments of labeling text had been sent to translators and affiliate reviewers as soon as they were ready. We developed a standard process by which batches of 10,000 English words would be translated and laid out (using standard desktop-publishing software such as QuarkXPress). A larger volume of text to work on yielded immediate economies of scale:

- It became easier to recruit top translators for highly specialized linguistic work. The qualified pool of talent is already very small, and the pool of those willing to drop everything for 500-word assignments is minuscule. Without batching, top vendors can easily be busy with other assignments and, even if available, might charge hefty minimum fees for short translations. Batching enhanced recruitment and retention of top vendors, which bolstered consistency and quality.

- Project-management costs dropped dramatically as a percentage of total revenue. One could manage 10,000 words in seven languages in about the same time as one could manage 1,000.

- Batching enhanced translation consistency and quality. In the past, J&J tech writers would send an insert text for translation, and six months later J&J packaging engineers might send for translation the text that would appear on the outer box for that same product. The danger could exist, absent a rigorous process to ensure consistency, for the Spanish or Japanese product name to appear differently on the outer box than it did on the instructions inside. Such a translation error would surely send off alarm bells in the case of an audit, and could potentially trigger a recall. Batching significantly reduced such risks, since a batch included most if not all translation related to a product.

Batching also ushered in a streamlined affiliate-review process. HT worked closely with J&J to forecast workflow as much as possible. Knowing that 10,000 words were scheduled for receipt at HT on a given date, HT could schedule resources, and inform J&J's affiliate reviewers when they could expect that batch for approval.

At the same time, HT implemented a *standardized review process*. Reviewers would receive packages of approximately equal volume and format, and thus grew comfortable with the "look and feel" of the text. They were given standard instructions on how to mark up translations, reinforcing that they were part of a process. This further reduced affiliate-review politics.

There is no shortcut for creating credibility in a process, to say nothing of creating belief in translation quality among in-country reviewers. Reviewers in a country who had become used to seeing mediocre translations could hardly be expected to suddenly "see the light" that translations were now on track. Credibility had to be built up over time, but proceduralizing the review was an important factor in accelerating affiliate buy-in. The procedures also helped set common expectations, without which complaints about quality are far more prevalent.

One improvement was instituting standard means of recording affiliates' comments, including a form for their global preferences in style and terminology (e.g., the French affiliate's desire for using a certain term for "extra large" when referring to an orthopedic device, or the wording for a standard warning statement). One should hardly accept at face value statements such as "the Czech reviewer said the translation was bad." Such forms helped localize the source of the comments—they might be politically motivated (was the translation that used to be done in their country now being outsourced to an "upstart" US firm?), or caused by procedural flaws rather than by poor translators. (One phenomenon that emerged over the years was a *change in reviewer personnel*—a Korean reviewer might have preferred a given term, and his replacement three years later might have been upset at the existing "mistranslation" requested by the predecessor.)

Much of the solution rests in setting the right expectations: we began by advising J&J that they should *expect* reviewers to be skeptical at first, that we would have to win their approval. The decision to centralize, batch, and proceduralize affiliate review yielded impressive results:

- Previously, it had taken up to eight months to complete a standard, 2,000-word insert.

- Now, it took a predictable six weeks for batches of up to 10,000 words, which included multiple inserts and labels.

Challenge 2: Controlling Translation Quality

With a basic process in place for creating foreign-language text and artwork in a predictable timeframe, J&J moved to a more subtle question: How can US headquarters evaluate the quality of foreign-language labeling? To put it in terms to which we can all relate: "How do I know that my Japanese label isn't saying something wrong or offensive, when I don't speak Japanese?"

Because so much is riding on the accuracy of labeling, regulatory experts require robust systems, typically ISO- or GMP-compliant, for generating the text associated with a product. In their view, there is a clear right or wrong in labeling text. On the other side are individual linguists or translation companies, which traditionally see more grey areas in a text. A good translator is a good writer, and writing involves substantial creativity and right-brain activity. How does one bridge this gap, in an era where ISO or similar compliance is deemed a prerequisite?

Further complicating the matter is the very nature of ISO, which was designed for a manufacturing environment. For example, ISO 9000 Section 4.11 covers "Control of inspection, measuring, and test equipment." Clearly this section and others are difficult to apply to a language solution.

In the end, J&J needed a *language process* that dovetailed with its own labeling procedures, and that could be understood by reasonably intelligent, but non translation-savvy, regulatory auditors. The language vendor would ideally demonstrate a structured framework, consisting of the following:

- a standardized, auditable process, integrated with the client's workflow;

- resources that are properly qualified;

- close integration with Regulatory Affairs;

- project components that are fully traceable, in case of an audit;

- a feedback mechanism for improving the process.

Solution: A Standardized Process

The solution was to treat quality as a *process*, with standard procedures and quantitative measures. The alternative was untenable over the long term— namely, an anecdotal approach to quality, where the parties "get comfortable" with translation style and accuracy. A translation vendor might sail along without significant customer complaints for a given period, but ultimately the lack of a commonly understood and agreed standard with quantitative measures will come back to haunt both parties.

We agreed with J&J that the ISO quality framework would be most suitable for their language solution. Gearing up for ISO compliance entailed a substantial investment of time and money on both sides, but this longer-term commitment proved modest in comparison with the return.

As part of its own ISO or GMP certification, a company typically audits its language vendors (under ISO 4.6, "Purchasing," or comparable section in another standard). Below are select ISO 9000 sections with some notes on the criteria we applied, and which any firm may use in evaluating and auditing a translation process. Although ISO was designed for manufacturers and not language-service companies, it can help control the foreign language on many firms' labeling and documentation.

Section 4.3, Contract Review

Many problems in translation go back to poor communication and specification of scope of work. Typical problems: lack of specificity of deliverables and lack of communication on technical details of delivery (e.g., a client might have asked for Japanese text files, but did not understand that a Japanese operating system is needed to read the files).

Section 4.6, Purchasing

Under this section, clients audit their suppliers, including language vendors. The same section covers how those language vendors qualify their own linguistic resources. Given the worldwide web of translators, it is critical to document how a vendor qualifies any subcontractors who are not in-house. Acid-test: a client should pull individual vendor files. Do they document the proper level of education and experience to understand difficult labeling text and translate it accurately?

Section 4.8, Production Identification and Traceability

The paper or electronic trail of a project is specified and stored under this section. If there is ever a problem with foreign-language labeling, there must be a way of tracing where the error occurred, when, and by whom. Acid-test: a client should select an old labeling project and ask to see the record of each step, from initial translation to final layout.

Section 4.9, Process Control

This is the trickiest section to implement—the heart of the quality system. The ISO standard provides little explicit guidance, as the actual language of the section is very brief and general: "the production, installation, and servicing of processes which directly affect quality." In auditing a company's process control, perform this acid test: does the supplier have a clearly documented process that is easy for the layman to understand? Does the process include cross-checks? Who controls the process and what are these people's qualifications? In an audit, a client should talk with a translation project manager to validate written procedures.

Section 4.13, Control of Nonconforming Product

It is easy to imagine an assembly line where a widget does not meet a certain threshold value for tensile strength. But can a translation be pulled from a figurative assembly line for failing to meet critical values? Some companies have devised ingenious methods for an analogous approach.[2] If the editors find problems in the translation, how is their feedback handled? Can substandard work be returned for rework? How is this documented? Note that nonconformances include not only errors in translation, but also any non-adherence to a stated procedure that affects quality.

Section 4.18, Training

This is one of the most critical sections. It is not sufficient for a translator, for example, to be well schooled and experienced. She or he must also be trained for the task at hand. Acid test: a client should ask to see documented requirements for an individual task (e.g., translation, editing, layout), as well as the training records that show that an individual is qualified. Under a separate section, a language supplier must have internal auditing of its own systems. Are internal auditors qualified? (Pull their training records.)

Section 4.20, Statistical Techniques

At first blush, this section seems to have little to do with translation. However, a client and vendor should consider whether meaningful metrics might not be devised, particularly if they have a large volume of foreign-language copy. What is the error rate per 10,000 words? How is throughput measured? Together with J&J, we developed standard quality metrics, included error rates per given volume of translation, with a classification of errors ("nonconformances") as major or minor. By gathering these data over time, we could track trends in quality.

Challenge 3: Database Labeling

With a basic process in place, JJPI next had technical problems to solve. Specifically, how could its label design, storage, and printing systems be optimized for a multilingual environment?

The company, which prints thousands of medical labels within its facilities throughout the US and the world, now had to print foreign-language text on those labels. How would quality be controlled on those labels? How would existing printers output Japanese—and how would an operator know whether the label had printed properly, or with incorrect characters?

J&J's wish list included:

- support for foreign character sets (for languages currently needed, like Finnish and Japanese, and for languages with complex character sets that might be added, such as Czech or Korean);

---

2. Consider the Quality Assurance model proposed by the LISA organization, outlined in a separate case study in this volume.

- a relational-database structure (a flat-file structure, such as a single Excel spreadsheet, creates inefficiencies through redundant data, and increases the potential for error by having many translations where one will do);

- reduction of overlabeling (the need to overprint or apply supplementary labels in certain target markets).

Solution: A Custom Application

The solution was a custom application that HT designed and programmed. Its features may interest many in labeling or regulatory fields; more generally, it illustrates that custom technology solutions are often needed to solve complex language problems.

J&J wished to retain its Zebra-brand printers, with which it had printed labels for years. A software solution would save hundreds of thousands of dollars in new hardware. In the end, HT provided an on-demand printing system with the following features:

- The system supported 12 languages, including Japanese and other double-byte languages.

- The system was multiuser: many could use it simultaneously, whether entering labeling text, reviewing translations, or printing labels.

- The system allowed remote access: label operators around the world could log in and print labels.

- The database structure was normalized and relational, using an off-the-shelf application. This eliminated redundancy (for example, if the term "Store above 20° C" appeared on 10,000 product codes, it was stored once in the database—which would not be the case with an old-line, flat-file structure). This made it much easier to control quality on translations ("put all your eggs in one basket—and watch that basket"), while dramatically cutting translation cost.

- Foreign languages are preserved as "live" text, not static artwork. Many systems store double-byte text as art files (EPS, BMP, or PDF) embedded into the database structure. This "freezes" the artwork, preventing manipulation by a labeling operator. On the downside, any change to a term in the database would require new artwork to be created for every piece of Japanese text that might appear on a label. For a company with 15,000 discrete labeling elements, this might cost a small fortune in artwork expenses alone.

- Label text goes through the same quality process as insert text, with a complete paper trail and J&J-internal approvals. We found that many companies have one team dealing with packaging text and another with instructional inserts. We have already mentioned the potential danger of not integrating translation of the two—inconsistencies of such basic information as the product's name can arise. Text that appears on packaging is *the most critical* in terms of quality and recall potential. Its translation, though not extensive in volume of words, requires the same rigor as translation of a 2,000-word insert.

- The system produced output in all languages (including Japanese and Greek) to a Zebra labeling printer, including barcodes.

CASE STUDY 2: ETHICON ENDO-SURGERY (EES)

Baseline Situation (1994)

Ethicon Endo-Surgery, based in Cincinnati, Ohio, is a spin-off of Ethicon, Inc., the world's leading supplier of sutures. EES specializes in state-of-the-art endoscopic and laparoscopic instruments.

The differences between the EES and JJPI corporate structures and growth strategies had profound implications on translation requirements. JJPI, while rolling out some new products, had a product line of million-sellers that had sold well for decades. EES's growth was fueled primarily by new-product development. This meant even greater pressure on translations—every week saved could have a major impact on product sales. Hence, translation was viewed from the outset as having a major strategic role for the company.

Another complicating factor was EES's aggressive acquisition strategy. When a company acquires another, it faces these basic language issues:

- Does the acquired company require translation? If little has been translated, a large volume of new work is possible, since management often needs to rapidly bring both companies' product lines into conformity, which includes translation.

- Does the acquired company have existing standards for translation? In a worst-case scenario, the acquired company's translations are poor, produced without the acquirer's rigorous processes, and thus requiring substantial rework. Even if translation had been done well, inconsistencies in terminology, style, and graphics are inevitable, necessitating at least a careful review of any translated materials from the acquired company.

Challenge 1: Communications

EES benefited from the translation process already developed for J&J. Still, they desired to explore whether time could be cut from the process in the age of such technological breakthroughs as the Internet.

One must keep in mind the nature of regulated industries. The medical industry treads very cautiously when it comes to replacing traditional practices such as a paper trail and handwritten signatures; the regulatory apparatus will not adopt such innovations as electronic signatures or a virtual paper trail until they are rigorously tested and foolproof.

Nonetheless, each existing means of communication presented an obstacle or bottleneck:

- *Fax* was deemed unreliable, messy, and time-consuming.

- *FedEx* or similar overnight service was expensive (a company could spend hundreds of dollars a month shipping text for review to 10 affiliate offices). Further, at least two days were lost *in each direction*. Although FedEx was reliable, if there were six shipments in a month to 10 affiliate offices, at least one or two packages would experience some sort of delivery problem, yielding painful delays in the final translation.

- *Email* presented security and conversion problems, particularly in the early days. File formats remain a challenge when people use programs on different platforms (including Mac-to-PC issues, font problems, and PDF format issues).

Solution: A Corporate Translation Intranet

EES, working with HT, developed a state-of-the-art technology solution. The Global Translation Process System, or GTPS, is a corporate intranet, housed at EES headquarters, that serves as a central clearing house for the entire translation process.

GTPS has a central server that allows EES, its affiliate reviewers, and HT to store, upload, and download project files. It grants varying access levels to the parties involved. The system tracks and controls all project components—indispensable in a mission-critical activity where all parties, from translators to reviewers, must be held accountable for performing on schedule. Here are some key system features:[3]

- *State-of-the-art global approval.* EES affiliates log directly into the system, and work in a common file format. This solved several problems. First, cumbersome and expensive overnight deliveries were a thing of the past. (By some estimates, these savings alone rationalized the entire programming effort.) Second, the standard file formats and conventions for modifying and marking up translations ensured minimal problems with conversion, diacritical marks, etc. EES technical staff worked with affiliates to ensure that they had common hardware and software. Third, the polished GTPS interface and process solidified relationships with the affiliates and heightened their confidence in the translation process.

- *Real-time communications between headquarters/affiliates/translation vendor.* Files were transmitted instantaneously between all parties. There were suddenly few, if any, transmission errors, while previously any FedEx glitch added significant time tracking the problem, making new copies, alerting parties, and adjusting schedules.

- *Published schedule and approval status.* A major problem had been adherence to schedules. By publishing schedules and tracking results, EES reined in the process and held people accountable. In the past, if an affiliate had said review time was insufficient, the company had no recourse. Now, EES was collecting performance data, with which the company could truly manage and control the process.

- *Official glossary continually updated and available.* A key to good translation in regulated industries, as we have seen, is consistency. Terminology must be kept in a continually updated glossary. By posting this live document on an intranet, all parties can access the same terminology.

Challenge 2: Conflicting Priorities

The single greatest challenge in translating for highly regulated industries is arguably the following: On the one hand are forces demanding economy and efficiency (do it faster, cheaper); on the other are equally powerful forces for quality (embodied by Regulatory Affairs). We stress *powerful* when discussing Regulatory Affairs. These are the people who—whether inside the client company or from an outside agency like the FDA or SEC—can literally shut down an operation that they feel is not in compliance.

---

3. A more thorough description can be found in a story about the GTPS and Ethicon Endo-Surgery published in *Pharmaceutical and Medical Packaging News*, ISSUE January 1997.

The basic question is: How do we reduce translation cost and turnaround time while satisfying Regulatory Affairs?

Solution: Process Integration

The solution rested in applying a process orientation, as discussed under "Standardized Process" above, but going one step further—actually ingraining translation in the organization so that all parties, including Regulatory, have a say in work processes, and understand what *will be* happening (as opposed to a reactive mode, where people are suddenly confronted by translation outputs).

In the proactive, strategic model that EES and HT jointly developed, these were some of the benefits:

- Work forecasts became more common, so that all parties became aware of how translation worked, and how to budget and schedule for it.

- Translation became more integrated into the production cycle, with technical writers who produced the original English as well as engineers who designed the product starting to think more internationally, thus simplifying translation and rendering the final product more user-friendly around the world.

- There was greater information-sharing among all parties. Rather than fostering an antagonistic relationship, the processes and systems reinforced cooperation. Audits were collaborative efforts that helped educate the parties that were new to translation.

- Regulatory Affairs became more comfortable with some of the cutting-edge solutions, and also had significant input in them. For example, parts of the review process became essentially paperless, while preserving electronically a rigorous "virtual paper trail." This safeguarded the critical traceability required, for example, under ISO 4.8.

- Regulatory Affairs' function became proceduralized and standardized. Rather than acting as an arm's-length third party with little knowledge of the process (common at many companies), Regulatory was involved early, minimizing 11th-hour surprises and allowing translation to proceed more smoothly.

- All other roles were clearly defined, including that of the translation vendor and the affiliates. Explicit roles meant fewer surprises, with clear goals and accountability.

Summary

The results of the above process and technology improvements have been substantial. Qualitatively, they included:

- reduced time-to-market;

- reduced costs;

- improved quality;

- improved communications.

But these advantages were not left in the realm of the anecdotal and qualitative. Most regulated industries share a drive to develop metrics and quantify results for key systems, and this was also the case with the language solutions implemented here. The following are some manifestations of the *strategic*, rather than *tactical*, view of language that J&J embraced:

- Key procedures for translation were documented, using an ISO- and GMP-compliant quality system.

- Quality metrics were applied to the language solution, such as tracking nonconformances, with an appropriate mechanism for taking corrective action.

- Performance data were recorded and analyzed, including standard turnaround, throughput, and efficiency of all parties.

Given tremendous time-to-market pressure—which will only get more acute with the arrival of the Internet—these solutions represent a sane approach for the company going global that sees overcoming language barriers as a strategic advantage.

Machine Translation and Controlled Authoring at Caterpillar

Rose Lockwood
Equipe Consortium Ltd.

SUMMARY[1]

Caterpillar is a pioneer in the implementation of machine translation based on controlled-English documentation. An already huge publishing volume is expanding as the company globalizes into new markets. To handle increased volumes, more languages, and the need for electronic distribution, Caterpillar has completely reengineered its documentation and publishing processes, implementing an innovative system combining SGML databases with automatic translation.

COMPANY BACKGROUND

Caterpillar, based in Peoria, Illinois, USA, is a growth-oriented, high-tech global company, and the world's leading manufacturer of construction and mining equipment, natural gas engines, and industrial gas turbines. It is a leading global supplier of diesel engines and also offers varied financing options through its Financial Products Division. The company had 1997 revenues of US$18.9 billion, with US$1.7 billion profits.

Throughout the 1990s, Caterpillar has been engaged in a corporate reengineering program aimed to create a decentralized, function-oriented organization. Part of that strategy is to operate with a global perspective, and to target growth markets worldwide, particularly in emerging markets with high demand for construction equipment. About half of Caterpillar's sales are outside the US (51 percent in 1997).

---

1. This case study is based on material previously published in: Lockwood, et al., *Globalisation: Creating New Markets with Translation Technology* (Ovum, 1995); Kamprath, et al., "Controlled Language for Multilingual Document Production: the Experience of Caterpillar Technical English," *Proceedings of the CLAW '98 Conference*; Nyberg, et al., "The KANT Translation System—From R&D to Large-Scale Deployment," LISA Newsletter, March 1998. The latter two articles can be viewed at www.lti.cs.cmu.edu/Research/Kant (research articles number 20 and 21). The opinions expressed in this case study are those of the author, and not of Caterpillar or CMT/CMU.

Caterpillar has a significant manufacturing presence outside the US, for better access to its key markets. Manufacturing sites include:

- Australia
- Belgium
- Brazil
- Canada
- China
- France
- Germany
- Hungary
- India
- Indonesia
- Italy
- Japan
- Mexico
- Northern Ireland
- Poland
- Russia
- Sweden
- United Kingdom

Caterpillar pursues its globalization strategy in partnership with companies located in emerging markets. For example, joint-venture agreements have been reached with AMO-Zil and Kirovsky Zavod in Russia, and Shanghai Diesel and Zuzhou Construction Machine Group in China. With nearly half the world's mineral wealth, these two countries are important markets for Caterpillar's products. Countries where Caterpillar operates have 74 percent of the world's land area and 81 percent of its population; the company has a strong position in infrastructure development and electrification of emerging markets. Despite difficulties in Asia in 1998, the company has continued to show strong sales.

Caterpillar has established a strong product-support system to service its dealership network worldwide. Extending to nearly 200 countries, the company considers the network a key competitive edge, and meeting the language needs of that network has been one of the drivers of the translation-automation program. Most of the company's 197 dealerships are locally owned independent businesses, and many dealers have been with Caterpillar for 50 years. This network operates in over 35 languages; providing product information in local languages is a strategic issue for Caterpillar as it pursues its globalization strategy.

CATERPILLAR'S DOCUMENTATION NEEDS

Caterpillar produces a large volume and variety of technical publications, including documentation for over 350 current products and older products still in use. Documentation must be available for the life of a product, which tends to be long. Each Caterpillar product incorporates several complex subsystems, such as an engine, hydraulic system, drive system, implements, and electrical systems, for which a variety of technical documents must be produced. They include operation and maintenance manuals, testing and adjusting instructions, disassembly and assembly manuals, and specifications, as well as bulletins regarding service procedures and new service offerings.

This information is provided to all dealerships. Moreover, the volume is always increasing. Many dealers have found it difficult to locate the information they need, when they need it—whether at the parts counter, in the service bays, or in the field where equipment is often serviced. To solve this problem, Caterpillar launched a project called the Service Information System (SIS), an electronic delivery system supplying documentation to dealers on CD-Rom.

In non-English-speaking markets, dealers require as much documentation as possible in translation. Therefore, in developing SIS, Caterpillar planned to improve its translation program and increase the amount of information supplied in local languages. Documentation is routinely translated into Spanish, French, German, Italian, Portuguese, Danish, Dutch, Finnish, Swedish, Norwegian, Greek, and Russian. Some material is also translated into Hungarian, Thai, Arabic, Chinese, Japanese, Icelandic, Turkish, Bahasa, Vietnamese, and Korean. Caterpillar now runs a substantial publishing operation, generating over 800 pages of new material a day and shipping over 110 tons of printed materials to dealers every month (since some material is still required on paper). The company maintains the largest CD-Rom library in the world, and generates over 50 CD-Rom masters every month.

Product-development cycles are getting shorter at Caterpillar, putting additional strain on the documentation system. Five years ago, the entire product development cycle was 18 months to two years; it is now six months or less.

Documentation requirements at Caterpillar can be summarized as:
- large volumes with frequent updates;
- electronic delivery and print formats;
- multiple-language versions;
- shorter documentation cycle times.

THE CATERPILLAR SOLUTION

Caterpillar has made a long-term investment in innovative technologies and processes to solve language problems. The current solution has been in development for a number of years, and is based on the use of controlled-English authoring with Caterpillar Technical English, an SGML database for file and document management, and automatic translation. The Caterpillar system has been granted a US patent, and international patents are pending.[2]

Caterpillar Technical English and the Language Environment

The company began to face the problems of a multilingual customer base in the early 1980s. This problem was originally addressed through the creation of Caterpillar Fundamental English (CFE)—a set of around 1,000 English words which authors attempted to use in all documentation. The company developed a CFE training program for overseas dealers and staff to eliminate the need to localize documentation.

Over time, it became clear that CFE was not a total solution. Authors were forced to use elaborate and lengthy descriptions of concepts that were not in CFE, and English users sometimes found the material unreadable. As Caterpillar's product base became more complex, adding high-tech features such as high-pressure hydraulics and electronics, the limited vocabulary of CFE became increasingly inadequate for technical publishing. High staff turnover and low levels of English literacy in the field-service staff made the increasing complexity even more difficult to support with CFE training alone. As Caterpillar moved into more markets, some with languages using non-Roman alphabets, and a growing number demanding product localization, it became clear that more translation was required.[3]

Caterpillar has reestablished controlled English as a technique which supports both document management and the translation needs of the publications department. In researching options for automatic translation to meet the ever-growing volume of translated material, it became clear that having a constrained set of inputs would greatly improve the possibility of achieving high-quality machine-based translation. In the early 1990s the company launched a project with The Carnegie Group, Inc. (CGI in Pitts-

---

2. US Patent 5,677,835—"Integrated Authoring and Translation System," Carbonell et al., granted October 1997—covering a wide range of functions of the system.
3. Use of CFE was discontinued by Caterpillar in 1982. The technology was subsequently licensed by Smart Communications, who have developed it further for their clients; the Communication Studies Unit of the University of Wales Institute of Science and Technology have also used CFE in R&D projects. See Nyberg, et al.

burgh, Pennsylvania) to develop controlled-English documentation and automatic translation into a subset of their 15 target languages. CGI served as a systems integrator for linguistic tools developed at Carnegie Mellon University (CMU).

Rather than attempting to limit text to an extremely small number of terms (as had been the case with CFE), the company started from scratch to reduce all terms and phrases to a standard, if much larger, set. They selected 900 Caterpillar documents representative of all types of technical publications and all existing product types. Using linguistic analysis tools developed by the Center for Machine Translation (CMT[4]) at CMU, CGI parsed this large volume of material and reduced the text to some one million unique words and phrases. Caterpillar staff then pared this set down, eliminating redundant terms (where different authors had used different terms for the same concept or object), and reduced the set to approximately 70,000.

This set of terms, along with a grammar that defines acceptable usage, is Caterpillar Technical English (CTE), and forms a fundamental part of Caterpillar's multilingual solution. CMT and Caterpillar staff worked together to devise guidelines for using CTE in authoring, and wrote usage examples for each CTE term. CTE consists of these 70,000 terms and a large subset of the structures of standard English in the CTE grammar.

Over 100 technical authors access CTE from a central server, using a CGI-developed "Language Environment" (LE) interface. The system provides a full linguistic sentence-by-sentence analysis of each document written by the authors. The LE user-interface provides definitions of terms and usage examples to authors; it controls the use of terms and provides interactive "disambiguation" to assure consistency and accuracy in English source text, and more accurate automated translation. The LE software interacts with the machine-translation engine as a co-process, while managing interactions with the user and the SGML text-editing environment, ArborText.

Initial training for CTE authors began in 1994, with bimonthly "brown-bag seminars" throughout the year in advance of initial CTE implementation. Formal author training began in 1995. The entire staff of authors was brought into the system gradually, while document types have been added incrementally. Standard training for authors has included:

- two weeks training to use ArborText (and its Unix environment), the file-management system, and graphics tools;

---

4. The CMT was expanded in 1996 to become the Language Technology Institute, LTI (see www.lti.cs.cmu.edu).

- three weeks of mentoring by a CTE expert.

SGML Database for File Management

While the CTE solution was being developed, the Caterpillar publications department began to develop a text- and document-management system that would support the new electronic delivery systems needed for SIS. The old document formats, based on a proprietary generic coding system developed many years prior for input to an ATEX typesetting system, were not easily converted to formats appropriate for CD-Rom and electronic publishing. Caterpillar decided to develop the new system as an SGML database to generate both print documents and elements for CD-Rom and online delivery.

SGML—Descriptive vs. Presentational Coding

Proprietary text-editing formats (such as those used by word processors or desktop-publishing systems) address the layout and appearance of a document on a page. This limits their usefulness as coding schemes for documents which will be presented in other formats (help screens, for example)—and especially for documents that may be presented in a number of *different* formats, such as Caterpillar requires. An alternate approach to document coding is *descriptive*, and much more akin to database coding. It describes the structural elements of a document such as headings, body text, and sections. The most commonly used descriptive coding system is Standard Generalized Markup Language (SGML).

SGML was published as ISO 8879 in 1986, and has since been adopted by a number of vendors (including a longer-term commitment from Microsoft) and, most significantly, was incorporated into the CALS (computer-assisted logistical support) standard required by the US Department of Defense for all documentation in systems supplied to them. This requirement has been extended to all US-government tendering documents, ensuring that SGML will be an important standard.

SGML is a tagging methodology whereby the structure of any text (including graphics and other nonlinguistic elements) can be maintained independently of the devices and software used to create the document. Parallel and nested information structures can be maintained, and can be format- and content-related, so that SGML actually extends the concept of markup into new areas.

Strictly speaking, markup is everything in a document that is not content-related, and the term comes from marking up typed text with instructions for the typesetter or compositor about aspects such as how to fit the text on a page, what typeface to use, etc. SGML takes this generic concept a step further and specifies a method for setting up document-hierarchy models where every element fits into a logical, predictable structure. It includes a syntax for defining document data elements and the overall framework. SGML is not a set of tags or document types—it is a method for designing tags and rules for any type of document. In other words, it is a programming language.

The heart of an SGML application is a *document type definition* (DTD) that defines the structure of a document in the same way that a database design describes the structure of a database. Elements defined by a DTD might include chapters, chapter headings, sections, and topics. It also defines rules—e.g., "A chapter heading tag must be the first element after a chapter tag." The DTD accompanies the document wherever it goes in a publishing system.

The DTD also provides a framework for the content of a document. Tagging identifies the role of content within a document and tags mark the beginning and end of each content type. Creating an SGML document thus involves adding text and inserting tags around it. The DTD is written in a rigorously defined language which is handled by an SGML parser. The parser is used to develop DTDs and verify that documents conform to the standard.

The elegance of the SGML solution is that it does not restrict document definitions to any particular type of output, and this is one reason it is seen as the standard of choice for electronic publishing. Output styles are defined in *formatting output specification instances* (FOSIs), which are a special kind of DTD. A FOSI is like a large style sheet which specifies the formatting characteristics for each tag in each of its contexts. Alternatively, one may use proprietary editing systems for coding the descriptive structure provided by SGML.

SGML turns "unstructured information"—which constitutes 90 percent of information stored electronically—into "structured data." In effect, document resources can be handled like data because they are in a database environment. This has highly significant implications for publishing and information provision, especially in multilingual environments.

In the world of online or electronic publishing, variants of SGML have evolved—starting with HTML (Hyperlinked Text Markup Language), which is a standard DTD for use with hyperlinked Web pages, and is used on most Web pages now published. This standard will, however, give way to XML, a more sophisticated variant capable of handling the complex multimedia documents published on the Web.

Caterpillar's SGML Solution—Information Elements

To support an SGML database, Caterpillar had to introduce a new authoring platform. The new system uses an SGML editor developed by ArborText to create the DTDs and FOSIs needed for the new file-management environment. SGML editors facilitate definition of DTDs and FOSIs, and creation of SGML-compliant documents. These editors provide a friendly editing environment with visual cues about the structure of the document, which removes the burden of knowing SGML programming.

The most revolutionary innovation in Caterpillar's document-management approach may well be the adoption of "information elements" to replace documents in the publishing system. Instead of writing books or manuals, authors now write information elements (IEs) that describe a specific concept or procedure. IEs are usually two or three pages long and are reused whenever possible. An author only writes what is specific to a particular information element. These elements are combined with other IEs and with shared objects (which can be graphics, tables, etc.) to build books or CD files as needed. This "write once, use many" approach produces substantial time and cost savings.

One requirement for CTE development was that it should support modular creation of documents as part of these reusable information elements, to improve consistency in English documentation as well as create a common look-and-feel for Caterpillar's technical publications. Since documents are created by combining different IEs, the CTE system needs to make IEs consistent, despite different levels of expertise and experience among authoring staff. It needs to incorporate SGML tagging for both paper publishing and electronic delivery of multilingual texts, and its grammar needs to handle complex and variable types of markup within information elements, including grammatical markup for target-language output in translation.

These IEs are combined into one of the dozen different document types identified for Caterpillar technical publications. Each document type has a DTD that defines the internal document structure in English and 15 other languages, and includes general style guidelines.

A File Management System (FMS) is a system that controls the creation, update, and translation of IEs. It is an integrated set of document-management tools (incorporating some 60 different software elements), managed by a custom-built workflow-management tool. Using workflow management, IEs are passed through tasks assigned to various authoring and translation staff.

Automatic Machine Translation (AMT) System

With expanding volumes of translation at Caterpillar, a machine-based translation system was an integral part of the solution. However, a review of available systems revealed none that would provide adequate quality without the need for extensive post-editing. Caterpillar's goal is to do as much "pre-editing" as possible at the authoring stage of the document cycle, to reduce the time and costs of translation. They decided to work with the CMT at Carnegie Mellon University to develop a custom solution to exploit the benefits of controlled authoring. The system they developed is Caterpillar's AMT system, based on CMT's Kant technology.

Overview of Knowledge-Based Accurate Natural Language Translation (Kant)

CMT initiated the Kant project in 1989 for the research and development of large-scale, practical translation systems for technical documentation. The Kant translation engine uses a controlled vocabulary and grammar for each source language, and explicit semantic models for each technical domain, to achieve very high accuracy in translation. Designed for multilingual document production, Kant has been applied to electric power-utility management in addition to heavy-equipment technical documentation at Caterpillar.[5]

Kant is CMU's MT system for automatic translation in technical domains. Kant is dubbed "knowledge-based MT" because it makes use of lexicons, grammars, and mapping rules for each language. Users can define terminology for specific domains, where the meaning of terms is limited by relevance. This approach tends to produce more accurate translations of technical material than general-purpose MT systems and the output typically requires modest post-editing.

Kant supports use of controlled input language with explicit conformance-checking during text authoring, applying the same grammar used for translation. It also supports the use of SGML tagging within sentences—SGML is treated as an integral part of text to be translated.

Caterpillar's translation system was based on the original Kant architecture. However, the Kant development team at CMT is redesigning the software; the new version is called Kantoo (Kant object-oriented). Caterpillar is gradually replacing the initial modules of their system with the reengineered modules of Kantoo. The main purpose is to improve

---

5. CMT and CMU are forming a new commercial entity, Alantra Systems, Inc., which will be the primary vehicle for marketing Kant technology.

implementation and deployment of new Kant applications, rather than to change the language engines per se. Kantoo will include a Lexicon Maintenance Tool (LMT) to handle source-language terminology (i.e., CTE terminology at Caterpillar), and a Language Translation Database (LTD) for target-language terminology. Both tools are built on a PC-based Oracle database and forms applications, and are designed for rapid development and maintenance of linguistic resources.

The Kantoo Analyzer and Generator are reimplementations of the Kant tools—the Analyzer used for grammar checking and source-text analysis during translation, and the Generator a reimplementation of the target-language translation engine. The Knowledge Maintenance Tool (KMT) is a graphical user-interface   for real-time browsing, editing, and updating of lexica, grammars, domain models, and mapping rules—i.e., all knowledge sources used during analysis of source-language text and generation of target-language text. At present writing, development milestones are complete for all five modules of the Kantoo system and are now being integrated into the Caterpillar writing and translation environment.

The reengineering of Kantoo is driven principally by the need for better software-engineering procedures, such as reducing the cost and effort involved in maintenance through better database management. All elements of the system are being ported from LISP to C++, to make the system usable on more platforms, including standard desktop environments such as Microsoft Windows, more robust in operational environments, and easier to maintain.

Integrating Authoring and Translation Tools

The AMT system contains a database (or knowledge base) of CTE vocabulary and phrases, acceptable syntactic constructions, and relationships between concepts which constitute the Caterpillar domain knowledge. One of the tasks of the original CGI contract was to develop the interface tool which would give authors access to the linguistic processing modules of CMT's system, including this domain knowledge. Thus the same grammar system used to analyze text for translation is also used at the authoring stage to check whether new text conforms to CTE rules (for terminology and grammar). Where material does not conform, the editor suggests alternative vocabulary or offers examples of approved usage.

CTE terminology, which is also the dictionary resource for AMT, is too complex to control completely. Common terms with ambiguous meanings are the most difficult to control. Caterpillar uses the example of the English word "valve," which can have at least nine different meanings depending on the type of valve and the role it plays in various systems. Similarly, the verb "charge" can mean charging an electrical element such as a battery, or pressurizing a gas container such as an ether cylinder.

While CTE originally set out to define every term or phrase with a single meaning (to assure accurate translation), this did not prove possible. Around 2,500 terms in CTE are ambiguous and may cause translation errors in AMT. To overcome this problem, Caterpillar employs SGML codes to "disambiguate" these terms in the authoring process. When such a term is used, the CTE software prompts the author to indicate the intended meaning, and this information is tagged in the text. A similar technique is used to handle structural ambiguities—such as referents for prepositional phrases. At the time of translation, the AMT system selects the correct meaning based on the SGML codes.

After implementation of CTE, Caterpillar discovered that this disambiguation option could have negative consequences, where alternative meanings are irrelevant in a particular type of document. If an author is writing an IE pertaining to an electrical element, he or she doesn't want to be presented with the "pressurizing" definition for "charge" as an option in that document. A refinement was introduced, to attach subdomain codes to the IE; now only meanings relevant to the subdomain are offered in the interactive disambiguation session.

New IEs are filed in the File Management System, and the English version is subsequently submitted to the AMT system for translation. Authoring and translation are strictly separate. Translation itself is in two stages:

- the English version is analyzed and translated into a "language-independent" representation called an "interlingua"

- the target language is generated from the interlingua

The interlingua concept is central to the Carnegie-Mellon approach to machine translation. The advantage is that once the interlingua has been created, a new target language can be added by building a language generator for that language. No further parsing or analysis of the source text is required, as is the case with other approaches to MT (such as the so-called "transfer" method).

Both analysis and generation functions of the AMT system access the Caterpillar domain knowledge base. Each module accesses a base of information about whatever language is being handled; modeling target-language matches of CTE vocabulary is part of this language information.

Languages Implemented

The first AMT module became operational for French in 1996. With AMT, the translator's principal role is to check and do a final edit on the results of the automatic translation ("post-editing"). Prior to implementation, Caterpillar undertook an "acceptance evaluation" for French AMT, looking at various usability, performance, and quality factors. The result determined that improved post-editing productivity was the primary goal of the system. By some measures, productivity improvement for translators showed as much as a two-to-one gain. Caterpillar is cautious, however, about making definitive claims regarding productivity, since the new system is complex, and touches almost every aspect of the document creation, maintenance, translation, and publishing cycle. The results of the evaluation were sufficiently positive, however, to justify acceptance of AMT for French.

The next planned language, Spanish, was accepted for production use in 1997. Acceptance testing for Spanish was done somewhat differently. Rather than using a formal usability study (as with French), they used a specialist team, including a Spanish expert linguist and the CMT developers, to do rapid feedback and refinement over several months, in what was essentially alpha testing. Evaluation of Spanish in production mode is ongoing, and translators have reported that Spanish output requires little post-editing.

Caterpillar is currently implementing the German AMT system.

Maintenance and Costs

Caterpillar has gradually begun maintaining elements of the system. As of late 1998, they had taken on maintenance of source-text data (English terminology and grammar updates). They have developed a problem-reporting process, enabling authors to request term and grammar updates. Ongoing maintenance of CTE terminology controls new terms, removes redundant terms, and screens those requested by authors. Usage examples are also updated whenever CTE grammar is improved, and these examples must be revalidated.

Development of CTE, the LE interface, and target-language translation engines (for French and Spanish) all took place in parallel. The development phase for the system was relatively long, and the company committed five full-time equivalent staff per year over a five-year period. Participants from Caterpillar included linguists, pilot authors, trainers, mentors, and system developers. These resources were devoted principally to initial development of terminology and grammar, evaluation and refinement, and training. Ongoing operational costs include incremental updating of terminology for new products requiring new documentation, and refinement of the grammar as new document types are introduced or existing ones revised.

CHALLENGES

Caterpillar's new authoring and translation system has involved substantial reengineering of internal processes, as well as development and implementation of new technology, and no change of this magnitude can be trouble-free. Because various elements were developed in parallel, one challenge has been integrating the modules.

The CTE domain is too complex for lexicographers to anticipate all the ways authors will use terms. Since ambiguities cannot be defined in advance, terms and grammar must be constantly extended. Post-implementation support will be substantial, and the company will need to learn to shift skills from traditional translation roles to the more technical tasks of maintaining and interacting with the system.

The Caterpillar solution represents a complete change in the working paradigm of the publications division, and there has been understandable fear and worry on the part of authors because their jobs are now significantly different. Nevertheless, most authors have found the new system easier to use than they expected, and appreciate the ease with which they can pick up IEs to assemble new publications. Despite the sophisticated features of the CTE-checking tools, compliance by authors can be variable or difficult to enforce. Authors may use words with the wrong meaning, or select the wrong meaning during disambiguation. It is also possible to write syntactically correct sentences that are incomprehensible or inaccurate. Moreover, there are situations in which full CTE conformance is suspended—such as deadlines for product launches which preclude full coding of new terminology—and these can be used by authors to minimize the control of CTE on their writing.

In the course of implementing IE authoring with CTE checking, it became clear that sometimes an author would reuse an information element with only slight revisions, but the whole IE would have to be reparsed by CTE for compliance. A "region marking" feature has been added, to mark areas of text (usually sentences) that are CTE-approved and unchanged. This, combined with a batch-checking application for modified IEs, can quickly return only those sentences that fail to pass CTE, or require disambiguation.

Updating the CTE dictionary is a continuing challenge as new products emerge and little time remains between final engineering and shipment date. Unknown terms can now be temporarily protected from CTE analysis, and an automated process for requesting and screening missing terms has been introduced. This assures conformance of major parts of new texts, without requiring immediate new-term authorization.

The effort required for terminology work (especially during development) is usually underestimated. The ongoing maintenance load for CTE and target-language term development will naturally fluctuate, and be difficult to plan. Establishing translation equivalents for all new CTE terms requires ongoing vigilance to maintain consistency in the databases—a burden which will increase as new languages are added to AMT. Ambiguity in the English text can now be handled by coding during terminology development. As new AMT languages are implemented, all of which translate the same CTE input, it will become necessary to adjust the relation between English and target-language terminology.

Like many innovators in language engineering, Caterpillar finds it challenging to locate adequately skilled staff for some of the technical work, especially in terminology coding. The task needs a combination of detailed knowledge of the CTE domain, training in linguistics, and a thorough knowledge of the target language (i.e., translator skills). Caterpillar's solution requires highly skilled personnel at all levels, from authors and translators to terminologists, lexicographers, and system maintainers. In the medium term, they will probably continue to use outside services (such as those of CMT) to complement in-house skills.

Translators are being asked to move from traditional roles, where they are generally in control of the style and content of translation, to that of post-editor, and some are not enthusiastic about the change. The learning curve for effective post-editing is not trivial, and it implies a level of retraining for translator staff—a particular challenge where outside translators are used. The level of appropriate post-editing is still hard to define; editing to a standard of stylistic consistency is difficult to do efficiently (and not necessary where generated text is understandable), and some translators are reluctant to do minimal revision. Managers of translators will need new ways to measure translator effectiveness and make judgments about quality.

Finally, it is still a challenge to devise metrics for evaluation of AMT which are not influenced by factors outside the translation process, such as author compliance with CTE, the quality of the term database, knowledge of SGML, and system training. In the long run, Caterpillar will need to address the process improvements of the entire publishing system, as all elements in the document cycle are brought within an integrated environment.

Benefits and Strategic Directions

CTE has delivered benefits for both manual and automatic translation at Caterpillar. While consistent source-text authoring has been implemented principally to improve the output consistency of MT, it also improves the consistency and cost-effectiveness of manual translation. Controlled-English authoring also improves the quality and consistency of documentation for English-language users.

Caterpillar's solution has allowed the company to begin developing a full set of terminology resources for use in all company documentation—a benefit which was not initially a major goal for the system, but which may prove to be among the greatest it confers, as all elements of corporate publishing begin to leverage readily available and reusable terminology.

The implementation of the IE architecture has created substantial reusability in Caterpillar's publications database. IEs are now being reused across product lines, which increases production efficiency and cuts cost. The system has essentially delivered an author-memory system which eliminates redundant rewriting. Authors are increasingly skilled at reusing IEs for compiling new publications.

Implementation of CTE, IEs, and AMT have heightened awareness of language-related issues at Caterpillar. Close checking of authored text raises the profile within the organization of issues relating to documentation quality, such as the consistency that comes from conforming to authoring guidelines and standardization of processes.

Key benefits from the system include the following:

- technical publishing is shorter and more efficient;

- new document types that Caterpillar previously could not handle can be translated;

- documentation will be reusable in different formats, for different purposes, leveraging valuable corporate resources;

- electronic distribution of documentation will be simple and integrated with the mainstream processes;

- technical writing will be more closely integrated with production, as authors will be part of the new-product introduction team;

- products and translated documentation will ship simultaneously (in the past, translated versions lagged by eight to 10 weeks).

Although the system has required substantial investment and several years of development effort, overall costs for documentation will be lower, particularly considering the number of languages that will be handled. At the same time, costs will be substantially redistributed towards tools that support controlled authoring and editing, and management of documentation elements.

Expansion to other languages, particularly Asian languages, is under investigation. As an interim solution for other languages, Caterpillar uses translation memory, particularly for "high-reuse" documents such as updates of manuals. This remains the long-term solution for languages not automated through AMT.

The introduction of a multilingual document-management system has revolutionized publishing at Caterpillar. The company believes this system will give it a significant competitive advantage as it continues to pursue new markets worldwide.

14

Combining Machine Translation
with Translation Memory at Baan

Carmen Andrés Lange
Baan Development B.V.

Winfield Scott Bennett
Logos Corporation

INTRODUCTION

The demand for translation is currently rising dramatically, given the boom in international trade. Pressure on translators and translation companies to produce high-quality results in shorter times is likewise increasing. A major problem is the lack of qualified translators to meet the rising need. The dream of applying computer technology to assist in the translation process has been one of the earliest goals in the field of artificial intelligence. Long turnaround times for translation coupled with demand for translation services that outstrip the supply of human capital have again thrust technology into the forefront of the conversation.

What was once the realm of hype and fear—will machines replace human translators?—has emerged as a viable partner for the translation industry. Translators now routinely use a variety of tools, ranging from basic word processing and database-management systems to high-end translation memories and automatic-translation systems.

Two technologies are central to our discussion. *Machine translation* (MT) is typically the use of computers to perform first-pass translation. It is accompanied by the building of user-specific dictionaries, and is followed by "post-editing" by language professionals to verify accuracy and correct the translation. *Translation memory* (TM) is a translation tool that stores previously translated material and leverages it for new translations. Depending on the configuration and sophistication of the system, the TM solution may have varying degrees of sophistication in its "fuzzy matching" capability in relating new text to previously translated materials.

This case study reports how the integration of these two translation tools enabled both the process and the translators at Baan Company.

BACKGROUND

In 1997, having evaluated various MT systems, Baan Company decided to run a six-month MT-pilot project in Hanover, Germany, for English-into-German translation using the Logos MT system. Baan had already considered MT in 1994, but decided against it, based on these factors:

- A substantial investment would be required in manpower and technical equipment.

- New writing guidelines would be needed for source and target texts.

- Terminology would have to be used consistently to allow efficient machine translation.

- Integration of translation memory (reuse of previously translated material) was not straightforward.

- The return on investment was not clear.

While Baan postponed introduction of MT in 1994, the company began to pave the way for introduction of the technology. They streamlined terminology, recruited more employees for the documentation and translation department, and introduced Standard Baan English (a simplified and heavily rule-based subset of English that minimizes ambiguities—making machine translation much more accurate and efficient).

Because English and German are often among the most developed language modules in the MT industry and because English is Baan's source language and Germany one of Baan's key markets, Baan decided that the English–into-German translation team would pilot the use of MT in the organization.

By 1997 Baan was ready to implement MT. Management strongly supported the initiative and asked Carmen Andrés Lange (an author of this study) to lead the pilot project and integrate MT into the English-German translation procedure. Management established the following objective: reduce throughput time for translations by 50 percent through the use of automated translation.

Pilot Phase I: Text Analysis and Logos as a Stand-Alone System

Linguistic analysis demonstrated that Baan's standard online-help texts were the most suitable candidate for MT.

Baan obtained the Logos machine-translation package, and introduced terms, semantic rules, and pattern-matching rules to obtain optimal output. Interestingly, testing revealed that Baan's standards for formatting text proved problematic when those texts were submitted for machine translation. Written with editing software integrated into Baan's development system, the texts contained hard line breaks and numerous integrated codes. The codes represented either hyperlink-specific software components described in the online help, or phrases used to speed up manual translations. Text analysis showed that Logos' performance would be greatly enhanced if Baan could protect codes from being translated, and if hard line breaks could be removed where needed. This was accomplished manually during the pilot phase. Something as apparently trivial as removing hard line breaks proved problematic, and close collaboration between Baan and Logos was ultimately needed to resolve the issue.

Since Baan sought to implement a highly user-friendly solution for all involved, it was determined at the end of Pilot Phase 1 not to use Logos as a stand-alone solution, since too many issues remained open, not to mention challenges of internal "buy-in" for such a dramatic departure from Baan's traditional approach to translation.

Pilot Phase 2: Logos Combined with Translation Memory (TM)

The solution to Baan's formatting and other problems (e.g., Baan had not yet selected a post-editing tool) came unexpectedly. Why be concerned with removing hard line breaks if Star's Transit Translation Memory program could handle them? Baan had been using Transit for English-to-German translation since 1994. The idea was born to leverage both technologies in one solution.

This decision put the project back on track. An interface had recently been developed by Star and Logos, integrating Transit Translation Memory and Logos Machine Translation. Baan took a fresh look at the problem. During this phase, it was necessary to define clearly which system would carry out which tasks. It soon became obvious that Transit could support the following tasks:

- protect strings so that they are not translated or destroyed by the Logos system during translation processing;

- segment titles, subtitles, sentences, listings, etc.;

- automatically find and apply perfect (100-percent) matches embedded in previously translated reference material;

- leverage the company's core terminology already defined in TermStar, the terminological database integrated in Transit (the TermStar export profile allows Baan to export their company-specific terminology and import it into Alex, the Logos dictionary-management package);

- extract completely new segments and fuzzy matches, which are subsequently sent to Logos through the interface;

- incorporate a post-editing process.

The *only* task left for Logos is the translation of virtually every new or modified text segment.

Pilot Phase 3: Workflow

Once Baan recognized that MT could be integrated into their translation procedure through the TM system, they immediately began readjusting the entire workflow. What at first seemed very complicated and novel soon turned out to have notable similarities in structure to the prior approach of which the steps are listed and diagrammed below:

1. Text is imported into Transit.

2. Text is checked against reference material.

3. Multiple occurrences can be written into files called *extract.**

Transit Workflow Without MT

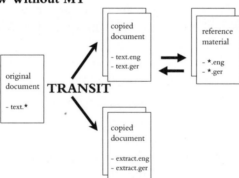

A dominant idea behind the new MT approach was, simply put, to create new reference materials. The new procedure (see Figure 2) was as follows:

1. The original text (in Figure 1 called *text.**) is imported into Transit.

2. Transit creates two file pairs named *text.eng/text.ger* and *extract.eng/extract.ger.*

3. The *text.eng/text.ger* file pair is compared with available reference material. Perfect (100–percent) matches are automatically inserted in *text.ger,* the file for the target language German.

4. *extract.ger* contains all untranslated segments (without redundancies) and is sent via the interface directly from Transit to the LogosClient where

the user may choose the appropriate Logos translation profile. The LogosClient sends the file to the LogosServer where the file is translated.

5. As soon as Logos has finished the automatic translation, the translated *extract.ger* is, again, automatically returned to Transit where it can be used as reference material.

6. If the translator opens the file to be translated in Transit (i.e., *text.eng/text.ger*) and activates the interactive TM function *Associative Net*, he or she always obtains not only the fuzzy matches of former translations, but also the Logos-translated segments from the *extract.ger* file.

7. Post-editing is done in the *Associative Net* window. After post-editing, the sentence or segment is sent to the *text.ger* file in the target-language window (see Figure 3).

Transit/Logos Interface

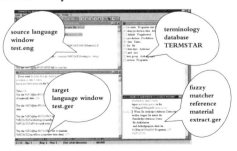

As shown in the following figure, this procedure allows human translators to control the entire process. The TM system ensures that translators review every segment and cross-check the terminology used by Logos with company-approved terminology in the TermStar master database.

Transit Translation Memory

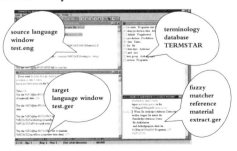

Pilot Phase 4: Enhancing Logos Output

Baan began to enhance the procedure by adding an extra Logos translation run, instead of immediately starting post-editing.

Translators can use the Transit *Insert Extract* feature to copy the content of *extract.ger* into *text.ger*. They then inspect each translated segment and forward comments to Baan's Superuser (the team member authorized to enter new terms and semantic rules into Logos). The original text is then run through the Logos system a second time, leveraging the new information.

Baan initiated training in the new approach for each member of the English-German team and simultaneously began to process "live" texts currently in the translation process. Finally, they compared the throughput times for manual, TM-based and TM/MT-based translations.

Based on the results, shown in the figure below, at the end of the pilot project, Baan came to several conclusions. They could reduce throughput times by 50 to 60 percent if all ran smoothly. However, this does not mean a procedure that runs without technical problems; it also assumes that everyone involved fully cooperates (a significant challenge, given the traditional resistance to MT in many environments). Note that MT productivity was markedly lower in the case of 350 text lines, actually taking longer than manual translation.

Initial Results

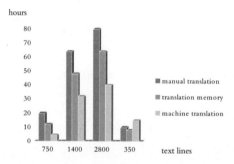

The Human Factor

Nearly every article about MT focuses either on linguistic aspects or on how fast large amounts of texts can be handled by MT. But they rarely explain how to motivate employees, and how to integrate MT into the translation business procedure. Introducing MT does not imply that everybody involved is excited to be part of a highly sophisticated technical procedure. Consider the impact on the translator: many of them are moved from a traditional translation role into that of post-editing—reviewing the output produced by the machine, which can be tedious and more "mechanical."

The chart above shows one result where MT took even longer than human translation would have taken. Analysis showed that the translator involved was very negative towards MT, and saw the pilot project as a temporary annoyance. Baan managers found they could generally predict the time a translator would need for post-editing by gauging his or her attitude towards MT.

Baan decided to move forward with MT implementation, but cautiously asked how far to go in imposing a new workflow. Baan proceeded with these conditions:

- To keep the whole MT procedure as simple as possible, they opted to go ahead with Transit, which each team member was comfortable with at that point.

- Everyone received training in entering terms and semantic rules in Logos.

- The role of each team member was clearly defined.

Baan noticed that motivation increased dramatically after individual training (including training of freelancers). This human factor will, however, remain a source of concern until professional translators are willing to use MT as a tool to assist them in their work. Baan's experience was that some finally overcame their reservations, while others were resistant and gained nothing from the system.

Starting in early 1998, Baan implemented an integrated TM/MT approach into its regular workflow, using the system for current and future online-help texts.

DETAILS

This section outlines a number of the issues and their solutions discovered in the course of the pilot project.

Baan online-help texts mainly contain three types of sentences, presented in the table below (strings in italics—red in the online version—are recognized dictionary entries in the Transit TM system; those in bold—blue in the online version—are protected tags in Transit TM system; question marks in the text are inserted by the MT system to mark phrases not in its dictionary and which it translated literally):

- Sentences without encoding that must be protected from being overwritten during the MT run (1a–1c).

- Sentences with nonencoded software components (program names, commands, field names, etc.) (2a).

- Sentences with encoded strings for software components protected from being translated and highlighted in bold (3a–3c).

Category I: Plain Text Without Hypertext Encoding		
1a	English	For example, if the *ordered quantity* is large, *machine*s with higher production capacities are used.
	Logos Output in German	Zum Beispiel wenn die bestellte Menge groß ist, werden Maschinen mit höheren Produktionskapazitäten verwendet.
	Desired Output	Wenn die Bestellmenge zum Beispiel groß ist, werden Maschinen mit höheren Produktionskapazitäten verwendet.
	Possible Human Translation	Ist die Bestellmenge beispielsweise sehr hoch, werden Maschinen mit höheren Produktionskapazitäten eingesetzt.
1b	English	Use this *session* in order to copy *project* data to a new or existing *project*.
	Logos Output in German	Verwenden Sie dieses Programm, um Projektdaten in ein neues oder bestehendes Projekt zu kopieren.
	Desired Output	– no modification necessary -
	Possible Human Translation	Mit diesem Programm können Sie Projektdaten in ein neues oder bestehendes Projekt kopieren.
1c	English	You must *specify* the *ledger account* to which the *transaction amount* must be *posted*.
	Logos Output in German	Sie müssen das Sachkonto angeben, auf das der Buchungsbetrag gebucht werden muß.
	Desired Output	– no modification necessary -
	Possible Human Translation	Geben Sie das Sachkonto an, auf das der Betrag gebucht werden soll.

Category II: Plain Text with Nonencoded Software Components		
2a	English	You must select multiple *records*, then use the Assign Automatic *command*.
	Logos Output in German	Sie müssen verschiedene Datensätze auswählen, dann verwenden Sie den Zuweisen Automatischen Befehl.
	Desired Output	Sie müssen verschiedene Datensätze auswählen, dann verwenden Sie den Befehl 'Automatisch zuordnen'.
	Possible Human Translation	Wählen Sie zunächst die gewünschten Datensätze aus, und führen Sie anschließend den Befehl 'Automatisch zuordnen' aus.

Category III: Plain Text with Encoded Software Components (Hyperlinks)		
3a	English	Select the *check box* **%TF@tiipd001.oqdr** in the **%SE@tiipd0501m000** *session.*
	Logos Output in German	Markieren Sie das Kontrollkästchen**%TF@tiipd001.oqdr** in**%SE@tiipd0501m000** Programm.
	Desired Output	Markieren Sie das Kontrollkästchen **%TF@tiipd001.oqdr** im Programm **%SE@tiipd0501m000.**
	Possible Human Translation	Markieren Sie das Kontrollkästchen **%TF@tiipd001.oqdr** im Programm **%SE@tiipd0501m000.**
3b	English	Use this *session* in order to enter the *default project* **%HC(tiGL000053,***calculation office*) by the *project* **%HC(tcGLSeries.tc,***series*) that is used for automatic numbering.
	Logos Output in German	Verwenden Sie dieses Programm, um das Standardprojekt einzugeben**%HC(tiGL000053,**Abteilung für Auftragsbearbeitung) vom Projekt**%HC(tcGLSeries.tc,**Nummernkreis), das für automatische Numerierung benutzt wird.
	Desired Output	Verwenden Sie dieses Programm, um das Standardprojekt für die **%HC(tiGL000053,**Abteilung für Auftragsbearbeitung) pro Projekt**%HC(tcGLSeries.tc,**nummernkreis), der für die automatische Numerierung benutzt wird, einzugeben.

Category III: Plain Text with Encoded Software Components (Hyperlinks)		
3c	English	**%FF@tffas0108s0001tffas008.deli** *field* is a combination of *degressive depreciation*, where the depreciation *base* is the **%HC(tfGLBookValue.tf,***book value*), and **%ENtffas.desy.fix.perc.base,** where the *depreciation base* is **%HC(tfGLPurchaValue.tf,***purchase value*).
	Logos Output in German	**%FF@tffas0108s0001tffas008.deli** das Feld ist eine Kombination aus ?degressive Abschreibung, wo die Abschreibungsart ist**%HC(tfGLBookValue.tf,**Buchwert) und**%ENtffas.desy.fix.perc.base**Wo die Abschreibungsart ist**%HC(tfGLPurchaValue.tf,**Anschaffungs- und Herstellungskosten).
	Desired Output	Das **%FF@tffas0108s0001tffas008.deli** Feld ist eine Kombination aus degressiver Abschreibung, wobei die Abschreibungsbemessungsgrundlage der **%HC(tfGLBookValue.tf,**Buchwert) ist, und die **%ENtffas.desy.fix.perc.base,** wobei die Abschreibungsbemessungsgrundlage die **%HC(tfGLPurchaValue.tf,**Anschaffungs- und Herstellungskosten) sind.

The human translator can more or less translate *around* the codes, given that translations into German in many cases do not require restructuring the sentence. When the translator is finished, all codes are replaced by the target text components.

Highlighting terms already in the terminology database (italic in the above examples, red in the online system) greatly speeds up the process. By simply pressing shortcut keys, translators can copy German target words into their documents.

Another conclusion: the greater the number of nonencoded strings in a text, the less attractive a purely human-translation approach, given that this is where the machine is most powerful.

The previous table shows the first Logos output without using pattern-matcher rules or macros. Only a few basic terms had been introduced into Alex, the Logos dictionary-management tool, and some semantic rules had been defined in Semantha, the Logos tool for semantic rules.

See example 3a where *select the check box* = *Kontrollkästchen markieren* is defined by the rule:

select (v) (tr) check box(n) = markieren (v) (tr) Kontrollkästchen (n) where v=verb, tr=transitive, n=noun

Translators confronted with the initial Logos output commonly reject it, stating that post-editing the sentence would entail a complete rewrite.

The first problem was to teach Logos the meaning of the encoded strings, which turned out to be virtually impossible, since dictionary entries in Alex could only be defined using alpha characters. The idea of encoding all available Baan text codes as term entries into Alex had to be abandoned. Apart from rejecting non-alphas, Logos unfortunately also destroyed the codes during the MT run. The solution was to define all codes as protected tags in Transit.

This produced the desired result, although translators had to live with two constraints: the protected strings are shifted one position to the left (see Logos Output in German for examples 3a–3c) and, more importantly, sentences could not be analyzed appropriately.

Example 3b:

the *project* **%HC(tcGLSeries.tc,***series)*...

is translated by Logos with

vom Projekt**%HC(tcGLSeries.tc,Nummernkreis)**

instead of

pro Projekt**%HC(tcGLSeries.tc,**nummernkreis)...

Logos overlooks the connection between *project* and *series* because of the protected code between them.

Example 3a may be the most typical online-help sentence, as it appears regularly only with other codes for field and program names.

Select the *check box* **%TF@tiipd001.oqdr** in the **%SE@tiipd0501m000** *session.*

is translated by Logos with

Markieren Sie das Kontrollkästchen**%TF@tiipd001.oqdr** in**%SE@tiipd0501m000** Programm.

In order to receive the desired output:

Markieren Sie das Kontrollkästchen **%TF@tiipd001.oqdr** im Programm **%SE@tiipd0501m000**.

the English sentence has to be rewritten before sending it to Logos.

If the sentence

Select the *check box* **%TF@tiipd001.oqdr** in *session* **%SE@tiipd0501m000**.

is sent to Logos, the output becomes:

Markieren Sie das Kontrollkästchen**%TF@tiipd001.oqdr** im
Programm**%SE@tiipd0501m000**.

To brush up the output, a macro can be run shifting the protected strings
one position to the right. Now the output becomes:

Markieren Sie das Kontrollkästchen **%TF@tiipd001.oqdr** im Programm
%SE@tiipd0501m000.

No further modifications are needed if two data manipulations are performed: the noun *session* must be inserted before the code (a macro can be
run beforehand) and the protected codes must be shifted to the right before
post-editing (via a macro).

To this point, we have seen that text with encoded strings turns out to be
problematic for MT. Let us turn then to text that contains only natural
(human) language.

Example 2a:

The sentence

You must select multiple *record*s, then use the Assign Automatic *command*.

is translated by Logos with:

Sie müssen verschiedene Datensätze auswählen, dann verwenden Sie den
Zuweisen Automatischen Befehl.

Logos cannot recognize *Assign Automatic command* as a command button
with the description *Assign Automatic.*

Desired output ready for post-editing could be:

Sie müssen verschiedene Datensätze auswählen, dann verwenden Sie den
Befehl 'Automatisch zuordnen'.

Assign Automatic command can be defined in Alex as a noun with the German transfer *Befehl Automatisch zuordnen.* The output becomes:

Sie müssen verschiedene Datensätze auswählen, dann verwenden Sie den
Befehl Automatisch zuordnen.

What is left is to put the command description *Automatisch zuordnen* in quo-
tation marks by means of a pattern-matcher rule in Logos.

REPLACE TARGET 'Automatisch' 'zuordnen' WITH '\'Automatisch'
'zuordnen\"

Not every sentence in an online-help manual includes encoded strings or
predefined names of software components. Natural-language phrases can
sometimes be time-consuming for human translations because of their

complex syntax. Standard English ensures simplified structure and reduces the length of sentences, thereby heightening MT accuracy and simplifying post-editing.

Example I a:

The sentence

> For example, if the *ordered quantity* is large, *machines* with higher production capacities are used.

is translated by Logos with

> Zum Reispiel wenn die bestellte Menge groß ist, werden Maschinen mit höheren Produktionskapazitäten verwendet.

Two constraints are immediately obvious to the translator. *ordered quantity* is not translated correctly. The desired German transfer should be *Bestellmenge* instead of *bestellte Menge.* And the word order *For example, if* is not changed in the German output.

The former problem can easily be solved by redefining the Alex entry for *ordered quantity.* Changing the word order for *For example* is trickier:

> Wenn die Bestellmenge zum Beispiel groß ist, werden Maschinen mit höheren Produktionskapazitäten verwendet.

There are clearly cases like this where it may be to cumbersome to change word order before MT processing, or where the rules of the MT system do not provide an ideal solution.

On the other hand, some Logos translation results require little further modification. One often hears of the "howlers" produced by MT, but a sampling of sentences in sound shape after MT such as the following shows the potential for an automated solution.

Example I b:

> Use this *session* in order to copy *project* data to a new or existing *project.*

is translated with:

> Verwenden Sie dieses Programm, um Projektdaten in ein neues oder bestehendes Projekt zu kopieren.

The errorless output could be achieved by defining two semantic rules telling the system that:

> *to use a session* should always be translated with *ein Programm verwenden* [use (vtr) session (n) = verwenden (vtr) Programm (n)] and

to copy sth to sth should always be translated with *etwas in etwas kopieren* [copy (vtr) n (acc) to (prep) n (acc) = *kopieren* (vtr) n (acc) in (prep) n (acc)

where v=verb, tr=transitive, n=noun, acc=grammatical case accusative, prep=preposition

The same goes for example 1c where no further modification is required:

You must *specify* the *ledger account* to which the *transaction amount* must be *post*ed.

Sie müssen das Sachkonto angeben, auf das der Buchungsbetrag gebucht werden muß.

EVALUATING THE RESULTS

Since typical times for human translations were known beforehand, we concluded that machine translation, in combination with translation memory, was able to speed up translation throughput times by up to 50 percent, but only if everything ran smoothly:

- The grammar of the input text must be correct.

- Translators must run the correct macros.

- The MT system must be provided with the correct terms and semantic rules to *understand* the text.

- Translators are properly trained and motivated to accept the style of an output free of grammatical faults as "acceptable."

Smooth runs also assume no system crashes and no problems with rules and terminology. In the study, the time for pre-editing, MT runs, post-editing, and dictionary work were carefully timed, as Baan was intent on quantifying the value of any savings, whether in terms of time or money.

As a result of the pilot, Baan concluded that translators' willingness was essential to success. The linguists' role changed drastically from that of an actor in the foreground who determines word-order, to one in the background who manipulates all available functions to force MT to produce an acceptable output.

Using trial-and-error during MT-test runs, translators discovered the following:

1. Phrases like *Use the session to* are translated without errors, if the English is changed to *Use the session in order to* prior to MT (solution: macro).

2. Encoded strings that are combined with natural words like *session, field, tab* are correctly translated simply by changing the code+word-order (solution: macro).

3. Encoded strings will not be destroyed by Logos if they are protected by translation memory (solution: project definition with regular expressions in TM Transit).

4. Sentences containing hard returns are not correctly parsed by Logos since Logos only analyzes the strings between two hard returns (solution: segmentation rules by means of regular expressions in TM Transit).

5. Nonencoded software-component descriptions can be translated without further modifications by defining them in Alex and writing pattern-matcher rules.

CONCLUSION AND FUTURE PROJECTS

During the MT pilot, Baan experienced the doubts typical of many with an interest in MT. For instance, at the end of the first pilot phase, Baan was disappointed and could barely believe that *formatting tags* could really be an insurmountable barrier to the use of MT in their environment.

What at first glance seemed to be a stopgap-solution (i.e., going through Transit and the Transit-Logos interface) emerged as the most suitable procedure for Baan and Baan's translators. Among the first to implement the Transit/Logos interface, Baan specifically implemented these processes:

- importing terminology into Logos;

- protecting strings by means of regular expressions in Transit;

- solving segmentation of phrases and sentences via regular expressions in Transit (even a missing period no longer hampers analysis);

- inserting previously translated material;

- integrating the post-editing environment through Transit's synchronized windows for source and target language;

- motivating team members.

At present writing, the LogosServer is established at Baan's subsidiary in Hanover, Germany, where the English-into-German team works.

Baan anticipates that an annual average of 1.5 million words in online-help files will be translated from English into German using the MT system. MT work currently involves five to six translators. The online-help files are specifically for Baan's Enterprise Requirements Planning (ERP) System, an administrative system that supports corporate-wide accounting, inventory control, production, and sales and purchasing departments. The ERP System is targeted at markets in the US, Germany, and Japan. Some 200,000 words of online help translated using MT are now part of the documentation for the ERP System in the field.

Current and future projects include further enhancements to Standard Baan English by means of a pre-editing tool and the introduction of more language pairs to be translated with MT. Baan currently uses Trados Translator's Workbench and IBM TranslationManager in addition to Star Transit; Logos MT is the sole MT system currently in use.

An open issue is implementing an authoring tool to enhance source text quality not only for MT, but also for implementing Standard Baan English. Also under consideration are:

- how to handle pre-edited English texts from former software releases that have been modified for the latest release, since TM will consider the modified English text as new text;

- knowledge transfer—a perennially open issue as team members leave and new ones join the group;

- recruiting appropriate translators with experience in MT and TM;

- reservations and reluctance for translators to use MT.

Language Automation
at the European Commission

Colin Brace

In the mid-1970s, at the instigation of a far-sighted European Union official, Loll Rolling (now retired), the European Commission made its first incursion into the world of machine translation (MT). It acquired a license to exploit Systran, a commercial machine-translation system, and began beefing up the system's dictionaries with EU terminology and developing additional language pairs that the Commission required. While sharing its origins, the Commission's system, for practical purposes, has scarcely more than name in common with the commercial PC-based software developed and marketed by California software company Systran.

REVERSE-ENGINEERING BABEL AT THE EC

With 11 official languages to contend with, the collective institutions at the helm of the European Union are probably the largest producer and consumer of translation in the world today. The most familiar of these is the European Commission, the enormous administrative wing of the EU divided between Luxembourg and Brussels. Others include the European Parliament, the Council, the Court of Justice, the Court of Auditors, the Economic and Social Committee, and the European Investment Bank.

Because the EU is committed to "linguistic equality" among its member states, all Union legislation needs to be translated into the 11 official languages. But it doesn't stop there. Countless calls for proposals, internal reports, and intermediary drafts need to be translated on an ad-hoc basis, not to mention the need for live interpreting of meetings. Moreover, as new countries join the Union and additional languages need to be reckoned with, the translation burden expands exponentially.

The major EU institutions all have their own internal translation departments, the largest of which is the Commission's Translation Service (SdT). With an army of some 1,500 full-time professional translators divided between Luxembourg (one third) and Brussels (two thirds), the SdT is the largest single translation organization in the world, producing over one million pages a year.

MACHINE TRANSLATION JOINS THE EC

Since the early 1990s, use of MT at the Commission has soared, primarily due to the adoption within the organization of email, which simplifies submitting and retrieving texts, but also thanks to some judicious internal promotion. In 1996, some 220,000 pages were run through the system, making the Commission by far the most prolific user of MT in the world in terms of shear volume. The Commission's Translation Service (SdT) accounted for slightly less than a third of this volume, with the remainder being nonlinguists in the many administrative departments.

Until now, funding for development and maintenance of Systran has been provided by DG XIII under the Multilingual Action Plans (MLAPs), but the success of the system within the organization placed the Commission in a quandary. DG XIII's raison d'être is funding research in telecommunications and language engineering, and it could no longer continue to justify subsidizing development of the system if it had truly passed from being an advanced research topic to a fully operational concern. So in 1995, DG XIII announced its intention to phase out its support by the end of 1997, and over the past two years the SdT has been contemplating the way forward.

IN-HOUSE MT USER SURVEY

One option is for the SdT to allocate funds from its own operational budget to support the use of MT within the Commission. To determine whether this would be appropriate, an extensive feasibility study was undertaken last year, encompassing a user survey, practical experiments with in-house translators, an examination of legal issues, a market study, and a cost-benefit analysis.

More than 1,500 users—both translators and nonlinguists alike—responded to the survey, providing a very detailed snapshot of how machine translation is used within the Commission. With an eye on objective information, the SdT also surveyed a number of nonusers, people who for one reason or another do not avail themselves of the system. The results of the survey provide a unique picture of the use of MT within this vast organization.

Among its users in the administrative departments, the vast majority turn to MT for urgent translations that they might otherwise have sent to the SdT, for browsing, and for preparing draft versions of documents. Within the SdT, some translators consider that MT does not help them in their work, or remain opposed to the use of MT on principle. But many value the system's fast turnaround times, and find its vast terminological resources and its preservation of formatting to be important benefits. While post-editing machine output can be tedious, some translators, as Dorothy Senez of the MT Help Desk wryly notes, find consolation in the system's unintentional sense of humor.

Of course, the system is not cut from the same technical cloth in every detail, and the quality of its translations varies greatly among the language pairs. At the moment, the French-English, French-Spanish, French-Italian, and English-French language pairs are considered by users to be the best.

Feedback from the practical experiments carried out by the SdT shows that on average a translation time saving of 35 percent can be achieved, provided a number of conditions are met. Documents have to be of the appropriate type, post-editors should be experienced, and MT dictionaries prepared in advance. And the actual results will still depend on the quality of the language pair in question.

The study acknowledges that SdT users and administrative users have different requirements, but the general consensus is that the primary value of MT lies in its immediacy—MT is fast. They also perceive the need for improved linguistic coverage as well as better promotion within the Commission.

So where does this leave the SdT with regard to the future of MT within the institution? While the exact details have yet to be hammered out, it appears that the SdT and DG XIII have reached a happy compromise. Now that the SdT's cost-benefit analysis has demonstrated to its satisfaction that the MT system both directly and indirectly benefits not just the Service itself but also the Commission as a whole, the SdT will now support the mature, operational language pairs.

DG XIII meanwhile has agreed to continue funding the development of other language pairs, under the famous subsidiarity principle—development will depend on cofinancing by the relevant Member States. In other words, if a Finnish-English language pair is deemed a priority, the government of Finland will have to be prepared to partly underwrite the effort.

COMMERCIAL ARENA

The Commission will be issuing calls for tenders for the maintenance of the most promising language pairs as well as for systems or services for languages not covered by the Commission's system, or for language pairs which are of lesser quality. Keeping an eye on developments in the commercial arena, the Commission could conceivably license a language pair not covered by Systran from a third-party developer, should such a product become available.

By virtue of both its substantial internal translation requirements and its commitment to linguistic diversity, the European Commission is in many ways an exemplary test bed for language technology such as MT. As such, it is in the unique position of playing the roles of both user and mover. What lessons can be drawn from the Commission's experience by other, albeit smaller organizations?

Euramis General Architecture

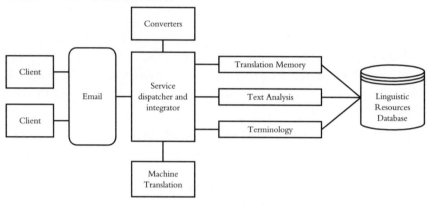

INTEGRATING MT INTO WORKFLOW

For one, the MT development team and the MT user base (the SdT in particular) have enjoyed close proximity; feedback from the latter to the former has ensured practical results. Since few organizations can justify development of their own MT system (the Pan American Health Organization being an exception that comes to mind), this is admittedly an exceptional albeit pertinent factor.

In addition, the Commission has striven to integrate MT within the document flow of the organization. That means a substantial investment in the software- engineering side of things—such as document format filters and integration with email—admittedly prosaic matters which have all too often been given short shrift by language technologists in the past. This task has been neither easy nor trivial (see "Euramis Tools Up" below).

The Commission has also expended tremendous effort building up the Systran dictionaries. The four top-rated language pairs boasted nearly 700,000 entries—and that was before the Eurodicautom data were imported. Currently, Systran has more than four million entries distributed across the 16 extant language pairs. This is a lesson that applies to both small and large MT users alike.

Given the Commission's needs and resources, any inability to leverage this technology would have sent out a warning message to the MT community in general. As Dorothy Senez puts it, "If we can't make it work, who can?"

EURAMIS TOOLS UP

One way in which Systran is expected to integrate into the EC's SdT is via the Euramis project (short for European Advanced Multilingual Information System). Launched in 1994, and due to become semioperational for a pilot user group in the near future, Euramis aims to provide a single client interface to a panoply of server-based translation tools and resources for the Commission's translators, but also other end-users of translated documents. If it reaches its long-term goals, Euramis will very likely be the most comprehensive attempt ever to integrate 25 years of natural-language processing and tool development into a heavy-duty workflow architecture for translators and their "customers."

The key components of Euramis include a translation memory (TM) facility (presumably based on the Trados Workbench—Trados recently confirmed that it is providing their product to the European Union institutions for use by some 2,000 in-house translators, a terminology extraction tool, the Systran MT facility, and a Linguistic Resources Database containing the system's complete linguistic entries, with links to Eurodicautom, among other term bases. Users with a document to translate will send an email request to Euramis which will automatically convert the document into SGML format with a Unicode character set, process it using selected TM and MT resources and email back a text with automatic candidate translations in the target language. Translators will then post-edit the result to deliver a final version.

Euramis Workflow

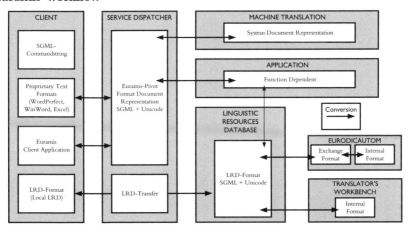

INSIDERS ONLY

Unfortunately, for interested parties outside the Union's institutions, the Commission's Systran is likely to remain an attractive product but out of reach for the foreseeable future. Access to the Commission's MT system is restricted to users within the EU institutions, the rationale being that the Commission should avoid distorting the competitiveness of the free market.

In any event, Systran, which originated from research at Georgetown University (Washington, DC) in the 1950s, looks poised to enjoy a rosy future well into the 21st century. If language is the soul of a culture, then the soul of a unified but multicultural Europe lies in its multilinguality, symbolized imperfectly yet impressively by Systran.

About the Contributors

Carmen Andrés Lange received a degree in technical translation at the University of Hildesheim, Germany, where she studied Spanish and English in combination with mechanical engineering, electronics, and applied linguistics. In 1991 she began working for Space GmbH in Hanover, Germany as a translation engineer and technical author. Space GmbH later became Baan Germany (1995). Andrés Lange has translated software programs, user manuals, and product information. She became team leader for the German translation group in 1994. In March 1997, she came to the Netherlands to investigate and lead a pilot project in machine translation for Baan Development. Since 1997 she has worked as a translation consultant, offering terminology workshops and presentations on Baan's innovations in translation memory, machine translation, and terminology. Her current project is a 16-language database to be implemented on the Internet.

Winfield Scott Bennett received a Ph.D. in Germanic linguistics from the University of Texas at Austin in 1978. After a year on the faculty at UT-Austin he began research and development on the Siemens-sponsored Metal machine-translation project at the University of Texas. During this period he was instrumental in the research-and-development effort to create a production machine-translation system from the existing theoretical system developed at the University of Texas from 1959 to 1979. This system, named Metal, was marketed by Siemens beginning in 1987. Siemens stopped funding the R&D effort in 1993, at which time Bennett moved to Logos Corporation. During his time at Logos he has served as director of linguistics, director of institutional and government relations, director of marketing, and now director of strategic relations. He has been active in the international translation community for a number of years, including holding offices in the Association for Machine Translation in the Americas and the International Machine Translation Association, as well as membership in the ATA. Bennett has written a number of articles and contributed to books on machine translation and related issues.

Colin Brace is a journalist based in Amsterdam who writes regularly about language technology. From 1991 to 1996, he published the *Language Industry Monitor*, a newsletter dedicated to this field.

David Brooks joined Microsoft in 1990 as the manager of transfer pricing, and since then has held a variety of jobs with an international focus. Today he is senior director of international product strategy for Microsoft, and his mission is to support and coordinate the creation of international versions.

Prior to joining Microsoft, Brooks was a management consultant with KPMG Peat Marwick. There, he was an early advocate of activity-based costing and worked extensively with technology companies on strategic planning and cost analysis. Brooks's first "real job" was with Ford Motor Company, where he was a financial analyst in International Automotive Operations. After graduating from Cornell University in 1969 with a degree in English literature, he spent three years in Japan teaching English. After returning to the US, he completed his MBA degree at the University of Washington and passed the CPA exam several years later. Brooks lives in Seattle with his wife and two teenage children. He is an active outdoor enthusiast who enjoys biking, hiking, and skiing, and is also an active amateur astronomer and cosmologist. His favorite saying is, "Anything that doesn't kill me makes me a better man."

Susan Cheng is the cofounder and vice president of marketing for Idiom Technologies. She completed her A.B. in history and science at Harvard University. While completing her undergraduate work, Cheng was program director and community-relations director for Partners for Empowering Neighborhoods, an organization that offers English as a Second Language classes in Boston-area housing developments. Cheng also cofounded and directed the Health Advocacy Program at Boston Medical Center, a volunteer program that improves access to health care and welfare for low-income children and their families. She has also held leadership positions at numerous benevolent organizations, including the Rockefeller Foundation and Project New Life in Boston, a literacy program for adults. Cheng was a recipient of the 1995 Action for Boston Community Development Award. Contact her at scheng@idiomtech.com.

Karen Combe is president of Combe Consulting, which offers consulting in internationalization and localization. Prior to establishing her practice, Karen worked for nearly 10 years at International Language Engineering, a localization service provider. At ILE she led the development of each of the company's production departments during its growth from 12 people to a staff of over 125. As senior vice president she managed both the client-services and sales and marketing departments. Karen holds a B.A. in linguistics from the University of California at Berkeley, and a post-graduate degree in social anthropology from Cambridge University. She spent two years in the Peace Corps in Senegal, West Africa, and two years with International Voluntary Services in Algeria. Subsequent work experience includes two years in the financial-services industry and eight years working as a cowboy on a ranch in northwestern Colorado.

Cornelia Hofmann has been working in technical communications for over 10 years. She started as technical writer in 1987 with AEG (now Schneider Automation) in Seligenstadt, Germany, and became manager of technical communications in 1993. Since then, her team has been working on multilingual information management aimed at improving the processing of information in multiple languages. In 1993, a first single-source publishing project started. Her team developed a tool based on Interleaf which allows the creation of paper documentation and help files from a single source. Currently, this tool is used to create more than 7,000 pages of documentation in multiple languages each year. In 1997, her team started a new single-source publishing project based on SGML. Since mid 1999, she is partner and managing director of Ovidius Gesellschaft für Technische Kommunikation mbH in Hanau, Germany. Ovidius offers translation and documentation services as well as consulting for international companies, with focus on the implementation of information management projects.

Gary Jaekel is currently managing director of TNC, the Swedish Centre for Technical Terminology, after having served on the board of that organization for several years. From 1987 to 1997, Gary was manager, then managing director, of Ericsson Language Services, a wholly owned Ericsson subsidiary. Language work was subsequently outsourced to Interverbum, a language-services company, at the end of 1997, where Jaekel was responsible for vendor relations. Jaekel was also a founding member and former president (1990-1995) of the Swedish Association of Professional Translators (SFÖ). Gary is also a member of the Steering Committee for Language Technology in Sweden, and has been a member of the Regional Centre Europe steering committee under the auspices of FIT. Jaekel writes and presents frequently on the areas of translation, localization, terminology, and language training.

Andrew Joscelyne has been closely involved in promoting the emerging language industry for the past decade. After an academic career in linguistics in Europe and North Africa, he began to explore the impact of the digital revolution on language and business in Europe in the mid 1980s. He helped pioneer the reporting of language technology, taught technology awareness to trainee language professionals, and set up a translation and communications consultancy in Paris, where he now lives. He has reported extensively on language-industry issues for a number of publications ranging from *Intermedia* to *Wired*, including a column in *Language International*. As an associate of the UK-based Equipe Consultancy, he is currently working on a number of European Commission projects for the multilingual information society.

J.H.G. (Harold) Kinds, Certified Public Accountant (1960) has worked in accountancy for the last 20 years. At present he is head of the Technical Department at Van Zwol Wijntjes, Accountants in Amersfoort, the Netherlands and the Cooperating Certified Public Accountants in Bunnik, the Netherlands. He teaches auditing at the Catholic University in Tilburg (Netherlands) and is a member of the Statistical Auditing Committee at the Interuniversity Limperg Institute.

Bernhard Kohlmeier studied technology and cartography, earning a degree in 1985 from the Fachoberschule für Technik in Munich, Germany. He embarked on a career in electronic data-processing by starting his own company when IBM introduced its first personal computers. In 1989 he joined Software Products International GmbH, the German subsidiary of SPI, the San Diego-based developer and publisher of Open Access, an early, DOS-based application that integrated database, spreadsheet, business graphics, word processing, and communications applications. In 1992, Kohlmeier joined Gesellschaft für Technische Information mbH (Gecap), a pioneer in Germany in computer-aided word and graphics processing. Kohlmeier eventually became director of localization at Gecap. As vice president of strategy and planning, Kohlmeier guided localization strategies for Gecap's subsidiaries and customers, including the first German version of the Microsoft *Encarta Encyclopedia*, as well as other Microsoft products such as Office 97. Kohlmeier now lives in Seattle where he serves as executive vice president for strategic development at Bowne Global Solutions.

S.L. Koo, an aeronautical engineer (1965), has worked in localization for the last 15 years. At present she is director of L&L Gebruikersinformatie B.V., a localization company based in the Netherlands. She is a member of the Executive Committee of the Localisation Industry Standards Association (LISA).

Rose Lockwood is a founder and managing director of Equipe Consortium Ltd., based in Cambridge, England. After over 15 years as a management consultant (with Booz-Allen and Butler-Cox in New York) and market analyst (with Ovum in London), she established Equipe in 1996 to offer specialized services in the language industries. One of the original analysts of the office-automation market in the 1980s, she has published market studies covering a wide range of IT and software topics, including networking, groupware, messaging, and document management. Her Globalization report, published by Ovum, was the first comprehensive study of the localization market. Since 1991 Lockwood has carried out around 30 different studies of various aspects of the market for language technology and services, for suppliers, users, investors, and the public sector. She is currently engaged in assessing the impact of language in the digital-content industries, and in global e-commerce.

Thorsten Mehnert studied computer science and business administration in Hamburg, Baton Rouge, and Karlsruhe and holds a diploma (Dipl.-Inform.) from the University of Karlsruhe. After graduation, he joined Gemini Consulting where he worked as a management consultant on several reengineering projects for clients in telecommunications, trade, and public administration. Since 1996, Mehnert's independent consulting work has focused on information and process management in the documentation and translation industry. As a senior information architect at Tanner Documents, he currently supports clients in optimizing the creation, management, and distribution of technical information often hidden in publications such as pre-sales and spare part catalogs, user manuals, technical data sheets, etc. Thorsten's goal is to increase the impact of technical information on a company's competitiveness by synchronizing information engineering with the product life cycle and EDM/ERP systems, by utilizing object-oriented and SGML/XML-based methods, and by integrating technical information into corporate information management. He can be contacted at mehnert@tanner.de or tm.wordnet@scm.de.

Ricky P. Thibodeau joined MapInfo Corporation of Troy, New York in 1995 and has worked there as software localization engineer, quality assurance supervisor, and international localization manager. He currently serves as international product release director at MapInfo, where he oversees localization in 20 languages. Previously, he worked in the information technology department for the New York State Department of Social Services, and network operations for the Department of Taxation and Finance. Thibodeau holds a bachelor of science degree in computer science and associate degree in data processing from the State University of New York. He lives in Albany, New York with his wife and has his roots in Quebec. Contact him at rthibodeau@mapinfo.com.

Suzanne Topping is the owner of Localization Unlimited, which provides localization consulting and training services. Prior to starting her own business in October 1998, Suzanne spent 10 years with Eastman Kodak, where she founded two localization groups, which managed localization for a range of products including thermal printers, digital printing kiosk systems, inkjet printers, digital scanners, and digital cameras. At Kodak, Suzanne focused on localization process improvement and on educating project teams about localization. She began an Internationalization Special Interest Group, authored a Localization Quick Reference Guide, developed content for a corporate Internationalization Web site, and coordinated the creation of development guidelines for easily localizable software. She is currently the localization editor for the Open Directory Project (http://directory.mozilla.org/about.html), and is founder and moderator for the Northeast Localization Special Interest Group (nelocsig@egroups.com). Contact her at stopping@rochester.rr.com.

Alberto Vourvoulias-Bush is deputy editor for Time Latin America. Before entering journalism he was a research associate at the Council on Foreign Relations, a public policy think-tank, and a lecturer on Latin American politics at Yale University and New York University. He has published in both Latin America and the United States, in English and Spanish, and is coeditor of *The City and the World: New York's Global Future* (Council on Foreign Relations Press, 1997).

ABOUT THE EDITORS

Robert C. Sprung is chairman and founder of Harvard Translations, Inc., a Cambridge, Massachusetts–based foreign-language translation solutions provider and consulting firm. Sprung is editor of *Language International*, a trade magazine for the language professions (translation, localization, globalization). He writes and speaks regularly on language and translation, including engagements at the computer show Comdex, a column on language issues in the magazine *Pharmaceutical and Medical Packaging News*, and a chapter in *Designing User Interfaces for International Use* from Elsevier. Sprung holds an A.B. from Harvard College, *summa cum laude*, in classics and German. He received an M.A. in modern languages from the University of Cambridge (England) with first-class honors, under a George C. Marshall scholarship. Contact him at rsprung@htrans.com; www.htrans.com, www.language-international.com.

Simone Jaroniec holds a bachelor of arts degree in French and international relations from Kent State University. She was awarded an internship at the Center for Human Rights of the United Nations in Geneva. She holds a master of arts in German translation from Kent State University, where she concentrated on terminology management. Jaroniec is currently manager of linguistic services at Harvard Translations, Inc., where she also oversees research and application in language tools and technologies.

About the Sponsors

AMERICAN TRANSLATORS ASSOCIATION (ATA) OFFICERS AND BOARD OF DIRECTORS, 2000

Ann G. Macfarlane, President
Thomas L. West III, President-Elect
Courtney Searls-Ridge, Secretary
Eric Norman McMillan, Treasurer

Allan W. Adams, Kirk Anderson, Beatriz A. Bonnet, Scott Brennan, Gertrud Graubart Champe, Jo Anne Engelbert, Alan K. Melby, Izumi Suzuki, Timothy Yuan

RECIPIENTS OF THE ALEXANDER GODE MEDAL

1964 Alexander Gode
1965 Kurt Gingold
1966 Richard and Clara Winston
1967 The National Translations Center (University of Texas)
1968 Pierre-François Caillé
1969 Henry Fischbach
1970 Carl V. Bertsche
1971 Lewis Bertrand
1972 Lewis Galantière
1973 Jean-Paul Vinay
1974 Eliot F. Beach
1975 Frederick Ungar
1977 Eugene A. Nida
1978 Royal L. Tensley, Jr.
1980 Gregory Rabassa

1981 Georgetown University, Monterey Institute of International Studies, State University of New York at Binghamton
1983 Françoise Estac
1984 Charles M. Stern
1985 Ludmilla Callaham
       Richard Ernst
1986 William I. Bertsche
1987 Patricia E. Newman
1988 Marilyn Gaddis Rose
1990 Ben Teague
1992 Deanna L. Hammond
1993 Karl Kummer
1996 Javier Collazo
       William Gladstone
1997 Danica Seleskovitch

PAST PRESIDENTS OF THE ATA

1995-97 Peter W. Krawutschke
1993-95 Edith F. Losa
1991-93 Leslie Willson
1989-91 Deanna L. Hammond
1987-89 Karl Kummer
1985-87 Patricia E. Newman
1983-85 Virginia Eva Berry
1981-83 Ben Teague
1979-81 Thomas R. Bauman
1977-79 Josephine Thornton
1975-77 Royal L. Tinsley

1973-75 William I. Bertsche
1971-73 Thomas Wilds
1970-71 William I. Bertsche (completed Moynihan's term)
1969-70 Daniel Moynihan (resigned in June 1970)
1967-69 Boris Anzlowar
1965-67 Henry Fischbach
1963-65 Kurt Gingold
1960-63 Alexander Gode

ATA CORPORATE MEMBERS (1 MARCH 1998)

A2Z Printing Center
A L Madrid & Associates
A & M Logos International, Inc.
Able International, Inc.
Academy of Languages Translation & Interpretation Services
Academy of Legal and Technical Translation, Ltd.
Academy Translations
Accent Typography & Translation
Accento, The Language Company
Accents
Access Language Experts
Accu Trans, Inc.
Accura International Translations
Accurapid Translation Services, Inc.
Accurate Spanish Translations by Spanish Business Services, Inc.
Accurate Translation, Inc.
Accuword International, Inc./dba inlingua International
Ace Translation Center
Acentos, Marketing & Advertising & Translations
Adams Translation Services
Adaptive Language Resources, Inc.
AD-EX Worldwide
Advance Language Studios
AE Inc. - Translations
Agnew Tech-II
AIM Translations, Inc.
Albanian Translation Services
Albors and Associates, Inc.
Alexandria Translations
Allen Translation Service
Allied Languages Cooperative
Ambassador Translating, Inc.
America Translating Services
Amway Corporation
Andalex International, Inc.
Antiquariat Literary Services, Inc.
Arabic Scientific Alliance
Argo Translation, Inc.
ASET International Services Corporation
Asian Translations, Inc.
ASIST Translation Services, Inc.

Astratec Traduções Técnicas Ltda
ATG Language Solutions
ATL Ultrasound
AT&T Language Line Services
Auerbach International, Inc. dba Translations Express
Avant Page
Babel, Inc.
Babel Translation Services
Baker & McKenzie
Banta Information Services Group
BCBR - Business Communications Brazil
Benemann Translation Center - BTC
Berkeley Scientific Translation Service, Inc.
Berlitz Interpretation Services
Berlitz Translation Services
Bilingual Services
Bowne Translation Services
Bradson Corporation
Bureau of Translation Services, Inc.
Burg Translation Bureau
C. P. Language Institute
CACI Language Center
Calvin International Communications, Inc.
Cambridge Translation Resources
Canadian Union of Professional & Technical Employees
Carioni & Associates, Inc.
Carolina Polyglot, Inc.
Caterpillar, Inc.
Center for Professional Advancement/ The Language Center
Chicago Multi-Lingua Graphics, Inc.
Cial Lingua Service International
Ciba Corning Diagnostics Corporation
CinciLingua, Inc.
CITI-Translation Center, Inc.
Cogtec Corporation
Columbia Language Services
ComNet International
Computain, Inc.
Contact International
Continental Communications Agency
Copper Translation Service
CopyGroup, Inc.

Corporate Language Services, Inc.
Corporate Translations
Corporate Translations, Inc.
Corporate Translation Services, Inc.
Cosmopolitan Translation Bureau
Coto Interpreting, Translating & Graphics
Course Crafters, Inc.
Crestec (UK) Ltd.
Crimson Language Services
Crossword Translation Services
Cybertec, Inc.
CyraCom International, Inc.
Czech Translation Services
Delta Translation International
Die Presse Editorial, Ltd.
Digital Publishing, Inc.
Diplomatic Language Services, Inc.
Direct Language Communications
Diversified Language Institute
Documents International, Inc.
DocuTrans
Dynamic Language Center, Ltd.
East-West Concepts, Inc.
Echo International
Edimax, S.A. de C.V.
Elite Language Productions
Elucidex
Eriksen Translations Inc.
Escalante Translations
Euro - Translation
Excel Translations, Inc.
Executive Linguist Agency, Inc.
Expert Language Services
First Translation Services
FLS, Inc.
Foreign Ink Ltd.
Foreign Language Center
Galaxy Systems, Inc.
Garjak International, Inc.
Geonexus Communications
Geotext Translations
GeoText Translations & Typesetting
Services
Global Advanced Translation Services Inc.
The Global Institute of Languages and
Culture, Inc.

Global Language Services, Inc.
Global Language Solutions/
The Russian Word, Inc.
Global Languages & Cultures, Inc.
Global Translation Services, Inc.
Global Translations & Interpreters
Services, Inc.
The Global Word, Inc.
GlobalDoc, Inc.
Globalink, Inc.
Glorbet Consultants, Inc.
Harvard Translations, Inc.
Health Outcomes Group
Heitmann of America, Inc.
HG Translations
Hightech Passport Limited
Honda R&D North America, Inc.
HSN Linguistic Services Ltd.
i. b. d., Ltd.
IBS-International Business Services
ICN Language Services
Idem Translation
in French only inc./in Spanish too!
Information Builders, Inc.
Inlingua International Services
Inlingua Language & Intercultural Services
Inlingua Language Services Center
Institut für Fremdsprachen und
Auslandskunde
Intel Corporation
Interclub, Inc.
Intercontact - Peru
Interlanguage SNC Di Abbati A. E C.
InterNation Inc.
International Communication by
Design, Inc.
International Communications, Inc.
International Contact, Inc.
International Effectiveness Centers
International Language Engineering Corp.
International Language Services, Inc.
International Translation and
Publishing, Ltd.
International Translators International &
Typesetters, Inc.
International Access/Ability Corp.
Interpretations

Interpreters International & Translations
Interpreters Unlimited
Interpreting Services International Inc.
InterSol, Inc.
Interspeak Translations, Inc.
Intertech Translations, Ltd.
InterTrans, Inc.
Inwords, Inc.
IRU International Resources Unlimited
Iverson Language Associates, Inc.
J.D. Edwards & Company, Inc.
Jackson Graphics, Inc.
Japan – America Management, Ltd.
Japanese Language Services, Inc.
JKW International, Inc.
JLS Language Corporation
John Benjamins Publishing Company
Josef Silny & Associates, Inc.
JTG, Inc.
K & L Language Services
Korean Technical Communications
Langua Translations, Inc.
Language Company Translations, L.C.
The Language Connection
The Language Exchange, Inc.
Language Innovations, LLC
Language Intelligence, Ltd.
Language Interface, Ltd.
The Language Lab
Language Link Corporation
Language Management International
(The Corporate World, Inc.)
Language Matters
The Language Network, Inc.
Language Plus
The Language Service, Inc.
Language Services Associates
The Language Solution, Inc.
Languages International
The Languageworks, Inc.
Latin American Translators Network, Inc.
Legal Interpreting Services, Inc.
Liaison Language Center
Liaison Multilingual Services
Lingo Systems
Lingua Communications Translation Services
Linguae Translation & Interpretation Bureau

Lingualink Incorporated
LinguaNet, Inc.
Linguistic Consulting Enterprises, Inc
Linguistic Systems, Inc.
Localization Associates of Utah
Logos Corporation
LRA Interpreters, Inc.
Lucent Technologies–ILT Solutions
Luz
M2 Limited
Magnus International Trade Services Corp.
Master Translating Services, Inc.
MasterWord Services, Inc.
Gene Mayer Associates
McDonald's Corporation
Ralph McElroy Translation Company
McNeil Technologies, Inc.
ME Sharpe, Inc., Publisher
Mercury Marine
Metropolitan Interpreters & Translators Worldwide, Inc.
Mitaka Limited
Morales Dimmick Translation Service Inc.
Morgan Guaranty Trust Company
Multilingual Translations, Inc.
N.O.W. Translations
NCS Enterprises, Inc.
New England Translations
Newtype, Inc.
NIS International Services
Ntext Translations
Occidental Oil & Gas Corporation
Okada & Sellin Translations, LLC
Omega International
OmniLingua, Inc.
Oriental Communication Services, Inc.
O'Sullivan Menu Corporation
Pacific Interpreters, Inc.
Pacific Ring Services, Inc.
Paragon Language Services
Peritus Precision Translations, Inc.
Peters Translation, Inc.
Planning S.N.C.
Polyglot International
Precision Translating Services, Inc.
Premier Translation Services, Ltd.
Prisma International
Professional Translating Services
ProTrans, Inc.

PSC, Inc.
Quantum, Inc.
Quark, Inc.
Quintana Multi-Lingual Services, Inc.
R.R. Donnelley Financial Translation Services
Rapport International
Rennert Bilingual Translations
Resource Network International, Inc.
Richard Schneider Enterprises, Inc.
Rosetta
Routledge, Inc.
RussTech
Sally Low & Associates
Schreiber Translations, Inc.
SH3, Inc.
Shoreline Translations, Inc.
Showorks, Inc.
Simulacrum LLC/Context
SinoMetrics International, Inc.
Slovak Translation Services
Sohsei, Inc.
Spectrum Multilanguage Communications
Sputnik Translation Services
Square D Company
Suzuki, Myers & Associates, Ltd.
Sykes Enterprises, Incorporated
Tech Link, Inc.
Techlingua, Inc.
Technik-Sprachendienst Gmbh
Techno-Graphics & Translations, Inc.
TechTrans International, Inc.
Techworld Language Services, Inc.
Terra Pacific Writing Corporation
TEXTnology CORPoration
TIICO-Translating Interpreting International Company
Total Benefit Communications, Inc.
Trade Typographers, Inc.
Trados Corporation
Traducciones LinguaCorp
TransACT
Trans-Caribe Communications
Transcript Communications, Inc.
Transemantics, Inc.
Transglobal Translations & Immigration Services, Inc.
TransImage

Translation Company of America, Inc.
Translation Services International Inc.
TranslationPlus
Translingua, Inc.
TransLingual, Ltd.
Transperfect
Transperfect Translations International, Inc.
Universal Translations, Inc.
Universe Interpreters and Translators Corporation
University Language Center, Inc.
U.S. Technical Translations, Inc.
U.S. Translation Company
Vanguard Academy
Victory Productions, Inc.
Vormbrock Translating, Inc.
West-Star Consultants
Whitman Language Services
Winter Wyman Contract Services, Inc.
WKI International Communications
Wordnet, Inc.
World Trade Center Portland
Worldwide Translations
YAR Communications, Inc.

ATA INSTITUTIONAL MEMBERS (I MARCH 1998)

Academy Interpreting and Translations International

American Education Research Corp.

American Institute of Physics

An-Nahda Educational Office

Binghamton University (SUNY)

Boston School of Modern Languages, Inc.

California State University

Center for Applied Linguistics

Chitco

Christian Science Publishing Society

The Church of Jesus Christ of the Latter-day Saints

Community Interpreter Services Catholic Charities/Greater Boston

Community Management Staff

Eureka - Foreign College Evaluators & Translators

Executive Office for Immigration Review

FBIS

Florida A&M University

The French Library & Cultural Center

Gallaudet University

Georgetown University

Georgia State University

Instituto Superior de Interpretes y Traductores, S. C.

Inter-American Development Bank (IDB)

Inter-American Air Forces Academy

International Refugee Center of Oregon-International Language Bank

International Institute of Connecticut, Inc.

International Institute, Inc.

Kent State University

Language Interpreter Services and Translations/WA State Department of Social and Health Services

The Language School

M. D. Anderson Cancer Center

Marygrove College

Mayo Medical Center

Monterey Institute of International Studies

New York University

Northern Illinois University

Ordre des Traducteurs et Interprètes Agréés du Québec

Purdue University

Quba Institute of Arabic and Islamic Studies

Queen of the Valley Hospital

Rose-Hulman Institute of Technology

San Diego City Schools

School District of Palm Beach County International Student Support/Multicultural Awareness Department

Southwest Washington Medical Center

Summer Institute of Linguistics

Thammasat University

Translation & Critical Languages Institute of Florida A & M Univ.

Tucson Unified School District Title I Program/School-Community Relations Dept.

University of Hawaii

University of Idaho

University of Miami

University of Nebraska at Kearney

University of La Verne

The University of Texas Medical Branch at Galveston

University of Washington

Western Michigan University

Western Wisconsin Technical College

World Bank

For Further Reference

ORGANIZATIONS

American Translators Association (ATA). www.atanet.org

Localisation Industry Standards Association (LISA). www.lisa.org

Society for Technical Communication (STC). www.stc.org

LANGUAGE-INDUSTRY PUBLICATIONS

Language International Amsterdam: John Benjamins. www.language-international.com

Multilingual Computing & Technology. Sandpoint, Idaho: Multilingual Computing. www.multilingual.com

Technical Communication, Journal of the Society for Technical Communication. www.stc.org

CROSS-CULTURAL ADAPTATION

Axtell, R. *Do's and Taboos of Using English Around the World.* New York: John Wiley, 1995.

——————. *Gestures: The Do's and Taboos of Body Language Around the World.* New York: John Wiley, 1991.

The Parker Pen Company. *Do's and Taboos Around the World.* Elmsford, New York: The Benjamin Company, 1985.

Usunier, J. *Marketing Across Cultures.* New York: Prentice Hall PTR, 1996.

GLOBAL COMMUNICATIONS

Barrett, E., ed. *Text, ConText and HyperText: Writing with and for the Computer.* Cambridge, Massachusetts: MIT Press, 1988.

Brusaw, C., et al. *Handbook of Technical Writing,* 2nd ed. New York: St. Martin's Press, 1982.

Burnett, R. *Technical Communication,* 3rd ed. Belmont, California: Wadsworth Publishing Company, 1994.

Hoft, N. *International Technical Communication: How to Export Information about High Technology.* New York: John Wiley & Sons, 1995.

Leki, I. "The Technical Editor and the Non-Native Speaker of English." *Technical Communication* Vol. 37 No. 2 (1990): pp. 148-152.

Sanderlin, S. "Preparing Instruction Manuals for Non-English Readers." *Technical Communication* Vol. 35 No. 2 (1988): pp. 96–100.

Schur, N. *British English, A to Zed.* New York: Harper, 1991.

SOFTWARE LOCALIZATION AND INTERNATIONALIZATION

Carter, D. *Writing Localizable Software for the Macintosh.* Reading, Massachusetts: Addison-Wesley, 1992.

Esselink, B. *A Practical Guide to Software Localization.* Amsterdam: John Benjamins, 1998.

Hall, P. and R. Hudson. *Software Without Frontiers: A Multiplatform, Multicultural, Multinational Approach.* New York: Wiley, 1997.

Jones, S., et al. *Developing International User Information.* Bedford, Massachusetts: Digital Press, 1992.

Kano, N. *Developing International Software for Windows 95 and Windows NT.* Redmond, Washington: Microsoft Press, 1995.

Luong, T., et al. *Internationalization: Developing Software for Global Markets.* New York: John Wiley & Sons, 1995.

Nielsen, J., ed. *Advances in Human Factors/Ergonomics, vol. 13: Designing User Interfaces for International Use.* Amsterdam: Elsevier, 1990.

O'Donnell, S.M. *Programming for the World: A Guide to Internationalization.* Englewood Cliffs, New Jersey: Prentice Hall PTR, 1994.

Taylor, D. *Global Software: Developing Applications for the International Market.* Springer-Verlag, 1992.

Uren, E., et al. *Software Internationalization and Localization: An Introduction.* New York: Van Nostrand Reinhold, 1993.

LANGUAGE TOOLS AND MACHINE TRANSLATION

Asian Association for Machine Translation (AAMT). www.jeida.or.jp/aamt/index-e.html

Association for Machine Translation in the Americas (AMTA). www.isi.edu/natural-language/organizations/AMTA.html

Center for Machine Translation and Language Technologies Institute. www.lti.cs.cmu.edu

European Association for Machine Translation (EAMT). www.eamt.org

European Language Resources Association (ELRA). www.icp.grenet.fr/elra/home.html

Gingras, B. "Simplified English in Maintenance Manuals." *Technical Communication* Vol. 34 No. 1 (1987): pp. 24-28.

Hearne, V. "Controlled English and Poetic Common Sense." *Language Technology* 9 (1989): pp. 17-20.

Machine Translation Journal. http://admin.ccl.umist.ac.uk/staff/harold/mtjnl

MT News International. www.lim.nl/eamt/mtni

Strong, K.I. "Kodak International Service Language." *Technical Communication* Vol. 30 No. 2 (1983): pp. 20-22.

The Unicode Consortium. www.unicode.org

LANGUAGE-INDUSTRY ANALYSIS AND MARKET STUDIES

Language Translation: World Market Overview, Current Developments and Competitive Assessment. Oyster Bay, New York: Allied Business Intelligence, 1998.

Lockwood, Rose. *Globalisation 1998.* Cambridge, UK: Equipe Consortium, 1998.

——————. *Globalisation: Creating New Markets with Translation Technology.* London: Ovum, 1995.

Mason, J. and A. Rinsche. *Translation Technology Products.* London: Ovum, 1995.

American Translators Association Scholarly Monograph *Series* ISSN 0890 4111

I. GADDIS ROSE, Marilyn (ed): *Translation Excellence.* 1987. Out of print.

II. VASCONCELLOS, Muriel (ed.): *Technology as Translation Strategy.* 1988.

III. KRAWUTSCHKE, Peter W. (ed.): *Translator and Interpreter Training and Foreign Language Pedagogy.* 1989. Out of print.

IV. BOWEN, David and Margareta BOWEN (eds): *Interpreting - Yesterday, today and tomorrow.* 1990. Out of print.

V. LARSON, Mildred L. (ed.): *Translation: Theory and practice, tension and interdependence.* 1991.

VI. WRIGHT, Sue Ellen and Leland D. WRIGHT Jr.: *Scientific and Technical Translation.* 1993.

VII. HAMMOND, Deanna L. (ed.): *Professional Issues for Translators and Interpreters.* 1994.

VIII. MORRIS, Marshall (ed.): *Translation and the Law.* 1995.

IX. LABRUM, Marian B. (ed.): *The Changing Scene in World Languages. Issues and challenges.* 1997.

X. FISCHBACH, Henry (ed.): *Translation and Medicine.* 1998.

XI. SPRUNG, Robert (ed.): *Translating Into Success: Cutting-edge strategies for going multilingual in a global age.* 2000.

All titles available from John Benjamins Publishing Company, Amsterdam/Philadelphia. Out of print titles can be supplied as "Publishing on Demand" documents.